Revising
AS Accounting
By June Baptista M.Ed, M.Com

Welcome to Revising AS Accounting. This book will be an invaluable tool to students who wish to gain mastery of the syllabus, as well as to teachers as a resource to set homework and class work to supplement those available in the student book. The question and answer format is intended to help both teachers and students write better answers.

Contact the author for answers at: junebaptista@hotmail.com

Contents

1   Double Entry Bookkeeping 1

2   The Trial Balance 6

3   Books Of Prime Entry 9

4   Income Statements of Sole Traders 18

5   Statement of financial position for Sole Traders 23

6   Accounting Principles 25

7   Accruals and Prepayments (Other Payables and Receivables) 30

8   Depreciation Of Non-current Assets 35

9   Irrecoverable and Doubtful Debts 42

10 Bank Reconciliation Statements 49

11 Control Accounts 55

12 Suspense Accounts 62

13 Incomplete Records 69

14 Valuation Of Inventory 77

15 Partnership Accounts 83

16 Partnership Changes 89

17 Accounts Of Limited Companies-An Introduction 98

18 Analysis And Interpretation 113

19 Total or Absorption Costing 123

20 Unit, Job and Batch Costing 133

21 Marginal Costing 136

22 The Application of Accounting to Business Planning 146

23 Appendix 148

Double Entry Bookkeeping

1.1 | What happens when a business transaction takes place?

Since we are studying 'Double-entry' bookkeeping, there will be two effects when a transaction takes place:
One account will be debited and one account will be credited.

1.2 | What is meant by 'an account'?

An account is where all information about a particular person, firm, asset, liability, expense or income is collected. It has a debit side and a credit side. When an account is to be debited, an entry is made on the debit side of the account and when an account is to be credited, an entry is made on the credit side of the account. Accounts are maintained in Ledgers.

1.3 | How many types of Ledgers are normally maintained by a business?

There are three types of Ledgers:
The Sales Ledger in which all the personal accounts of a business's customers are found.
The Purchases Ledger in which the personal accounts of a business's suppliers are found.
The Nominal or General Ledger in which all the other accounts are found (excepting the cash and bank account which are found in the Cash Book).

1.4 | How does one know when an account is to be debited and when an account is to be credited?

All accounts can be classified into three classes:
Personal Accounts: Accounts dealing with people or firms are included in these types of accounts e.g. W Smith's Account, ABC Ltd's Account
The rule to be followed is : Debit the 'receiver' and credit the 'giver'.
Real Accounts: Accounts dealing with tangible or animate objects are included in these types of accounts e.g. Machinery Account, Furniture and Fixtures account
The rule to be followed is: Debit 'what comes in' and credit 'what goes out'.

Nominal Accounts : Accounts dealing with intangibles, things that exist as an idea only, are included in these types of accounts. E.g. Rent account, Salary account.
The rule to be followed is: Debit the expenses and losses and credit the gains and incomes.

√ **Tip:** *It should be remembered that the money with which rent is paid is 'real' and can be touched and felt, but the idea of 'rent' cannot. Hence the **cash** with which rent is paid is a real account whereas **rent** is a nominal account*

√ **Tip:** *Print out these rules on a sheet of paper and display them prominently above your desk etc. so that you can revise them again and again.*

The RULES in action:

EXHIBIT
Transaction: Paid W. Smith $400 cash.

Step one: Underline the two accounts that will be affected:
√ **Tip:** *Underline the nouns*
Paid W. Smith $400 Cash.

Step two: Decide to which class the accounts belong:
W. Smith is a person hence it is a 'Personal' account
Cash is tangible so it is a 'Real' account

Step three: Decide whether the accounts are to be debited or credited:
W. Smith is the 'receiver' and hence her account should be debited.
Cash is 'going out' and hence the Cash account should be credited.

Transaction: Paid $ 40 Rent by cheque.

Step one: Underline the two accounts:
Paid $40 Rent by Cheque.

√ **Tip:** *They are normally the NOUNS in the sentence*

Step two: Decide the types of accounts:
Rent is intangible, it exists in name only and hence it is a Nominal account

<u>Cheque</u> involves a 'Bank', a firm, and hence it is a 'Personal' account.

Step three: Decide which account to debit and which to credit:
<u>Rent</u> is an expense and hence it will be Debited.
<u>Bank</u> is the 'Giver' and hence it will be Credited.

» EXERCISE 1.1

For each of the following transactions, decide which account will be debited and which account will be credited :

20x6	Transaction	Debit	Credit
Jan 1	The proprietor introduced $6,000 cash into the business.		
Jan 4	$2,000 cash was deposited into the business bank account.		
Jan 6	Bought furniture $670 from Mogambo Furniture on credit		
Jan10	Took a loan from Gallagher $3,000 in cash.		
Jan16	Paid salaries in cash $1,200.		
Jan20	Received $200 cash as commission.		
Jan25	Paid Gallagher $2,000 cash in respect of loan owing to him.		

» EXERCISE 1.2

For each of the following transactions, decide which account will be debited and which account will be credited :

20x1	Transaction	Debit	Credit
Jan 1	Bought a car paying $ 300 by cheque		
Jan 4	M. Smith paid us $ 3500 cash.		
Jan 6	Took a loan from J. Jamal $ 2800 cash		
Jan10	The proprietor introduced $3400 cash into the business.		
Jan16	The firm bought stationery $76 paying cash.		
Jan20	Paid a creditor, M. Gallagher, $400 by cheque.		
Jan25	Deposited $450 cash into the bank.		

» EXERCISE 1.3

For each of the following transactions, decide which account will be debited and which account will be credited :

20x2		Debit	Credit
Aug 1	The proprietor put $3500 into the firm's bank account.		
Aug 4	Borrowed $600 cash from Emad.		
Aug 6	Put $600 cash into the bank.		
Aug10	Bought a car for $340 on credit from Daljit.		
Aug16	Smithers, a debtor, paid us cash $4500.		
Aug20	Bought a computer for $450 paying by cheque.		
Aug25	Sold furniture for $600 cash.		

» EXERCISE 1.4

For each of the following transactions, decide which account will be debited and which account will be credited :

20x2		Debit	Credit
Aug 1	The proprietor introduced $5,000 cash into the business.		
Aug 4	$1,500 cash was deposited into the business bank account.		
Aug 6	Bought furniture $980 from Maxine Furniture on credit.		
Aug10	Took a loan from Jinny $2,300 in cash.		
Aug16	Paid salaries in cash $1,000		
Aug20	Received $500 cash as rent.		
Aug25	Paid jinny $2,300 cash in respect of loan owing to her.		

1.5 | What is 'Inventory' (or 'Goods' or 'Stock')?

Inventory is goods bought for resale.

NOTE:
Any one of the following accounts is usually affected:
Purchases: When the inventory is bought
Sales: when the inventory is sold
Sales returns or Returns inwards: When the inventory that you have sold is returned by your customers
Purchases returns or Return Outwards: When the inventory that you have purchased is returned by you to your suppliers

√**Tip:** *Buying/Selling transactions can be either for cash, cheque or on credit. When cash is paid or received, then the cash account is affected, when a cheque is involved, then the bank account is affected and when it is a credit transaction, then the supplier's/customer's account (Personal Account) is affected.*

1.6| What is a cash discount?

A Cash Discount is a discount given or received to encourage early payment of debts. It is recorded in the books as 'Discount Received' or 'Discount Allowed'

1.7 | Define: Discounts Received

Discounts Received is the amount we deduct when paying our suppliers. E.g. We owe our suppliers $450 for goods bought on credit. If we pay $435 in full settlement of that debt, then $15 is the 'Discount Received' from our suppliers.

1.8 | Define: Discounts Allowed

Discounts Allowed is the amount our customers deduct when paying us. E.g. Our customers owe us $345. If they pay us $335 in full settlement of this debt, then $10 is the Discount we have allowed.

EXHIBIT
Transaction: Bought inventory from M Saleem $3400 on credit.
Step one: (Underline)

Bought inventory from M. Saleem $3400 on credit.
(Since the transaction is a credit transaction, M. Saleem's account will be affected. He is your creditor now.)

Step two: (Identify the class)
Inventory (Purchases account) is a real account
M. Saleem is a personal account

Step three: (decide which account is to be debited and which account is to be credited.)
The Purchases account is debited and M. Saleem's account is credited.

THE 'T' ACCOUNT:

EXHIBIT
Enter the following transactions in the Nominal ledger:
20XX
June 5   Paid rent $ 45 by cash
June 18 Paid rent $36 by cheque.
June 28 Received a rent refund $12 cash.

THE NOMINAL LEDGER

Rent Account					
Dr.			Cr.		
Date	Details	Amt.	Date	Details	Amt.
20xx		$	20xx		$
Jun5	Cash	45	Jun28	Cash (refund)	12
"18	Bank	36	"30	Balance c/d	69
		81			81
July 1	Balance b/d	69			

1.9 | What steps should be taken to balance a 'T' Account?

Steps to be taken to balance a 'T' account are:
—Total up the columns on the debit side (81) and the credit side (12).
—Write the totals at the top of the Amount columns in pencil on their respective sides (81 and 12).
—Write the bigger total (81)after leaving one line on the side that has more entries e.g. in this case the debit side has more entries.
—Draw the 'calculating line' (one horizontal line)above these totals and 'ruling out lines'(two horizontal lines) below them.
—Subtract the smaller of the two totals from the bigger one and write the difference on the side that has the smaller total – in this example: the credit side.
—Write the words 'Balance c/d' in the details space on the same line as this difference. The date in the date column will be that of the last day of that month/year.
—On the line after the 'ruling out' lines write the words 'Balance b/d' on the opposite side of the 'Balance c/d' in the

details column. In the amount column the amount that was to be carried down is to be written – in this example $69. In the date column the first day of the next period is to be written.

» EXERCISE 1.5
Enter the following transactions into the Sales ledger.

√*Tip:* *Remember that only credit transactions will appear in the Sales Ledger. Hence the cash transaction on July 5 will not be entered in the Sales Ledger.*

20XX
July 1   Sold inventory $390 on credit to M. Malik.
July 5   Sold inventory for cash $ 450.
July 7   M Malik returned inventory to us $30.
July 28 M. Malik paid us by cheque to settle the account after we gave him a cash discount of 10%.

√*Tip :* *Discounts allowed on July 28th = 10% x (390-30) = $..............*

M.Malik's A/C					
Dr.			Cr.		
Date	Details	Amt.	Date	Details	Amt.

» EXERCISE 1.6
Enter the following transactions in the Purchases Ledger.
2003

Jan 1   Bought inventory from Howie on credit $560.
Jan 5   Bought inventory from Janice for cash $340.
Jan 7   Bought inventory from Kasi on credit $400.
Jan 8   Returned inventory to Howie $12.
Jan 18   Returned inventory to Kasi $34.
Jan 25   Paid Howie $548 by cheque in full settlement of his account.

Howie's Account

Dr.			Cr.		
Date	Details	Amt.	Date	Details	Amt.

NOTE: The phrase 'in full settlement' means that the person (Howie in the transaction on Jan 25) does not owe any more money. Hence, the difference between what he owed and what he paid is a cash discount.

Kasi's Account

	Dr.			Cr.	
Date	Details	Amt.	Date	Details	Amt.

NOTE: When a proprietor injects money into a business, the Capital account is credited. When she withdraws money (or an asset) the Drawings account is debited.

» EXERCISE 1.7

Enter the following transactions in the Sales Ledger.

2003

Jan 1   Sold inventory to Homie on credit $500.
Jan 5   Sold inventory to Kim for cash $380.
Jan 7   Sold inventory to Kim on credit $500.
Jan 8   Homie returned inventory to us $32.
Jan 18   Kim returned inventory to us $36.
Jan 25   Homie paid us by cheque in full settlement of his account.

Homie's A/C

	Dr.			Cr.	
Date	Details	Amt.	Date	Details	Amt.

Kim's A/C

	Dr.			Cr.	
Date	Details	Amt.	Date	Details	Amt.

» EXERCISE 1.8

Enter the following transactions in the Rent A/c in the Nominal Ledger.

2004

June 3   Paid rent by cash $300.
June 7   Paid rent by cheque $280.
June 20 Received a rent refund $10 cash.

» EXERCISE 1.9

Enter the following transactions in the Purchases Ledger.

20x4

May 1   Bought inventory from Nina $350 on credit.
May 13   Bought inventory from Nina $450 paying by cheque.
May 20   Returned inventory worth $20 to Nina.
May 25   Bought inventory from Nina worth $700 on credit.
May 31   Paid Nina, on account, $300 by cheque.

NOTE : The phrase 'on account' means that the business still owes Nina money

» EXERCISE 1.10

Enter the following transactions in the Nominal Ledger. **20x5**

June 2   Paid insurance $340 by cheque.
June 7   Paid insurance $340 in cash.
June 27 Received refund $20, cash, from insurance company .

» EXERCISE 1.11

Open the necessary ledger accounts and post the following transactions to them. (Posting is the act of transferring data from one book to another)

20XX

May 1   The proprietor started his business with $7500 cash in the business bank account.
May 3 $ 1,300 cash was withdrawn from the bank for business use.
May 4   Bought a Motor Van for $4300 paying by cheque.
May 5   Bought Stationery paying by cash $25.
May 8   Sold inventory for cash $640.
May 9   Bought inventory on credit from Ali $350.
May 12   Goods worth $45 were returned by us to Ali.
May 14   Sold a car for $560 cash.
May 15   Bought inventory for cash $600.
May 18   Sold inventory to Mina on credit $370
May 21   Paid rent $50 by cheque.
May 25   Paid Salary by cheque $300.
May 26   The proprietor withdrew cash from the bank $250for his personal use.
May 28   Borrowed from Alice $650 cash.
May 30   Sold inventory for cash $ 600.

» EXERCISE 1.12

Open the necessary ledger accounts and post the following transactions to them.

20x6

Jan 1   The proprietor introduced $5600 cash into the business.
Jan 4 $4500 cash was deposited into the business bank account.
Jan 6   Bought furniture $780 from Juline on credit.
Jan 10   Took a loan from Abraham $2,300 in cash.
Jan 16   Paid salaries in cash $150.
Jan 20   Received $250 cash as commission.
Jan 25   Paid Abraham $2,300 cash in respect of loan owing to him.

Jan 26   Bought inventory $450 on credit from Kelly.
Jan 27   Returned inventory $50 to Kelly.
Jan 28   Sold inventory for cash $600.
Jan 29   Sold inventory on credit to Larry $670.
Jan 30   Larry returned inventory worth $50.
Jan 31   Larry paid us $600 by cheque for goods bought on Jan 29.

Points to remember:
- *Put yourself in the place of a business, not a customer or supplier when you are recording transactions.*
- *A full entry on the debit or credit side should contain the date, details and the amount.*
- *Two entries are required per transaction, one is made on the debit side and one on the credit side of their respective accounts.*

1.1   Multiple Choice questions

i) Manny, a trader, sold inventory to Ace and company on credit. Which entries in Manny's books record this transaction?

	Debit account	Credit account
A	Sales	Ace and company
B	Sales	Manny
C	Manny	Sales
D	Ace and company	Sales

ii) Manny, a trader, sold some used furniture to Ace and company on credit. Which entries in Manny's books record this?

	Debit account	Credit account
A	Ace and company	Sales
B	Manny	Sales
C	Manny	Furniture
D	Ace and company	Furniture

iii) Manny, a trader, deposits cash into his business bank account. Which entries record this in his books?

	Debit account	Credit account
A	Cash	Bank
B	Bank	Capital
C	Bank	Cash
D	Drawings	Cash

iv) Manny, a trader, receives $450 as rent from Wilma in cash. Which entries record this in Wilma's books?

	Debit account	Credit account
A	Cash	Rent
B	Cash	Rent receivable
C	Rent	Cash
D	Drawings	Cash

v) Manny, a trader, purchases inventory from Ace and Company, paying by cheque. Which entries record this in Manny's books?

	Debit account	Credit account
A	Bank	Goods
B	Bank	Purchases
C	Purchases	Bank
D	Purchases	Ace and company

1.2   For each of the following transactions, decide which account will be debited and which account will be credited.
20XX

May 1   The proprietor started his business with $6000 cash in the business bank account.
May 3 $ 2500 cash was deposited into the bank.
May 4   Bought a car for $450 paying by cheque.
May 5   Bought stationery paying by cash $34.
May 8   Sold inventory for cash $600.
May 9   Bought inventory on credit from Mason $200.
May 12   Goods worth $45 were returned by us to Mason.
May 14   Sold some old furniture for $340 cash.
May 15   Bought inventory for cash $540.
May 18   Sold inventory to Neena on credit $340
May 21   Paid rent $46 by cheque.
May 25   Paid Salary by cheque $450.
May 26   The proprietor withdrew cash from the bank $380 for his personal use.
May 28   Borrowed from Glenn $ 500 cash.
May 30   Sold inventory for cash $ 750.

1.3   Draw up Ledger Accounts for the following transactions. First fill in the debit and credit columns. (The first one is done for you):

20XX		DEBIT	CREDIT
May 1	The Proprietor invested $6900 by cheque in the business.	Bank	Capital
May 3	Bought inventory from L. Larry $670 on credit		
May 5	Sold inventory to Kelly $780 on credit		
May 7	Returned inventory to L. Larry $45.		
May10	Sold inventory and deposited the money in the bank $890.		
May17	Bought stationery for $76 paying by cheque.		
May20	Kelly returned inventory worth $89 to us.		
May24	We paid L. Larry by cheque in full settlement.		
May27	Kelly paid us by cheque what she owes us.		
May29	Paid wages $ 67 by cheque.		
May31	The proprietor withdrew $40 from the bank for his personal use.		

The Trial Balance

2.1 | What is a 'Trial Balance'?

The Trial Balance is a statement of accounts' names and their balances recorded in Debit and Credit columns as on a particular day.

2.2 | What are the uses of a Trial Balance?

A Trial Balance is used to check the accuracy of the books of accounts : that for every debit entry there was a corresponding credit entry recorded.

2.3 | What are the reasons why a Trial Balance does not balance sometimes?

If the Trial Balance does not Balance i.e. the debit side total exceeds that of the credit side and vice versa, then it may be due to the following errors:
1) An error in calculation.
2) Recording a debit entry and not recording the corresponding credit entry.
3) Recording one figure in the debit entry and a different one in the credit entry.

NOTE: A debit balance in a personal account means that that person or business owes the business money and is a *debtor*.
A credit balance in a personal account means that that person or business is owed money and is a *creditor*.

EXHIBIT
The following is an example of a trial balance.

Trial balance as at 31st May 20XX	Dr	Cr
	$	$
Capital		6900
Cash	6308	
Purchases	670	
Sales		1670
Stationery	76	
Return Outwards		145
Return Inwards	89	
Wages	67	
Drawings	40	
Bank	1465	
	8715	8715

NOTE:
1) Kelly's and Larry's accounts do not appear in the trial balance since their accounts were closed.
2) The balances on accounts in the Purchases Ledger (suppliers' account credit balances) are listed and totalled separately; the total is entered in the Trial Balance as Trade Payables.
3) The balances on accounts in the Sales Ledger (customers' debit balances) are listed and totalled separately; the total is entered in the Trial Balance as Trade Receivables.

√**Tip** If the Balance b/d was on the debit side then it is called a debit balance and should appear on the debit side of the Trial Balance.

√**Tip** If the Balance b/d was on the credit side of the account, then it is called a credit balance and should appear on the credit side of the Trial Balance.

» EXERCISE 2.1

Decide whether the following items will appear in the debit or credit column of the Trial Balance (the first one is done for you):

Solution:

Purchases	Debit
Sales revenue	
Return outwards	
Cash	
Drawings	
Capital	
Trade receivable	
Trade payable	
Motor Van	
Rent	
Discounts allowed	
Return inwards	
Carriage outwards	
Rent receivable	
Carriage inwards	
Bank overdraft	
Stationery	
Opening Inventory	

NOTE:
1) Closing inventory **does not** appear in a trial balance.
2) 'Bank' will be either a debit balance or a credit balance. This is due to the fact that certain banks offer an overdraft facility whereby the firm can withdraw more than they have deposited. Cash, however, can never be a credit balance since one cannot pay off cash that one does not have. Cash is tangible and one cannot have a negative 'tangible'.

» EXERCISE 2.2
Draw up ledger accounts for the following transactions. Balance the accounts and with the balances, draw up a trial balance.
20x6

December 1	The proprietor introduced $6,000 cash into the business.
December 2	Deposited $1,000 cash in the bank.
December 4	Bought Inventory $450 paying by cash.
December 12	Bought Inventory $340 paying by cheque.
December 16	Bought Inventory $200 on credit from Jacques and sons.
December 20	Returned Inventory to Jacques and sons $30.
December 22	Paid Jacques and sons $100, on account in cash.
December 25	Paid salaries $2,000 in cash.
December 26	Deposited $500 cash in the bank.
December 27	Bought a Typewriter paying $600 by cheque.
December 29	Paid rent $370 by cheque.
December 30	Bought Inventory $600 from Jacques on credit.
December 31	Paid Jacques and sons $200, on account in cash.

» EXERCISE 2.3
The following balances have been extracted at 31st December 20x5 from Hema's books.

	$
Purchases	45,000
Sales revenue	100,000
Trade receivable	6,000
Trade payable	2,000
Sales returns	1,600
Purchases returns	1,780
Salaries	5,500
Rent receivable	3,400
Advertising	10,000
Rent	11,000
Postage and Stationery	340
Discounts allowed	460
Discounts received	550
Fixtures and fittings	34,500
Machinery	25,000
Bank	12,000
Drawings	23,000
Land and Buildings	112,000
Delivery Van	36,700
Inventory at 1st December 20x5	24,000
Inventory at 31st December 20x5	34,000
Capital	?

Required:
Prepare a Trial Balance at 31st December 20x5 from the balances extracted from Hema's books and calculate the balance on her Capital Account (It is the difference between the debit and credit columns.)

» EXERCISE 2.4
The following balances have been extracted at 31st December 20x4 from Hesham's books.

	$
Purchases	56,000
Sales revenue	90,000
Trade payable	12,000
Trade receivable	14,000
Sales returns	2,600
Purchases returns	780
Salaries	3,400
Rent receivable	1,200
Advertising	11,000
Rent	12,000
Postage and Stationery	1,340
Discounts allowed	420
Discounts received	450
Fixtures and fittings	45,000
Machinery	27,000
Bank	22,000
Drawings	20,000
Land and Buildings	104,000
Delivery Van	26,900

	$
Inventory at 1st December 20x4	25,000
Inventory at 31st December 20x4	55,000
Capital	?

Required:
Prepare a Trial Balance at 31st December 20x4 from the balances extracted from Hesham's books and calculate the balance on his Capital Account.

2.4 |Why is closing inventory not entered in a trial balance?

Closing inventory consists of inventory bought during the year that remained unsold. Hence, it is already included in purchases in the trial balance.

2.5 |When would closing inventory be included in the trial balance?

When a trial balance is prepared after the preparation of the trading account.

2.1| Multiple Choice questions

i) Which of the following accounts will normally have a credit balance?
a) Trade payable
b) Stationery
c) Drawings
d) Purchases

ii) Which of the following accounts will normally have a debit balance?
a) Capital
b) Rent
c) Rent receivable
d) Purchases returns

iii) Which of the following errors do NOT affect the Trial Balance?
a) An error in calculation.
b) Recording a debit entry and not recording the corresponding credit entry.
c) Recording one figure in the debit entry and a different one in the credit entry.
d) An account that should have been debited has been credited and the account that should have been credited has been debited.

2.2| An inexperienced bookkeeper has extracted a Trial Balance at 31st December 20x2 from Eric's books. It contains some errors and does not balance.

	Dr	Cr
	$	$
Purchases		45,000
Sales revenue	34,000	
Trade payable	32,000	
Trade receivable		54,000
Sales returns	1,560	
Purchases returns	670	
Salaries		1,200
Rent receivable	3,400	
Advertising		14,000
Rent	22,000	
Postage and Stationery		2,140
Discounts allowed	220	
Discounts received	400	
Fixtures and fittings		50,000
Machinery	34,000	
Bank overdraft	12,000	
Drawings		19,000
Land and Buildings	84,000	
Delivery Van		25,500
Inventory at 1st December 20x4	20,000	
Inventory at 31st December 20x4	35,000	
Capital	290,150	
	569,400	210,840

Required

Re-write the Trial Balance and correct the errors so that it balances.

2.3| What is a trial balance?

....

....

....

....

Books Of Prime Entry

3.1 | What is meant by the term ' books of prime entry'?

These are books into which the first entries are made immediately after the transaction has taken place and *before* they are entered in the ledger . They are also known as 'books of original entry' or 'subsidiary books'. There are separate books for different kinds of transactions. E.g. Credit sales will be entered into the sales journal, a book of prime entry.

3.2 | What details would normally appear in such books?

Normally, the date, details, a cross-reference and the amount will appear in such books.

3.3 | Name the different types of books of prime entry.

The Books of Prime entry are:
a) The Sales Journal
b) The Purchases Journal
c) The Sales Returns Journal
d) The Purchases Returns Journal
e) The Cash Book
f) The General Journal.
g) The Petty Cash Book

3.4 | Outline two uses of subsidiary books.

The uses of Subsidiary books are:
a) They are used to enter transactions that occur very often during the course of a business day. Hence, the ledgers are saved from being cluttered with too many insignificant details. Only the totals are posted into the Nominal ledger at the end of the month.
b) They save frequent trips to the ledger.

3.5 | Write a short note on the 'Sales journal'.

The sales journal is also known as the 'Sales Day Book'. Only credit sales are entered in this book. The entries are made from copies of the sales invoices sent to customers. The rulings of a sales journal are:

Date	Name/Details	Invoice number	Folio	Amount
				$

The date on which the transaction occurred is entered in the date column. The name of the debtor (customer) is entered in the name/details column. The number of the sales invoice is entered in the invoice number column. The page number on which the Customer's account appears in the Sales ledger is entered in the folio column. The amount (net of trade discount) is entered in the amount column.

3.6 | How is double entry completed when a credit sale takes place?

When a credit sale takes place, the customer's account is debited in the Sales ledger. At the end of the month, the *total* of the Sales journal is credited to the Sales account in the Nominal Ledger. This total forms the double entry for all the individual debit entries in the personal accounts (in the Sales ledger).

3.7 | Write a short note on the 'Sales Returns Journal'.

The 'Sales Returns journal' is also known as the 'Returns Inwards Journal'. Details of goods returned by credit customers are entered in this journal. It is written up from copies of credit notes sent to the customers for goods they have returned. The rulings of a return inwards journal are:

Date	Name/Details	Note number	Folio	Amount
				$

The date column records the date of the transaction, the details column records the name of the customer, the note number column records the number of the credit note, the folio column records the page number of the sales ledger on which the customer's account is maintained and the amount column records the amount of the credit note (net of trade discount).

3.8 | Why do customers return inventory?

Goods are returned for any of the following reasons:
a) The inventory was damaged.
b) The inventory was the wrong colour.
c) The inventory was of the wrong size.
d) The inventory was faulty.
e) The customer ordered more than he needed.

3.9 | How is double entry completed when goods are returned by customers?

When the inventory is returned, the personal account of the customer is credited (in the sales ledger). At the end of the month, the total of the sales returns journal is debited to the sales returns (or returns inwards) account in the nominal ledger. The total forms the double entry for all the individual credit entries in the personal accounts.

3.10 | Write a short note on 'The Purchases Journal'.

The Purchases Journal is also known as the Purchases Day Book'. Only credit purchases are entered in this book. The entries are made from copies of the invoices received from suppliers. The rulings of a purchases journal are:

Date	Name/Details	Invoice number	Folio	Amount
				$

The date on which the transaction occurred is entered in the date column. The name of the creditor (supplier) is entered in the name/details column. The number of the invoice is entered in the invoice number column. The page number on which the supplier's account appears in the Purchases ledger is entered in the folio column. The amount (net of trade discount) is entered in the amount column.

3.11 | How is double entry completed when a credit purchase takes place?

When a credit purchase takes place, the supplier's account is credited in the Purchases ledger. At the end of the month, the *total* of the Purchases journal is debited to the Purchases Account in the Nominal Ledger. This total forms the double entry for all the individual credit entries in the personal accounts (in the Purchases ledger).

3.12 | Write a short note on the 'Purchases Returns Journal'.

The Purchases Returns Journal is also known as the Returns Outwards Journal. Details of inventory returned by the business to its suppliers are entered in this journal. It is written up from copies of credit notes received from suppliers or debit notes sent to suppliers, for inventory returned to them. The rulings of a returns outwards journal are: The date column records the date of the transaction, the details column records the name of the supplier, the note number column records the number of the credit note, the folio column records the page number of the purchases ledger on which the supplier's account is maintained and the amount column records the amount of the credit (or debit) note (net of trade discount).

Date	Name/Details	Note number	Folio	Amount
				$

3.13 | Name the business documents that are used to make entries in the following books of prime entry:

a) The Sales Journal
b) The Purchases Journal
c) The Sales Returns journal
d) The Purchases Returns journal

a) The source documents used to make entries in the Sales Journal are the sales invoices.
b) The sources documents used to make entries in the Purchases Journal are the purchases invoices.
c) The source documents used to make entries in the Sales Returns journal are the credit notes made out by the supplier receiving the returned goods.
d) The source documents used to make entries in the Purchases Returns journal are the credit notes received by the customer from the supplier or debit notes sent to suppliers.

3.14 | What is meant by the term 'posting'?

'Posting' is the act of using one book to transfer entries into another book.

NOTE: 1. Columns for Folio or Invoice number need not be included, if not specifically asked for.
2. Cash discounts are never entered in journals.

EXHIBIT:
Enter up the sales, purchases, the return inwards and the return outwards journals from the following details. Then post the items to the relevant accounts in the sales and purchases ledgers. The total of the journals should then be posted to the relevant accounts in the Nominal ledger.

20x3

June 1   Credit purchases: Susie $ 320, Aimee $150.
June 4   Credit sales: Jason $350, Mason $480.
June 7   Inventory returned to Susie $20
June 15 Inventory returned by Mason $60.
June 20 Credit sales: Mason $600.
June 28 Credit purchases: Susie $ 180.

Sales Journal

Date 20x3	Name	Invoice number	Folio	Amount $
June 4	Jason	xxx	SL 6	350
4	Mason	xxx	SL 8	480
20	Mason	xxx	SL8	600
			GL4	1,430

Purchases Journal

Date 20x3	Name	Invoice number	Folio	Amount $
June 1	Susie	xxx	PL16	320
1	Aimee	xxx	PL6	150
28	Susie	xxx	PL16	180
			GL7	650

Sales Returns Journal

Date 20x3	Name	Note number	Folio	Amount $
June 15	Mason	xxx	SL8	60
			GL6	60

Purchases Returns Journal

Date 20x3	Name	Note number	Folio	Amount $
June 7	Smith	xxx	PL16	20
			GL9	20

Sales Ledger

Date	Details	Debit	Credit	Balance
20x3	Jason's A/c (page 6)	$	$	$
June4	Sales	350		350(dr)
	Mason's A/c (page 8)			
June 4	Sales	480		480(dr)
15	Sales Returns		60	420(dr)
20	Sales	600		1,020(dr)

Purchases Ledger

Date	Details	Debit	Credit	Balance
20x3	Susie's A/c (page 16)	$	$	$
June1	Purchases		320	320(cr)
7	Purchases returns	20		300(cr)
28	Purchases		180	480(cr)
	Aimee's A/c (page 6)			
June 1	Purchases		150	150(cr)

General Ledger

Date	Details	Debit	Credit	Balance
20x3	Sales A/c (page 4)	$	$	$
June30	Total for the month		1,430	1,430(cr)
	Purchases a/c (page7)			
June 30	Total for the month	650		650(dr)
	Sales Returns a/c (page 6)			
June 30	Total for the month	60		60(dr)
	Purchases Returns a/c (page 9)			
June 30	Total for the month		20	20(cr)

NOTE : The above ledger Accounts are maintained in the 'Running Balance Method' - an alternate method to the 'T' Account method. Either method can be used in a business' ledgers.

» EXERCISE 3.1

Enter up the Purchases Journal and the Purchases Returns Journal from the following details. Then post to the Suppliers' accounts and show the transfers to the General ledger.

20x8

January 1   Credit purchases: Kasie $350, Selwyn $670
January 4   Credit purchases: Mala $270, Kelly $500.
January 8   Goods returned by us to the following: Kasie $60, Mala $70.
January 11 Credit purchases: Piper $680, Kasie $350.
January 27 Goods returned by us to the following: Piper $70.
January 30   Credit purchases : Piper $370.

» EXERCISE 3.2

Sambo is a sole trader who buys and sells on credit. His transactions for the month of August 20x7 include the following:

Date	Transaction	Customer's name	Amount($)
August 3	Inventory sold	Ace & co.	1,000
August 7	Inventory sold	Ali & Sons	450
August 14	Inventory returned	Ali & sons	50
August 25	Inventory sold	M. Ebrahim	2,000
August 29	Inventory returned	M. Ebrahim	300

Required:

a) Enter the transactions in Sambo's Sales Journal and Sales Return Journal and show the totals for the month.

b) Make the necessary entries in the ledger accounts.

» EXERCISE 3.3

Enter up the Sales Journal and the Sales Returns Journal from the following details. Then post to the customer's accounts and show the transfers to the General Ledger.

20x8

May 1   Credit sales to: Madan $230, Leo $670.

May 5   Credit sales to: Pete $260, Leslie $760

May 10   Inventory returned to us by: Leo $35

May 15   Credit sales to: Madan $500, Leo $290

May 23   Inventory returned to us by: Leslie $38.

May 25   Inventory returned to us by : Madan $56.

» EXERCISE 3.4

Enter up the Purchases and Purchases Returns Journals from the details that follow. Then post to the supplier's accounts and show the transfers to the General Ledger:

20x5

June 3   Credit purchases from: M. Kelly $560, Llyod $700.

June 8   Credit purchases from: June $230, Avril $670.

June 15   Inventory returned by us to: Llyod $36.

June 23   Inventory returned by us to; Avril $70.

June 24   Credit purchases from M. Kelly $700

THE THREE COLUMN CASH BOOK

3.15 | What is a Cash Book?

A cash book is a book of prime entry that acts as a ledger account for cash and bank transactions. The receipt of cash and cheques are recorded on the debit side and payments by cash and cheques are recorded on the credit side.

3.16 | What is meant by contra entries?

Contra entries, for cash book items, are where both the debit and the credit entries are shown in the cash book. E.g. $450 cash is withdrawn from the bank for business use: Cash account will be debited in the cash column and bank account will be credited in the bank column of the cash book.

3.17 | Is it possible for the cash column to have a closing credit balance?

This is not possible, since cash is tangible and one can only pay in cash when one has cash in hand. There is no such thing as negative cash.

Exhibit

The three column cash book has a column to record discounts. Discounts received are recorded on the credit side and discounts allowed on the debit side. The format is: Dr

Discounts allowed/received account											Cr
Dt	Details	F	Dis	Cash	Bank	Dt	Details	F	Dis	Cash	Bank

3.18 | What is the difference between the discount columns and the cash and bank columns?

The entries in the discount columns are not a part of double entry and have to be posted to the relevant accounts in the general ledger at the end of the period; whereas the entries in the cash and bank columns are part of double entry and do not have to be posted.

3.19 | What is the difference between a cash discount and a trade discount?

A trade discount is given to customers who buy in bulk, are loyal customers. or are in the same line of work. It is a reduction on the selling price and is given to enable the customer to make a profit. It appears in an invoice but not in the books of account.

A Cash discount is a reduction given at the time of payment of a debt. It is a percentage of the debt owing and given for prompt payment. It is usually mentioned in an invoice to encourage prompt payments. It is recorded in the books of accounts, either as 'Discounts received' – a benefit and therefore treated as income; or 'Discounts allowed' – a cost of debt collection and therefore treated as an expense.

Exhibit:

Mohammed started business on 1st June 20x8 with a capital of $4,500 deposited into the business bank account. Transactions for the month of June 20x8 were as follows:

20x8

June 5   Purchased **furniture** paying by cheque $2,000

June 8   Withdrew $650 cash from bank for business use.

June 10   Received cheque for $450 from Kao and paid it into the bank account.

June 15   Cash sales paid into bank $380

June 17   Paid Mabu by cheque $355 in full settlement of his account of $370

June 22   Cheque of $450 paid into bank on June 10th was returned dishonoured by the bank.

June 26   Received cash of $240 from Cally in full settlement of her account of $250.

Required:

a) Write up Mohammed's three column cash book for June 20x8. Balance the cash and bank columns and bring down the balances on July 1st 20x8.

Solution:

Date	Details	Folio	Dis	Cash	Bank	Date	Details	Folio	Dis	Cash	Bank
20x8			$	$	$	20x8			$	$	$
Jun1	Capital				4,500	Jun5	Furniture				2,000
Jun 8	Bank	c		650		Jun 8	Cash	c			650
Jun10	Kao				450	Jun17	Mabu		15		355
Jun15	Sales				380	Jun22	Kao				450
Jun26	Cally		10	240		Jun30	Bal c/d			890	1925
			10	890	5,330				15	890	5330
Jul 1	Bal b/d			890	1,925						

b) Mohammed is not sure how to treat the discount columns.

1. State to which ledger account, and to which side of that account, the total of the Discount column on the debit side (discounts allowed) is posted.

Ans. The total of the Discounts allowed column, $10, is to be transferred to the Debit side of the Discounts Allowed account in the Nominal Ledger.

2. State to which ledger account, and to which side of that account, the total of the Discount column on the credit side (discounts received) is posted.

Ans. The total of the Discounts received column, $15, is to be transferred to the **Credit side** of the **Discounts Received** account in the **Nominal Ledger.**

» EXERCISE 3.5

Frank maintains a three column cash book to record all cash and bank transactions. Balances at 1st July 20x6 were:

	$
Bank	2,300
Cash in hand	500

His transactions for the month of July were as follows;

July 3   Received and banked a cheque from Jason in full settlement of his account of $100 after deducting cash discount of 5%

July 5   Cash sales banked $600.

July 10 Frank brought further capital in cash $3,000. Paid cheques in full settlement of accounts owing to Gardener $600 and Mayor $400, in each case deducting 2% cash discount.

July 16 Paid rent in cash $200. Cash banked $350.

July 20 Paid wages by cheque $100. Paid motor repairs in cash $270

July 22 Cash sales $1, 230

July 25 Received and banked cheque for $560 from Nasreen in full settlement of her account of $600 after deducting cash discount.

July 30 Frank withdrew $600 by cheque for personal use.

Required:

a) Record the above transactions in Frank's three column cash book. Bring down the cash and bank balances at 1st August 20x6.

b) Total the discount columns and show how the relevant discounts accounts would appear in the General Ledger at 31st July 20x6.

c) Explain why only the totals of the Discounts Received and Discount allowed are posted in these accounts.

√Tip: When 'cr' accompanies the opening bank balance , it means that the bank balance is an overdraft.

» EXERCISE 3.6

A three-column cash book is to be written up from the following details, balanced off, and the relevant discount accounts in the Nominal ledger drawn up.

20x7

June 1   Balances brought forward: Cash $3,000; Bank $200.

June 2   The following paid their accounts by cheque, in each case deducting 2% cash discounts: S.Nimble $500; G. Harper $600.

June 5   Paid salaries by cheque $400.

June 8   Mason lent us cash $270.

June 9   We paid the following accounts by cheque in each case deducting a 5% cash discount: J. Monto $300; L Lissom $700.

June 11 Withdrew $50 from the bank for business use.

June 14 I. Moony paid his account of $450, by cheque $430, deducting a cash discount of $20.

June 20 Cash banked $500.

June 25 Paid repairs to Motor van $250 in cash.

June 29 Received commission by cheque $450.

» EXERCISE 3.7

Dolly maintains a three column cash book to record all cash and bank transactions. Balances at 1st July 20x6:

	$
Bank overdraft	1,500
Cash in hand	2,550

Her transactions for the month of July were as follows:

July 5   Received and banked a cheque from Jan in full settlement of his account of $500 after deducting cash discount of 2%

July 8 Cash sales banked $700.

July 15 Dolly paid further capital into bank $5,500. Paid cheques in full settlement of accounts owing to Henry $800 and Miron $500, in each case deducting 2% cash discount.

July 18 Paid rent in cash $600
Cash banked $300.

July 20 Paid wages by cheque $300
Paid motor repairs in cash $130.

July 22 Received and banked cheque for $370 from

Nena in full settlement of her account of $400 after deducting cash discount.

July 30 Dolly withdrew $590 by cheque for business use.

Required:

a. **Record the above transactions in Dolly's three column cash book. Bring down the cash and bank balances at 1st August 20x6.**

b. **Total the discount columns and show how the relevant discounts accounts would appear in the General Ledger at 31st July 20x6.**

EXERCISE 3.8

A three-column cash book is to be written up from the following details, balanced off, and the relevant discount accounts in the Nominal ledger drawn up.

20x4

June 1 Balances brought forward: Cash $5,000; Bank overdraft $1,500.

June 2 The following paid their accounts by cheque, in each case deducting 5% cash discounts: Barry $2000 Polly $800.

June 5 Paid salaries by cheque $400.

June 8 Molly lent us cash $350.

June 9 We paid the following accounts by cheque in each case deducting a 2% cash discount: Lopez $4000 Koley $500.

June 11 Withdrew cash from bank $350.

June 14 Murthy paid his account of $360, by cheque $354, deducting a cash discount of $6.

June 20 Cash banked $400.

June 25 Paid repairs to Motor van $340 in cash.

June 29 Received commission by cheque $430.

THE GENERAL JOURNAL

3.20| What is meant by the term General Journal

The General Journal or, simply, the Journal, is a book of prime entry. It collects entries that cannot be entered in the other books of prime entry i.e. the Sales Journal, the Purchases Journal, the Sales Returns journal, the Purchases Returns Journal etc. The journal is a kind of diary and by recording a transaction in the journal, we know what account has been debited and which account has been credited. A narrative that follows each journal entry gives a description and explanation of the transaction. The journal is ruled like this:

Date	Details	Debit	Credit
		$	$

3.21| What are the uses of the General Journal?

The Uses of the General Journal or 'The Journal', as it is often referred to, are:

1) To write off Irrecoverable debts.
2) To record the purchasing and sale of items other than inventory on credit
3) To pass opening entries needed to open a new set of books.
4) To correct errors
5) Transfers between accounts and adjustments to accounts

EXHIBIT:

July 23, 20x5: An irrecoverable debt of $600 in 20x4 is now recovered in cash from the debtor S. Shetty. Pass the required journal entries to record this .

Date	Details	Debit	Credit
20x5		$	$
July 23	S. Shetty's Account	600	
	Irrecoverable Debts Recovered		600
July 23	Cash	600	
	S. Shetty's account		600
	(Being a irrecoverable debt now recovered)		

Tip: The amount in the Irrecoverable Debt Recovered Account is deducted from the irrecoverable debts account in the Income statement.

3.22| What is the entry passed in the Journal when a fixed asset is bought on credit?

The asset account is debited and the creditor's account is credited.

3.23| Name and explain the errors that do not affect the trial balance agreement.

Errors that do not affect the trial balance agreement are:

a) Errors of omission – Where a transaction is completely omitted from the books. E.g. The firm sold inventory $500 to Jerry, but did not enter it either in the sales account or Jerry's personal account. A correction entry would be to simply pass the original entry. In this case it would be: Debit Jerry's account and credit sales account with $500.

b) Errors of commission – This type is when the correct amount is entered in the wrong person's account. However, the error involves the same class of account. E.g. Where a sale of $100 to L Dan's entered in the account of M. Dan (note that both are personal accounts). Since we should have debited L. Dan we will now do that- Debit L Dan's account; and Credit M. Dan's account to cancel the wrong debit.

c) Errors of principle – This is when an item is entered in the wrong class of account. E.g Repairs to a motor van are debited to motor van account. 'Repairs' is a nominal account, whereas 'motor van' is a real account. To correct the error, we will Debit Repairs and Credit motor van account.

d) Compensating errors – This is when errors cancel each other out. E.g. When the sales account is overcast by $100 and the salary account is also overcast by $100. In such a case we will Debit the sales account to reduce the total sales and Credit the salary account with $100 to reduce the total purchases.

e) Errors of original entry – Where the original figure was incorrect. E.g. an error was made when totaling the amount of a purchases invoice as $340 instead of $430. This wrong figure was used to make a double entry. In this case we will Debit purchases with $90 in order to increase total purchases and Credit the supplier's account with $90 in order to increase our debt to her by $90.

f) Errors of complete reversal of entries – This happens when the correct amounts are used but entries are made on the wrong side of the accounts concerned. E.g. Samson paid us$350 by cheque and we debited Samson and credited bank. In order to correct this error we will now Debit Bank with $500 (250 x 2) and Credit Samson with $500, too. The amount is doubled in order to cancel out the original error and then to pass the correct entry.

g) Errors of Transposition – This is when the individual digits in a number are entered in a wrong sequence. E.g. We have debited bank and credited Massey's account with $450 instead of $540. In such a case it is important to firstly calculate the difference and then pass the journal entry with the difference. If the figure is more than that which should have been used then we pass an entry opposite to the one originally passed, if the figure is less than the original one, as in the example above, then we pass the same entry with the difference. We will thus Debit bank with $90, the difference and Credit Massey's account with $ 90.

» EXERCISE 3.9

Show the journal entries necessary to correct the following errors.
a) The purchase of furniture $6,700, had been entered in error in the furniture repairs account.
b) Discounts Allowed $400 had been entered in error on the debit side of the Discounts Received account.
c) Extra capital of $ 2000 paid into the bank had been credited to the Sales account.

d) Inventory taken for own use $760 had been debited to General Expenses .
e) Bank charges $35 had been debited to Salary account.
f) A purchase of inventory $123 had been entered in error on the debit side of the Drawings account.
g) A sale of $390 to Bella had been entered in the books, both debit and credit as $930.
h) Cash paid to S Rainer $60 entered on the debit side of the cash book and the credit side of S. Rainer's account.

» EXERCISE 3.10

Show the journal entries necessary to correct the following errors.
a) The purchase of machinery on credit from Gala Ltd. for $9800 had been completely omitted from our books.
b) The payment for repairs to the furniture $350 had been entered in error in the furniture account.
c) Goods taken for own use $30 have been debited to Purchases account and credited to drawings
d) Private insurance $100 had been debited to Insurance account.
e) Returns inwards $178 from Hadi had been entered in error in Ali's account.
f) A purchase of $350 from Kella had been entered in error, both debit and credit as $530.
g) Cash drawings of $500 had been credited to the bank column of the cash book.
h) A purchase of inventory from Norman $370 had been entered in the books as $730.

Exercise 3.11

Which of the following items would be posted from the books of prime entry to the ledgers if the business maintains a sales journal, a purchases journal, a general journal and a cash book?

a. A provision for doubtful debts
b. The writing off of an irrecoverable debt
c. Interest charged on overdue accounts
d. Discounts received

3.1| Multiple-Choice Questions

i) Maureen bought inventory from Frank at a list price of $4,500. Frank allows Maureen a Trade Discount of 2% and a Cash Discount of 10%, if Maureen paid within a month. Maureen did pay Frank within a month. What was the amount Maureen entered in her Purchases Journal?

A) $90
B) $4410
C) $441
D) $3969

ii) John sold inventory to Gayatri $450 on credit. He debited Gaya's account incorrectly but credited Sales correctly. Which journal entry should be passed to correct this error?

	Account to be debited	Account to be credited
A)	John $450	Gayatri $450
B)	Gayatri $450	Gaya $450
C)	Gayatri $900	Gaya $900
D)	Gaya $450	Gayatri $450

iii) Ebrahim received $345 cash in full settlement of a debt owing to him by Hussein of $350. How should this be recorded in Ebrahim's books?

	Account/s to be debited	Account/s to be credited
A)	Cash $345	Hussein $345
B)	Cash $345	
	Discounts Allowed $5	Hussein $350
C)	Hussein $345 Cash $345	
D)	Hussein $350 Cash $345	
	Discounts Received $5	

iv) Jim paid Agatha $230 by cheque. Agatha debited Jim's Account $230 and credited her bank account with $230 in error. Which of the following entries will correct this error?

	Account debited	Account credited
A)	Jim $230	Bank $230
B)	Jim $460	Bank $460
C)	Bank $460	Jim $460
D)	Bank $230	Jim $230

v) Sherman discovered that he had totaled his Sales Invoice to Malini incorrectly as $321 instead of $231. Which of the following entries should he pass to correct this error?

	Account to be debited	Account to be credited
A)	Malini $90	Sales $90
B)	Malini $231	Sales $231
C)	Sales $90	Malini $90
D)	Sales $ 231	Malini $231

The following exercise 3.2 is optional . Though the petty cash book is not listed in the AS syllabus, it is a good idea to know what a petty cash book is.

3.2| Balance and then restore:

Imprest amount $ 200

Extract of a Petty Cash Book

Receipts	Date	Details	Total	Expenses 1	Expenses 2
$	20XX		$	$	$
150	May 1	Bal b/d			
50	May 1	Cash			
4	May 25	Telephone call			
		Sundry expenses	170	100	70
			170	100	70
	May 31	Balance c/d			
	June 1	Balance b/d			
	June 1	Cash			

3.3| Madeline Jones has discovered the following:

a) Machinery was purchased from Jones &Co. for $4,600 but no entry has been made in Madeline's books.

b) $350 paid for Motor van has been wrongly debited to Purchases account

c) A cheque for $2,600 received from Sami has been debited to Sami's account and entered on the credit side of the cash book, in error.

Required: Prepare entries required in Madeline's Journal regarding each of the above matters. Narratives are required.

3.4| Draw up a three column cash book from the following information:

20x9

		$
June 1	Balances brought down from May :	
	Cash	200
	Bank	1,500
	Trade receivable accounts:	
	Mason	400
	Popcey	2,000
	Abraham	800
	Trade payable accounts:	
	Sulaiman	500
	Ali	400
June 3	Mason pays us by cheque	380
June 5	We pay Ali cash	384
June 10	We withdraw cash from bank for business use	400
June 15	Abraham pays us his account in cash	787
June 22	We pay salaries by cheque	300
June 25	We pay Sulaiman cash	479
June 29	Popcey pays us by cheque	1,982

3.5| Enter the sales and return inwards journal from the following details. Then post to the customer's accounts and show the transfers to the general ledger.

20x6

July 2   Credit sales to: Popsee $500, Omega & Sons $350, Preeti $260

July 3   Credit sales to: Manika Ltd. $2,000, Kesri & sons $670.

July 14   Inventory returned to us by: Omega & Sons $34, Kesri & sons $29.

July 26   Inventory returned to us by: Manika Ltd. $250.

July 27   Credit sales to: Popsee $700, Preeti $700

3.6| On 1st August 20x5 Milly sold goods on credit to Kelly, a new customer, for $1,200.

On 12th August 20x5, Kelly returned $300 worth of the goods . Milly made an allowance to Kelly for their cost.

a) Complete the following boxes to show in Kelly's books:

(I)The names of the business documents

(II)The books of prime entry used to record the above transactions.

		(I)	(II)
Date 20x5	Transaction	Business document to be used by Kelly	Kelly's prime entry book
August 1	Inventory bought		
August 12	Inventory returned		

b) On 22nd August 20x5, Kelly paid Milly the amount she owed for the above transactions by cheque, claiming a cash discount of 2%.

How much did Kelly pay? Show your workings.

....

....

....

....

....

Income Statements of Sole Traders

4.1 | What is meant by the term 'Financial Statements'?

The Financial Statements consist of:
1) The Trading Account section of the Income Statement.
2) The Profit and Loss Account section of the Income Statement.
3) The Statement of Financial position.
They are usually drawn up from the Trial Balance. These Accounts are prepared at the end of a financial period, usually, a year.

4.2 | What is meant by the 'Income Statement' or 'Statement of comprehensive Income'?

This is a 'profit calculation account' split into two:
1) The Trading Account in which the Gross Profit or Gross Loss is calculated.
2) The Profit & Loss Account in which the profit (or loss) for the year are calculated.
The Trading Account starts with Sales and ends with Gross Profit. Where the cost of sales is larger than sales, a Gross Loss results.
The Profit & Loss Account starts with Gross Profit and ends with profit for the year. The profit for the year consists of Gross Profit plus any revenue other than from sales, such as rent received or commission received, less total expenses during the period. When the total expenses exceed the Gross Profit and Revenue, a loss for the year results. A trader's profit is calculated only when goods have been sold and not before. The Account is known as a Period Statement as it covers a period of time; hence it should be described as 'for the year'.

4.3 | Which form of business structure is a Trading Account prepared for?

A Trading Account is only prepared for traders, people who buy and sell goods. The Trading Account is not required for people who sell their services, such as doctors, lawyers etc.

4.4 | What is Opening Inventory?

Last year's Closing Inventory is this year's Opening Inventory. It is almost always shown in the trial balance, whereas Closing Inventory is not. However, if the trial balance has been extracted after a Trading Account has been prepared, then it will *not* include Opening Inventory. In this case it will also not include Sales, Sales Returns, Purchases or Purchases Returns but will include closing inventory, if any.

4.5 | List the journal entries that should be passed to transfer balances to the Trading Account.

The following journal entries enable the balances of the Sales, Sales Returns, Opening Inventory, Purchases, Purchases Returns Accounts and Closing Inventory, to be transferred to the Trading account:

	Dr $	Cr $
Sales	xxxx	
Trading Account		xxxx
Trading Account	xx	
Sales Returns		xx
Trading Account	xx	
(opening) Inventory		xx
Trading Account	xxxx	
Purchases		xxxx
Purchases Returns	x	
Trading Account		x
Inventory (closing)	xxx	
Trading Account		xxx

(Narratives have been omitted)

4.6 | What is meant by the term 'Turnover'?

Turnover is Net Sales revenue and is Sales less Sales Returns.
Turnover=Sales revenue – Sales Returns.

4.7 | When a trader takes Inventory for his own personal use, how is this recorded?

The Inventory taken should be deducted from Purchases at Cost Price and added to the trader's drawings. The journal entry that records this transaction is:

	Dr	Cr
	$	$
Drawings	xxx	
Purchases(Ordinary goods purchased)		xxx

4.8 | What is the format of the Income Statement?

There are two formats:
a) The vertical format
b) The horizontal format (Examiners expect the vertical format, not the horizontal format)
The ⊠ertical format is :

EXHIBIT:
The Income Statement for the year ended……

	$	$	$
Sales Revenue			xxx
Less Cost of Sales:			
Opening inventory		xxx	
Add Purchases		xxx	
		xxx	
Less Closing inventory		xxx	xxx
Gross Profit			xxx
Add Income received		—	xx
			xxx
Less Expenses:			
Rent		xx	
Telephone		xx	
General expenses		xx	xxx
Profit for the year (Profit before tax)			xxx

4.9 | What is meant by : a) Carriage outwards? b)Carriage inwards?

a) **Carriage outwards** is the cost of transporting inventory to customers. It is included as an expense in the Profit & Loss account section of the Income statement.
b) **Carriage inwards** is the cost of transporting inventory from suppliers It should be included as a cost when calculating the Gross Profit. Hence it will appear in the Trading Account section of the Income Statement.

4.10 | What is meant by the term 'Revenue Expenditure'?

Revenue Expenditure is recurring expenditure incurred for the day-to-day running of the business. E.g. repairs to machinery, petrol costs.

4.11 | What is meant by the term 'Capital Expenditure'?

Capital expenditure is non-recurring expenditure that is incurred by the business when it buys or adds value to its fixed assets. e.g. purchasing machinery. It not only consists of the cost of purchasing non-current assets but includes other costs that are incurred to get assets up and running. Costs in addition to the purchase price of the non-current asset could be: Costs of delivering the asset, legal costs, installation costs etc.

4.12 | Why is it important to distinguish between Capital and Revenue Expenditure?

Capital Expenditure will affect the non-current assets in the statement of financial position whereas revenue expenditure is charged to the income statement. If Capital Expenditure is treated as Revenue Expenditure by error, then the income statement and statement of financial position will not show a 'true and fair view' of the business performance and position respectively.
E.g. If $400 paid for machinery repairs is treated as capital expenditure then the machinery account will be overstated by $400, less any depreciation that would have been deducted, if the error had not been made **and** the profit will be understated by $400, less any depreciation that would have been deducted, if the error had not been made.

» EXERCISE 4.1
For each of the following items place a tick in the correct box.

	Capital Expenditure	Revenue Expenditure
Wages paid to own building labourers to erect factory extension of a building firm.		
Accountant's salary		
Legal fees paid in connection with factory extension		
Petrol costs for motor van		
Repairs to office furniture		
Electricity costs of using machinery		
Painting sign on new business vehicle		
Repainting sign on old business vehicle		

» EXERCISE 4.2
A sole trader purchases a shop incurring the following costs:

	$
Purchase price of shop	230,000
Fees paid to solicitor related to purchase of shop	10,000
Cost of inventory bought to stock the shop	13,600
Costs of installing showcases	17,400

Required:
Calculate the amount that will be capitalised as the cost of the shop.

4.13 | Can Wages be included in Cost of Sales?

When wages are paid to workers to make goods suitable for resale, then it (wages) is included as an expense and added to Cost of Sales in the Trading Account section of the Income Statement. Otherwise, wages should be included in the profit and loss account section of the income statement.

» EXERCISE 4.3
Draw up a Income Statement from the following information:

a) Name of the business: Sandra's Bakery, Year end: 31st August 20x2.
Opening inventory $3,560, Closing inventory $2,000, Purchases $1,800, Return Inwards $120, Return outwards $100, Sales $6,700, Carriage inwards $100, finance costs $120, Rent $400, Telephone charges $210, Commission received $450, Salaries $190.

b) Name of the business: Baps Electricals, Year end: 31st December 20x0.
Opening inventory $1,000, Closing inventory $1,340, Purchases $1,000, Return inwards $100, Return outwards $160, Sales $7,900, Carriage inwards $250, Carriage outwards $40, Rent $200, Telephone charges $310, Sundry expenses $100, Commission received $470, Salaries $400.

c) Name of the business: Gita Traders, Year end: 31st December 2003.
Opening inventory $3,700, Closing inventory $2,500, Purchases $4,000, Return inwards $300, Return outwards $460, Sales $12,900, Carriage inwards $50, Carriage outwards $140, Rent $300, Telephone charges $490, Sundry expenses $200, Interest received $670, Salaries $300.

» EXERCISE 4.4
From the following details draw up Alison's Income Statement for the year ended 31st July 20x7.

	$
Inventory on 1st August 20x6	10,000
Purchases	30,000
Sales revenue	100,000
Returns inwards	500
Returns outwards	2,000
Carriage inwards	200
Carriage outwards	500
Wages	1,000
Rent	3,000
Inventory at 31st July 20x7	10,000
Sundry expenses	2,000
Rent received	3,000

Additional information:
a) 30% of the wages were paid to workers for packing prior to sale.

» EXERCISE 4.5
From the following information prepare:
a) A Trial Balance (The capital is to be deduced by you.)
b) An Income Statement for the year ended 31st December 20x0

	$		$
Inventory as at 1st Jan., 20x0	3500	Sales Revenue	4500
Bank Overdraft	500	Property	2300
Equipment	2400	Discounts received	300
Discounts allowed	400	Motor Van	3400
Ordinary goods purchased	400	Inventory at 31st December 20xx	2500
Rent	400	Wages	600
Telephone charges	70	General Expenses	250
Carriage inwards	30	Carriage outwards	45
Trade receivables	400	Cash and cash equivalents	100
Sales return	80	Trade payables	350
Purchases return	400	Drawings	65

Keep your answer; it will be needed in chaper 5

EXERCISE 4.6

The following is the trial balance of M Mala as at 31st December 20x0.

	Dr.	Cr.
	$	$
Inventory 1st January 20x0	1100	
Carriage outwards	36	
Carriage inwards	45	
Returns inwards	400	
Returns outwards		356
Purchases	1000	
Sales revenue		2459
Salaries	700	
Rent	200	
Insurance	670	
Motor expenses	137	
Office expenses	222	
Lighting and heating expenses	179	
General expenses	300	
Premises	4500	
Motor vehicles	1300	
Fixtures and fittings	450	
Trade receivables	1680	
Trade payables		2500
Cash at bank	300	
Drawings	470	
Capital		?
	13689	13689

Inventory at 31st December 20x0 was $1670 .

Required:

a) Calculate the Capital as 31st December 20x0.
b) Draw up a Income Statement for the year ended 31st December 20x0.
Keep your answer, it will be needed in chapter 5

Exercise 4.7

The following is the trial balance of Shetty at 31st December 20x1

	Dr.	Cr.
	$	$
Gross profit		47,000
Rent received		10,000
Carriage outwards	3,500	
Salaries	5,000	
Insurance	4,000	
General expenses	1,000	
Lighting and heating expenses	3,000	
Land and Property	130,000	
Fixtures and fittings	5,000	
Trade receivables	780	
Trade payables		20,000
Cash at bank	45,000	
Drawings	1,220	
Capital		?
	198,500	198,500

Inventory at 31st December 20x1 was $4,500

Required:

a. Calculate the Capital at 31st December 20x1.
b. Prepare the Income Statement at 31st December 20x1.
Keep your answer, it will be needed in Chapter 5

EXERCISE 4.8

A company has the following figures for years 20x4 and 20x5:

	20x4	20x5
	$	$
Profit for the year	40,000	50,000
Cost of sales	120,000	180,000

It discovers that at the end of 20x4 the value of inventory was overstated by $5,000.

Required:

Calculate the correct Cost of Sales and profit for the year for:

a. 20x4
b. 20x5

4.1| Multiple-choice questions

i) Which of the following does not appear in the Trading Account section of the Income Statement?
A) Carriage outwards
B) Sales
C) Opening inventory
D) Carriage inwards

ii) Calculate the Gross Profit and profit for the year from the following information:

	$
Sales	23,000
Purchases	10,000
Interest received	1,000
Expenses other than carriage	8,200
Carriage	800

Carriage inwards was 50% of total expenses for carriage.
Closing inventory was $2000 more than opening inventory.

	GROSS PROFIT	PROFIT FOR THE YEAR
A)	$15000	$7000
B)	$14600	$7000
C)	$14600	$6000
D)	$15000	$6000

iii) Which of the following is Capital Expenditure?
A) Expenses of repainting company sign on company car.
B) Cost of repairing company car after accident.
C) Legal fees related to buying new company car.
D) Cost of reconditioning engine of company car.

iv) Interest received amounted to $12,700 and interest paid amounted to $8,000. The interest paid has been credited to the Profit and Loss Account and the interest received has been debited to the Profit and Loss Account.
What is the resulting effect on the profit of the business?
A) Profit for the year overstated by $4,700
B) Profit for the year understated by $4,700
C) Profit for the year overstated by $20,700
D) Profit for the year understated by $20,700

v) Discounts received have been credited to the Profit and Loss account as $258 instead of $852. What effect will this error have on the profit for the year of the business?
A) profit for the year understated by $ 594
B) profit for the year overstated by $594
C) profit for the year understated by $852
D) profit for the year understated by $258

vi) Discounts received of $450 were recorded on the wrong side of the Discounts Received Account and Discounts Allowed of $670 was recorded on the wrong side of the Discounts Allowed

Account. If the trader's draft profit for the year was $27,890, what is the corrected draft profit for the year?
A) $ 27670
B) $28,110
C) $27440
D) $ 28,560

4.2| The following trial balance was extracted from the books of Hemant as at 30th September 20x0.

	Dr.	Cr.
	$	$
Opening Inventory	1090	
Purchases	4571	
Sales		7811
Carriage inwards	150	
Carriage outwards	70	
Purchases returns		500
Salaries	1000	
Rent and rates	170	
Trade receivables and payables	5600	4300
Discounts	48	17
Fixtures and fittings	6890	
Drawings	340	
Cash	230	
Bank overdraft		340
Premises	7300	
Capital		?

Required:
a) Calculate the Capital as at that date.
b) Draw up an Income Statement for the year ended 30th September 20x0.
Keep your answer, it will be needed again in chapter 5

Statement of financial position for sole traders

5.1 | What is the Accounting Equation?

The Accounting Equation is:
Assets – Liabilities = Capital.

5.2 | What is meant by the term 'Statement of financial position'?

It is a statement of Assets, Liabilities and Capital as on a particular day. It shows the financial position of the firm as opposed to the Income Statement that shows the financial performance of the firm. It is the embodiment of the Accounting Equation.

5.3 | What is meant by Working Capital?

Working Capital is the money used for the day to day working of a business.

Working Capital =Current Assets – Current liabilities

5.4 | How is the Capital Employed (Closing capital) in a Sole Trader's business calculated?

Capital Employed = Opening capital + Profit for the year – Drawings + Non-current liabilities
(or)
Capital Employed = Non-current Assets + Current Assets – Current Liabilities – Non-current Liabilities

5.5 | How are Non-current Assets listed in the Statement of Financial Position?

Non-current Assets are listed starting with the asset that will be with the firm the longest and ending with the asset which will be with the firm for the shortest time.

5.6 | How are Current Assets listed in the Statement of Financial Position?

Current Assets are listed according to the degree of their liquidity; starting with the least liquid and ending with cash itself.

5.7 | How are balances in the Profit and Loss section of the Income Statement and Drawings Account transferred to the Capital Account at the end of the year?

The balance of the profit for the year is transferred to the Capital Account by the following journal entry:

	Dr	Cr.
Profit and Loss A/c(Income Statement)	xxx	
Capital A/c		xxx

The balance of the loss for the year is transferred to the Capital Account by the following journal entry:

	Dr.	Cr.
Capital A/c	xxx	
Profit and Loss A/c(Income Statement)		xxx

The Balance on the Drawings account is transferred to the Capital Account by the following journal entry:

	Dr.	Cr.
Capital A/c	xxx	
Drawings		xxx

EXHIBIT

The following Statement of Financial Position is prepared from Exercise 4.5 in the previous chapter. Statement of Financial Position as at 31st December 20xx

Assets: $ $ $

Non-current Assets: Property   2,300
Equipment   2,400
Motor Van   3,400
                                          8,100

Current Assets: Inventory
Trade receivables Cash and cash   2,500
equivalents   400
                                  100   3,000
Total Assets   11,100
Capital and liabilities:
Capital: Balance at 1 January 20xx 8,390
Profit for the year   1,925   10,315
Drawings   65
                                          10,250

Trade payables   350
Bank overdraft   500   850
Total capital and liabilities   11,100

» EXERCISE 5.1
Prepare a statement of financial position at 31st December 20xx for M Mala from the trial balance given in exercise 4.6 in chapter 4.

EXERCISE 5.2
Prepare a statement of financial position at 31st December 20x1 for Shetty from the trial balance given in exercise 4.7 in Chapter 4.

EXERCISE 5.3
Kelly incurred the following costs when purchasing a new piece of equipment

                                          $
Purchase price   6,000
Installation cost   10,000
Manufacturer's list price   23,000
Testing the equipment before first use   500
Advertising new products to be made by
the equipment   12,000
Required:
Calculate the maximum intial cost of the equipment that would be recognised as an asset?

5.1| Multiple-choice questions

i) Repairs to Motor van have been debited to the Motor Van account in error. What effect will this have on the statement of financial position?

	Non-current Assets	Profit	Capital
A)	No effect	overstated	overstated
B)	Overstated	overstated	overstated
C)	No effect	no effect	overstated
D)	Understated	Overstated	No effect

ii) Which of the following statements is correct?
A) Capital employed = Current assets – current liabilities – fixed liabilities
B) Capital employed = Current assets – current liabilities + fixed liabilities
C) Capital employed = Opening capital + profit for the year -drawings
D) Capital employed = Non-current assets + current assets – current liabilities

iii) What will be classified as a current liability in a statement of financial position drawn up on 31st December 20x4?
A) A long term loan that is due to be paid on 30th June 20x5
B) A long term loan that is due to be paid on 30th June 20x6

C) Inventory bought on credit on 30th June 20x4
D) J. Juma who took a cash loan from us on 30th June 20x4

iv) A sole trader took goods from his warehouse for his own use. No entries were made in the books of accounts. What is the effect of this on the statement of financial position?

	Inventory	Capital
A)	No effect	Overstated
B)	No effect	No effect
C)	Overstated	Overstated
D)	Overstated	No effect

5.2 Prepare Hemant's statement of financial position as on 30th September 20xx from the trial balance given in Q4.2 (Test Yourself Chapter 4)

5.3| A sole Trader's current assets totalled $27,000 on 31 July 20x4. On 1 August the following transactions took place:

1) Inventory was bought for cash. The list price of the inventory was $3,000 and it was subject to a trade discount of 20% and a cash discount of 5%. Payment was made immediately.
2) A irrecoverable debt of $300 was written off.
What was the total of the current assets in on 2 August 20x4?

Accounting Principles

6.1 | What are Accounting Principles?

Accounting Principles or Concepts are necessary for businesses to provide reliable accounting information. They are standards that businesses adopt or rules that they follow when keeping their accounting records.

6.2 | What is meant by the Historic Cost Principle?

The Historical Cost Principle.

This principle requires that all **assets** are normally shown at cost price. It is the *cost price* that is used as a basis of valuation of an asset. This is done to avoid subjectivity when valuing an asset.

6.3 | What is meant by the Business Entity Principle?

The Business Entity Principle

This principle implies that the affairs of the business are treated as being **separate** from the non-business activities of its owner/s.

6.4 | What is meant by the Dual Aspect Principle?

The Dual Aspect Principle

This principle states that there are two aspects to every transaction. One account is always debited and another is credited. These two aspects are always equal to each other. The name given to this method of recording transactions is : The double entry method.

6.5 | What is meant by the Money Measurement Principle?

The Money Measurement Principle

Accounting information is concerned with facts that:
1) can be measured in money
2) most people will agree to that money value.

6.6 | Explain the 'Substance Over Form' Principle.

The Substance Over Form Principle

This is when the practical aspect (substance) is preferred to the legal aspect (the form) of a business transaction. For example, a car bought for business purposes on hire purchase remains the property of the seller, legally, until the final installment has been paid. This is the legal view (the form). However, the car is being used by the purchaser for business purposes and this is the practical aspect (substance). The accounting view is that the car is no different from other cars that have not been bought on hire purchase. Hence substance is preferred over form.

6.7 | What is meant by the Accruals (matching) Principle?

The Accurals (matching) Principle

This Principle states that all expenses and income relating to the financial period to which the accounts relate should be taken into account without regard to the date of payment or receipt, respectively.

6.8 | What is meant by the Prudence Principle?

The Prudence Principle

There are two aspects to this principle:
1) All assets should be understated rather than overstated and all liabilities should be overstated rather than understated. The accountant should choose the figure that will cause the capital of the firm to be shown at a lower amount rather than at a higher one. This ensures 'a true and fair view' of the statement of financial position
2) Profits should not be anticipated and all losses should be recorded. This ensures 'a true and fair view' of the Income statement.

6.9 | What is meant by the realisation Principle?

The Realisation Principle

Profits should be realized on a sale when the title has passed. Profits should be treated as realized only when realized in the form of cash or of other assets (e.g. Trade receivables). When a trader sends goods to a potential customer on 'Sale or return', for instance, the sale has not taken place until the customer informs the trader that she has decided to buy the goods.

6.10 | What is meant by the Going Concern Principle?

The Going Concern Principle

This principle implies that the business will continue to operate for the foreseeable future.

6.11 | What is meant by the Consistency Principle?

The Consistency Principle

Once a firm has fixed a method for the accounting treatment of an item, it will enter all similar items that follow in the same way. If the firm does change the method, it should be after a lot of consideration. If profits are affected by a material amount due to a change then, either in the income statement itself or in the reports accompanying it, the effect of the change should be stated.

6.12 | What objectives should be applied when selecting accounting policies?

The objectives are:
a) Relevance
b) Reliability
c) Comparability
d) Understandability

Relevance

The main objective of financial statements is to attempt to provide information about a business's financial performance and position. The information provided can be used as a means of assessing the stewardship of management. Such information is relevant to users if it can be used to:
1) Confirm or correct prior expectations about events in the past.
2) Help in forming, confirming or revising expectations about the future.

The information provided by financial statements is also used as the basis for financial decisions. However, such information must be timely, to be of any use.

Reliability

The information provided in financial statements must be reliable, to be of any use. To be reliable, the information must be:
1) capable of being depended upon as being a faithful representation of the underlying transactions and events which it is representing.
2) capable of being verified independently.
3) free from bias
4) free from errors of significance
5) prepared with suitable caution being applied to any necessary judgements and estimates.

Comparability

Information in the financial statements of a business can be of greater use if it can be compared with similar information about the same business for some other point in time, or at another period of time, or with similar information about other businesses.

Users of financial statements should be able to identify similarities and differences between the information in the statement and that relating to other businesses or other periods. In order to be able to make comparisons, the users need to be aware of the policies used in the preparation of these statements, changes in these policies, if any, and the effects of such changes.

Understandability

Financial statements must be capable of being understood by users.

The ability to understand the information depends partly on the users' capabilities and partly on the presentation of that information. It is normally assumed that the users have a reasonable knowledge of business and economic activities and accounting. It is also normally assumed that users are willing to exercise reasonable diligence when studying the financial statements.

Information should not be omitted from the financial statements simply on the assumption that it is too complex for the users to understand.

NOTE: Accounting policies are not included in the syllabus, but they are worth knowing about.

6.13 | What kind of information is not revealed by accounting?

Accounting can never reveal information about the following:

a) Whether a law is about to be passed by the government that will increase the firm's expenses in the future.
b) That a competitor is about to take away some of the firm's best customers.
c) Whether the firm has good or bad managers.
d) Whether the work force has low morale that threatens the smooth running of business in the future.

6.14 | When are sales recorded in the seller's accounts?

A sale is recorded when the goods are invoiced and the title has passed on to the customer in exchange for an asset: either cash or trade receivables – The Realisation Concept.

6.15 | Which transactions are kept separate from those of a business?

The owner's transactions are kept separate from those of the business — The Business Entity Concept.

6.16 | A Business continues to depreciate its fixed assets at the same rate as the previous years inspite of falling profits. Which concept is being applied?

The Consistency Concept is being applied.

6.17 | Which concept is being applied if insurance paid in advance is shown in the statement of financial position as a current asset?

The Matching (accruals) Concept is being applied.

6.18 | A provision for doubtful debts is being made in order to take into account foreseeable loses. Which principle is being applied?

The Prudence principle is being applied.

6.19 | What is meant by duality?

There are two aspects to every transaction – this is what duality means.

6.20 | Financial statements are prepared after an interval of a year. Which principle is being applied?

The Time Interval Concept is being applied.

6.21 | Accounts cannot use any other unit of measurement apart from money; which concept is being applied?

The Money Measurement Concept is being applied.

6.22 | Due to uncertainty about his business continuing, the proprietor is forced to make a large reduction in the valuation of his year-end stock. Which principle is being applied?

The Going Concern Principle is being applied here.

» EXERCISE 6.1

Calculate the amount to be credited to the Trading Account section of the Income statement as sales for the year ended 30th September 20x4 from the information given below:

	$
Credit sales invoiced during the year ended 30th September 20x4	45,000
Goods sent to customers during September 20x4 on sale or return basis but not sold by 30th September 20x4	4,600
Goods sent to customers on 12th September 20x4 but invoiced on 4th October 20x4	5,000

» EXERCISE 6.2

Calculate the amount to be credited to the Trading Account section of the Income Statement as sales for the year ended 30th June 20x5 from the information given below:

	$
Credit sales invoiced during the year ended 30th June 20x5	7,000
Goods sent to customers during June 20x5 on sale or return basis but not sold by 30th June 20x5	600
Goods sent to customers on 3rd June 20x5 but invoiced on 10th July 20x5	400

6.23 | A customer paid in advance $560 cash on 7th July 20x5 for goods that were to be supplied on 1st August 20x5. What are the entries to be made in the books of accounts?

The Cash account should be debited and the Customer's account should be credited with $560 on 7th July 20x5.

6.24 | What accounting principle is a sole trader following when she treats cash she withdraws from the business bank account for her own personal use as Drawings?

She is following the business entity principle.

6.25 | When a trader introduces cash into the business, the cash account is debited and the capital account is credited. What accounting principle is being followed?

The business entity principle is being followed. Capital is what the business owes the owner and hence is credited.

» EXERCISE 6.3

Kaligula bought a machine on hire purchase (interest free) on June 1 20x5. The price of the machinery is $65,000. Kaligula paid $25,000 as a down payment on June 1 20x5 and the remaining $40,000 was to be paid in monthly instalments of $10,000 on July 1,20x5; August 1,20x5; September 1,20x5 and October 1,20x5. Kaligula's financial year ends on 30th September 20x5.

How will the financial statements be affected?

» EXERCISE 6.4

Kassey bought some furniture for her business on hire purchase (interest free) on January 1 20x3. The price of the furniture was $34,000. Kassey paid $30,000 as a down payment on January 1 20x3 and the remaining $4,000 was to be paid in monthly instalments of $1,000 on February 1 20x3; March 1 20x3; April 1 20x3 and May 1 20x3. Kassey's financial year ends on April 30 20x3.

How will the financial statements be affected?

6.1| Multiple-choice questions

i) A trader has sold $450 worth of goods to a customer on a sale or return basis. At the time of drawing up his final accounts, which of the following concepts should the trader keep in mind so that his final accounts show a true and fair view of his business position and performance?

A) Going concern
B) Historical cost
C) Realisation
D) Money Measurement

ii) A trader withdraws $3500 from his business bank account to pay rates on his personal residence. The amount is debited to his Drawings account and credited to his business bank account. Which concept has been used?

A) Realisation
B) Substance Over Form
C) Historical Cost
D) Business Entity

iii) A company prepares its statement of financial position showing all amounts rounded to the nearest $000. During the course of the financial year the company bought a printer worth $367. This expenditure was treated as revenue expenditure. Which of the following concepts was applied?

A) Business Entity
B) Historical Cost
C) Materiality
D) Money Measurement

iv) Which concept is intended to prevent profit from being overstated?

A) Matching
B) Materiality
C) Consistency
D) Realisation

v) Which concept ensures that the profits or losses of different periods are compared meaningfully?

A) Consistency
B) Matching
C) Prudence
D) Going concern

6.2| A trader occupies a shop at an annual rental of $24,000. In the year ended 31st December 20x4, the trader paid $30,000 rent.

Using the Matching principle calculate the amount that will be shown as rental expenditure in the Income Statement.

6.3 List three things that, although being of significance to the stakeholders of a business, cannot be recorded in the accounts of the business.

Accruals and Prepayments

7.1 | What is an Accrued Expense?

An Accrued Expense is an expense that was due to be paid during the financial year of the business, but was not paid. Expenses owing at the end of the financial year are called Accruals or Other payables.

7.2 | How is an Accrued Expense treated?

The Matching principle states that payments for the current year, and for the current year only, whether paid or not, should be matched with revenue for the current year, and the current year only, whether received or not. If, for example, annual rent on premises is $1000 and only $900 has been paid, then $ 100 is still owing and is *accrued*. This is to be included in the year's expenses as a *charge against the profits*, as per the Matching principle. It is also treated as a *Current Liability* in the statement of financial position.

7.3 | What is meant by the term 'Prepaid Expense'?

A Prepaid Expense is an expense paid in advance. When expenses for the following year are paid in the current financial year, this expense is termed a prepayment or other receivables.

7.4 | How is a prepaid expense treated?

If the annual rent due on premises is $1000 and the rent paid was $1200, then $200 has been paid in advance for next year and should not be included in this year's expenses. It is treated as a *Current Asset* in the statement of financial position is termed a Prepayment or Other Receivables.

7.5 | What is meant by Accrued Income?

Accrued Income is income that is owing but not paid during the current financial year. E.g. If we rent out premises on an annual rent of $1,500 and we have received only $1,250, then our accrued income is $250.

7.5 | How is Accrued Income treated?

Accrued Income should be included as income in the Profit & Loss Account section of the Income Statement and is treated as a Current Asset in the statement of financial position.

7.6 | What is meant by Prepaid Income?

This is income that has been paid in advance. E.g. If the total annual subscriptions due to be paid to a Club is $3,000, and the club has received $3,500, then the prepaid income is $500.

7.7 | How is Prepaid Income treated?

Prepaid Income should not be included as income in the Profit & Loss Account section of the Income Statement and should be included as a Current Liability in the statement of financial position.

EXHIBIT:
Alistair's financial year ends on 31 July. He has premises for which he pays rent of $1500 a year.
During the financial year ended 31 July 20-8 made the following payments:

20-7	$
September 30	250
October 31st	250
December 4	250
20-8	
June 16	250

Required: Draw up the Rent Account, showing the amount transferred to the Income Statement.

Rent Account

Dr   Cr

Date	Details	Amt.	Date	Details	Amt.
20-7		$	20-8		$
Sept 30	Cash/Bank	250	Jul 31	Income st.	1500
Oct 31	Cash/Bank	250			
Dec 4	Cash/Bank	250			
20-8					
June 16	Cash/Bank	250			
Jul 31	Bal c/d (Accural)	500			
		1500			1500
			Aug 1	Bal b/d (Accural)	500

√Tip: Since $1,500 was the annual rent, that was the amount transferred to the Income Statement.

√Tip: 1) Get the financial year right.
2) Start with the balance b/d (if any). If the balance b/d is an expense owing from last year, then it will be a credit entry. The following table will be helpful:

	Expenses	Income
Opening balances		
Bal b/d (accrual)	Credit entry	Debit entry
Bal b/d (prepayment)	Debit entry	Credit entry
Closing balances		
Bal c/d (accrual)	Debit entry	Credit entry
Bal c/d (prepayment)	Credit entry	Debit entry

3) Go to what happened during the year. There may have been a payment or a receipt. A payment will appear in the debit column and a receipt will be entered in the credit column.
4) Go to the end of the financial year. This is the balance c/d referred to in the table above. Follow the rules set out in the table.
5) Don't forget to bring down (Bal b/d) in the new financial year whatever you have carried down(bal c/d) in the previous financial year. Do not bring down the figure transferred to the Profit & Loss account. This is a common error, consciously avoid it.

» EXERCISE 7.1

Show the ledger accounts for the following items, including the balance transferred to the necessary part of the financial statements and the balances carried down to 20-3. The financial year ended on 31st December 20-2.
a) Telephone charges: Paid in 20-2 $450, owing at 31st December 20-2 $45.
b) Rates: Paid in 20-2: $780, owing at 31st December 20-2:$20.

c) Motor Expenses: Paid in 20-2: $1000, owing at 31st December 20-2: $290.
d) Rent : Paid in 20-2: $1250, owing at 31st December 20-2: $340.
e) Salary : Paid in 20-2: $3050, owing at 31st December 20-2: $120
f) Motor Expenses: Paid in 20-2 $260, Prepaid as at 31st December 20-2 $50.
g) General Expenses: Paid during 20-2 $150, owing at 31 December 20-1 $30, Owing at 31 December 20-2 $40.
h) Rent receivable : Received during the year $560, Owing at 31 December 20-1 $360, Owing at 31 December 20-2 $70.
i) Rent: Paid during the year ended 31 December 20-2 $600, Prepaid as at 31 December 20-1 $45, Prepaid as at 31 December 20-2 $50.
j) Rates : Owing as at 31 December ,20-1 $35. On March 31,20-2 paid $600 for twelve months.

» EXERCISE 7.2

Show the ledger accounts for the following items, including the balance transferred to the necessary part of the final accounts and the balances carried down to 20-3. The financial year ended on 31st December 20-2.

a) Rent: Owing at 31 December 20-1 $88
    January 31 20-2 :   Paid rent by cash $150.
    July 31 20-2:   Paid rent by cheque $150
    October 31 20-2:   Paid rent by cash $180.
    November 30 20-2   Paid rent by cash $250.
The rent for the premises was $1000 per year.
b) Insurance : Owing at 31 December 20-1: $450.
    January 31 20-2 :   Paid by cash $190.
    March 31 20-2:   Paid by cheque $250
    October 31 20-2:   Paid by cash $90.
    November 30 20-2   Paid by cash $150.
The insurance charges were $990 per year.

c) Rates: Owing at 31 December 20-1: $90.
    January 31 20-2 :   Paid by cash $80.
    March 31 20-2:   Paid by cheque $350
    October 31 20-2:   Paid by cash $190.
    November 30 20-2   Paid by cash $170.
The rates for the premises was $1200 per year.

EXHIBIT:
1) Corina's financial year ends on 30 June 20-3. The trial balance on 30 June 20-3 included the following:

	Debit
	$
Rent	750
Insurance	50
Rates	140

At 30 June 20-3, Corina owed $45 for Insurance and $30 for Rates. $80 of the rent was prepaid.

Required:

a) Relevant extract of the Income Statement for the year ended 30 June 20-3

b) Relevant extract of the statement of financial position as at 30 June 20-3.

Solution:

a) Corina

Income Statement for the year ended 30 June 20-3

(extract)

	$
Gross Profit	xxx
Less Expenses:	
Rent (750 – 80)	670
Rates (140 + 30)	170
Insurance (50 + 45)	95

b) Corina

Statement of financial position as at 30 June 20-3 (extract)

Current Assets:	$
Inventory	xxxx
Trade receivables	xxx
Other receivables (Rent)	80
	xxxx
Current Liabilities:	
Other payables (30+45)	75

» EXERCISE 7.3

Hesham's financial year ends on 31 August. His Trial balance as at 31 August 20-1 had the following:

	$
Telephone Charges	890
Sundry Expenses	470
Rent	340

At 31 August 20-1, Hesham owed $50 to the Telephone company and $90 as sundry expenses. He had paid $ 30 rent in advance for the year ended 31August 20-2.

Required:

a) Relevant extract of the Income Statement for the year ended 31 August 20-1

b) Relevant extract of the statement of financial position as at 31 August 20-1

» EXERCISE 7.4

Harvey's financial year ends on 31 August. His trial balance as at 31 August 20-1 had the following:

	$
Telephone Charges	240
Sundry expenses	170
Rent	200

At 31 August 20-1, Harvey owed $40 to the Telephone company and $20 as sundry expenses. He had paid $ 50 rent in advance for the year ended 31August 20-2.

Required:

a) Relevant extract of the Income Statement for the year ended 31 August 20-1

b) Relevant extract of the statement of financial position at 31 August 20-1

» EXERCISE 7.5

Alan receives commission for jobs that he undertakes. His financial year ended on 31December 20-1. Information available:

Owing at 1 January 20-1 $35, Received during the year ended 31 December 20-1 $260, owing at 31 December 20-1 $50.

Required:

a) The commission receivable account.

b) An extract of the Income Statement.

c) An extract of the statement of financial position

» EXERCISE 7.6

Abe receives commission for jobs that he undertakes. His financial year ended on 31December 20-1. Information available:

Owing at 1 January 20-1 $35, Received during the year ended 31 December 20-1 $500, owing at 31 December 20-1 $45.

Required:

a) Commission receivable account.

b) Extract of the Income Statement.

c) Extract of the Statement of Financial Position.

» EXERCISE 7.7

A business paid $350 for salaries during the year ended 30 June 20-3, and owed a further $35 on that date.

Required:

a) Calculate the amount charged in the Income statement for salary for the year ended 30 June 20-3. (Draw up the account to show your workings)

b) An extract of the statement of financial position as at 30 June 20-3 showing the adjustment for salary.

» EXERCISE 7.8

A business's accounting year end on 30th June. It's insurance premiums are paid in advance on 1st April each year.

Premiums have been paid in the past four years as follows:

Year 1	$1200
Year 2	$1800
Year 3	$ 1500
Year 4	$1200

How much will be debited in the Income statement for insurance in year 4?

» EXERCISE 7.9

Radhika's financial year ends on 31st March. She provides the following information:

2005	$
April 1 Insurance prepaid for 3 months to 30th June 2005	90
July 1 Insurance paid by cheque for 12 months to June 2006	144

Required:
How much will be debited in the Income Statement for insurance for the year ended 31st March 2006?

» EXERCISE 7.10

Sammy is a sole trader who started business on 1st June 20x5. The following balances were remaining in his books on 31st May 20x6, after the preparation of his Income Statement:

	$
Trade payables	3,600
Premises	32,000
Machinery	5,900
Inventory	3,400
Cash in hand	100
Bank overdraft	500
Capital	38,800
Drawings	5,800
Profit for the year	4,300

It was found that the following items had been overlooked when calculating the profit for the year:
a) On 31st May 20x6 rent prepaid amounted to $350.
b) On 31st May 20x6 $100 was owing for electricity.

Required: Sammy's statement of financial position as at 31st May 20x6
NOTE: Adjustments such as the two mentioned above, will have a dual effect.

» EXERCISE 7.11

At 31 December 20x3 a business had a debit balance of $870 on its Rent account. Payments for rent in the following year ended 31 December 20x4 totalled $ 12,450. Rent prepaid at 31 December 20x4 was $ 2,300. How much rent was charged against profits in the year ended 31 December 20x4?

» EXERCISE 7.12

A business's financial year ends on 31 December. At 31 December of the first year of business the business carried forward a debit balance of $25,700 on the rent account. During year 2 payments made for 12 month's rent to 31 March of year 3, were $120,000.

What is the amount of rent to be charged against profit in the year ended 31 December year 2?

» EXERCISE 7.13

The following relates to rental income for the year ended 31 July 20x3:

	$
Rents owing at 31 July 20x2	2,000
Prepaid rent at 31 July 20x2	1,600
Cash received	10,600
Rents written off	400
Rents accrued at 31 July 20x3	1,250
Rents paid in advance at 31 July 20x3	1,340

Required:
Calculate the rental income that will appear in the Income Statement for the year ended 31 July 20x3.

Q. How should inventory of consumables be recorded?

Accounts of consumables such as stationery, lubricating oil, components and spare parts will often have a debit and a credit balance at the year end. The debit balance signifies unused consumable and are entered as a current asset in the statement of financial position. It should not be included with closing trading inventory but should have its own heading. If there is a credit balance, then this signifies amounts still owing for consumables purchased and will be shown as a current liability in the statement of financial position under the heading 'other payables'.

EXHIBIT
A business paid $490 for stationery in the year ended 31 December 20x7. At that date, they owed $60 and had unused stationery of $30.

Stationery account

20x7		$	20x7		$
Jan-Dec	Bank	490	Dec 31	Income statement	520
Dec 31	Accrual c/d	60	Dec 31	Inventory c/d	30
		550			550
20x8			20x8		
Jan 1	Inventory b/d	30	Jan 1	Accrual b/d	60

EXERCISE 7.14
Subodh bought $1,900 worth of heating fuel by cheque during the year ended 31 December 20x9. At 31 December 20x9, he had unused fuel of $800 and still owed Lala, a creditor, $400 for additional fuel purchased during the year ended 31 December 20x9.
Required:
a. Draw up Subodh's Heating fuel account.
b. How much will be shown as a current liability?
c. How much will be shown as a current asset?
d. What is the figure for expenses in the income statement?

7.1| Multiple-choice questions

i) On October 1 2004 Kelly had prepaid insurance of $ 230. On December 1 2004 she paid $1200 cash for one year's insurance to November 30 2005. What is the amount debited to the Income Statement for the year ended 30th September 2005.
a) $1200
b) $ 1230
c) $230
d) $970

ii) Calculate the profit for the year for the year ended 31st December 2003, given the following information:

	$
Gross Profit	12000
Operating expenses	7000

In addition:
$450 was owing for rent and $120 was prepaid insurance.
The profit for the year was:
a) $5000
b) $4670
c) $1900
d) $ 5330

iii) The accounts of a business have been prepared. However, no adjustments have been made for prepaid expenses at the end of the year. What effect will this have on the following:

	Current Assets	Current Liabilities	Capital
a)	No effect	Overstated	Understated
b)	No effect	Understated	Overstated
c)	Understated	No effect	Understated
d)	Overstated	No effect	Overstated

7.2| Amina rents her building to Billy. At 31st Dec 20x3, Billy owed $3,500 for rent. However, at 31st Dec 20x4 Billy had paid $2,300 in advance. During the year Amina had received $10,000 as rent from Billy.

Calculate the rental income to be shown in Amina's Income Statement for the year ended 31st December 20x4.

7.3| At 30th June 20x1, a company had a debit balance of $2,300 on its Rent Payable Account. Payments for rent in the year ended 30th June 20x2 totalled $12,000. Rent prepaid at 30th June 20x2 was $450.

How much rent should be charged against profits in the year ended 30th June 20x2?

7.4| The financial year of Moses ends on 31st December. On 1st April the business rents out part of its premises for an annual rent of $12,000 receivable in equal installments on 1st July, 1st October, 1st January, 1st April.

At 31st December what would the financial statements show?

7.5| The following information is extracted from the records of a sole trader:

	$
At 31 December 20x5 rent paid in advance	3,000
During the year ended	
31 December 20x6 rent paid	50,000
At 31 December 20x6 rent paid in advance	4,500

How much will be debited for rent in the Income Statement for the year ended 31 December 20x6?

Depreciation Of Non-current Assets

8.1 | What is meant by the term 'Depreciation'?

Most non-current assets lose value over time. Depreciation is the term used for this loss of value in the expected working life of a non-current asset.

8.2 | How is Depreciation treated?

Since this loss represents the cost of using the non-current asset in order to generate profits, depreciation is charged annually to the Income Statement in the form of an estimated figure.

8.3 | Why is a provision for Depreciation made annually by a business that has Non-current Assets that depreciate?

A provision for Depreciation is made annually for the following reasons:

1) To spread the cost of the non-current asset over the years it is used.

2) So that the Income statement shows a 'true and fair view' of the expenses for the period. Since the asset is being used to generate income, a figure representing the 'cost' of this asset should be charged to the profits of the period in question. This is in keeping with the 'Matching Concept'

3) So that the statement of financial position shows a 'true and fair view' of the Non-current Assets. The 'Prudence Concept' states that assets should not be valued too highly. The provision for depreciation is deducted from the historic cost of the Non-current Assets and hence the assets are shown at a Net Book Value which is a more realistic figure compared to the cost of the asset.

4) Since the provision for depreciation reduces the profit for the year, it is not overstated and this is also in keeping with the Prudence concept.

5) Since the profit for the year is understated to the extent of the provision for Depreciation, the owner is not encouraged to make excessive cash drawings which would be detrimental to the business.

METHODS OF CALCULATING DEPRECIATION

8.4 | What are the methods for calculating depreciation?

There are three methods for calculating depreciation. They are:
a) The Straight Line method
b) The Reducing Balance method.
c) The Revaluation method

8.5 | Write a short note on the Straight Line Method.

The Straight Line Method:
This method is also know as the Equal Installment method or the Fixed Installment Method. As the name suggests, an equal amount is charged to the Income statement every year. A certain percentage of the Cost of the Asset is normally charged. In the absence of a given percentage, the following formula is to be used:

$$\text{Annual Installment} = \frac{\text{Cost of the Asset} - \text{Residual Value}}{\text{Expected years of use}}$$

√ Tip: *Residual value or scrap value refers to the value the asset will have at the end of its life. Sometimes the asset is valueless. Hence, if the residual value is not mentioned in the question, assume that it is zero.*

Exhibit:
A machine is bought for $4500 . It is estimated that it could be sold for $500 after four years. Calculate the annual installment of depreciation using the Straight Line Method of Depreciation.

$$\text{Annual instalment} = \frac{\text{Cost} - \text{Residual value}}{\text{Years of use}} = \frac{4500 - 500}{4} = \$1000$$

Q. Why do assets depreciate?
Assets depreciate for the following reasons:
- Wear and tear
- Obsolescence - they have been replaced by more efficient assets
- Passage of time e.g. a lease
- Depletion - when an asset gets used up e.g. a mine

» EXERCISE 8.1

Calculate the annual provision for Depreciation charged to the Income statement of a van which costs 5000. It is estimated that the van will be used for 4 years and will then be sold for $600. (Use the Straight Line Method).

» EXERCISE 8.2

Ali bought a computer for $3000. He estimates that he will be able to sell it for $200 at the end of its life of 4 years. Calculate the amount for Provision for Depreciation using the Straight Line method.

» EXERCISE 8.3

A firm purchases furniture for $6000. They estimate that they will be using the furniture for ten years after which it will have a residual value of $100. What is the annual depreciation they will charge to their Income statement using the Straight Line Method?

» EXERCISE 8.4

A firm provides for depreciation on its furniture at 10% of the cost of the furniture in existence at the end of the financial year. They find that they have charged furniture repairs $ 300 to the furniture account. How would such an error have affected their profits of $8500? Does it have any other effect on the final accounts of the company?

NOTE: Not only are the *Expenses* in *the Income statement* understated thus affecting the correct valuation of the profit for the year, but the *Non-current Assets* in the statement of financial position would be overvalued too by the amount of $270 ($300 –$ 30)

» EXERCISE 8.5

The Profit for the year was $2000. However after the drawing up of the financial statements, the following error was discovered: $ 300 spent for repairs of Motor van was charged to the Motor Van account.
a) What type of error was this?
b) Which items in the financial statements will be affected?
c) If the rate at which the provision for depreciation of motor van was 20%, what is the correct figure for Profit for the year?

» EXERCISE 8.6

A firm purchases a car for $3500. They have decided to charge Depreciation at the rate of 10% of the cost every year. Calculate the annual depreciation charged. What is the name of the method they are using?

8.6 | Write a short note on

a) The Reducing Balance Method.
b) The Revaluation Method

a) The Reducing Balance Method:

This method is also called the 'Diminishing Balance Method'. The Annual Depreciation installment decreases as the asset becomes older. A certain percentage (the calculation of which is not in your syllabus) is used on the Net Book Value (also known as the carrying amount) of the asset at the end of the year and this is the amount charged to the Income Statement as Depreciation.

b) The Revaluation Method:

When full accounting records are not maintained the revaluation method of Depreciation is used. Assets are valued at the end of each year. The reduction in the value of the asset at the end of the year compared with its value at the start of the year is the depreciation of that asset for the year.
In the following example, the closing value of loose tools ($350) will be shown as 'Inventory of loose tools' after the usual inventory in the current assets.
Example: On January 1st 20x5 the value of loose tools was $450
On December 31st 20x5 the value was $350, hence the depreciation was $100

EXHIBIT (**Reducing balance method**):
A Machine is bought for $6000. It is decided to depreciate this machine using the Diminishing Balance Method @20%. Calculate the depreciation for the first three years of the life of the asset.

Solution:	$
Cost	6000
Less Depreciation for year 1 @20% of 6000	1200
Net Book Value (N.B.V.)	4800
Less Depreciation for year 2 @20% of 4800	960
N.B.V. (or Written down Value)	3840
Less Depreciation for year 3 @20% of 3840	768*
Net Book Value	3430

√**Tip:** *Since the figure for provision of depreciation is only an estimation, do not use decimals, round off to the nearest whole number.*

» EXERCISE 8.7

Machinery was bought for $7500 and it was decided to depreciate it @25% using the Reducing Balance method. What is the annual provision for Depreciation charged to the Income Statement for the first three years of its life?

» EXERCISE 8.8

Some furniture was bought for $3400 and it was decided to depreciate it @30% using the Reducing Balance Method. What is the annual provision for Depreciation charged to the Income Statement for the first four years of its life?

» EXERCISE 8.9

Depreciate Buildings which cost $25000 @20% using the Reducing Balance Method for five years, showing clearly the charge to the Income Statement every year.

» EXERCISE 8.10

Depreciate a computer which cost $5000 for three years:
a) Using the Straight Line method @ 10%
b) Using the Reducing Balance Method @ 25 %.

8.7 | What are the factors that would determine the choice of method between the Straight Line Method and the Reducing Balance Method?

The factors are:
• The asset should be depreciated according to how the asset is being used. If the asset is being used uniformly right through its economic life, then the Straight Line Method is suitable. However, if the asset is more useful when it is new compared to when it is older, then the Reducing Balance Method is more suitable.
• The repair and maintenance factor should be taken into consideration. If the asset incurs more repair and maintenance as it gets older, then the Reducing Balance Method is preferable since the amount charged to the Income Statement every year remains almost uniform.
• According to the concept of Consistency, the method in use should not be changed unless a thorough review is carried out.

8.8 | What is meant by 'Exceptional depreciation'?

When an event occurs that significantly reduces the value of a non-current asset as a result of which the asset's Net Book Value is more than the disposal value of the asset, then the asset is said to be 'impaired'. The procedure to follow in such an event is to reduce the Net Book Value immediately to its recoverable value. This is also called the 'carrying amount'. The reduction is treated as loss which is charged to the Income Statement and is called Exceptional Depreciation.

8.9 | How will depreciation be calculated for the remaining life of an impaired asset?

Depreciation is recalculated taking into account the new carrying amount which is divided by the remaining useful life of the impaired asset.

Exhibit
A car was purchased in 20x1 at a cost of $23,000. It was presumed to have a useful life of 10 years with a residual value of $4,000. Depreciation was to be provided in the year the car was bought but not in the year of disposal.

Required: Find the Net book Value of the car at 31st December 20x3.

Solution:
Annual Depreciation instalment $= \dfrac{23000 - 4000}{10}$
$$= \$ 1900$$

Net book value of car on
31st December 2003 = 23000 – (1900x3)
$$= \$17,300$$

In 20x4 it was found that the car had a recoverable value of only $10,000.

Required: What is the amount debited to the Income Statement on 31st December 20x4?

Solution:
Income Statement
should be debited with = Net book value – recoverable amount
$$= 17300-10000 = \$7,300$$

Required: If the car now has a useful life of 4 years with no residual value, what should be the Annual Depreciation for the next 4 years?

Solution:
The Annual Depreciation should be $= \dfrac{10,000}{4} = \$2,500$

» EXERCISE 8.11
A Machine was purchased in 20x0 at a cost of $100,000. It was presumed to have a useful life of 10 years with a residual value of $5,000. Depreciation was to be provided in the year the car was bought but not in the year of disposal. In 20x5 it was found that the machine had a recoverable value of only $40,000

Required:

a) Find the Net Book Value of the machine at 31st December 20x4.
b) What is the amount debited to the Income Statement on 31st December 20x5?
c) If the machine now has a useful life of 4 years with no residual value, what should be the Annual Depreciation for the next 4 years?

» EXERCISE 8.12

A car was purchased in 20x1 at a cost of $35,000. It was presumed to have a useful life of 8 years with a residual value of $3,000. Depreciation was to be provided in the year the car was bought but not in the year of disposal. In 20x3 it was found that the car had a recoverable value of only $20,000

Required: Find the Net book Value of the car at 31st December 20x2.

Required: What is the amount debited to the profit and loss account section of the Income Statement on 31st December 20x3?

Required: If the car now has a useful life of 5 years with a residual value of $500, what should be the annual depreciation for the next 5 years?

DISPOSAL OF ASSETS

8.10 | How is a disposal of an asset recorded in the books of accounts?

When an asset is sold, we need to delete it from our records. Two accounts will be affected:
1. The Asset account
2. Depreciation for that asset account.
The profit or loss on the sale will also have to be calculated. This is calculated in the Disposal Account.

Exhibit:
A car was bought for $5500 on January 4th 20x0. Depreciation is calculated on the assets in existence at the end of the year using the straight line method @10%. The asset was sold on 5th October 20x3 for $2000.

Required:
a) Car a/c
b) Depreciation for Car a/c
c) The Disposal of Car Account (which shows whether there was a profit or loss on disposal)

Dr   Car A/c   Cr

Date	Details	Amount	Date	Details	Amount
20X3		$	20X3		$
Jan 1	Bal b/d	5500	Oct 5	Car Disposals	5500

Dr   Depreciation of Car A/c   Cr

Date	Details	Amount	Date	Details	Amount
20X3		$	20X3		$
Oct 5	Car Disposals	1650	Jan 1	Bal b/d	1650

Dr   Car Disposals A/c   Cr

Date	Details	Amount	Date	Details	Amount
20x3		$	20x3		$
Oct 5	Car	5500	Oct 5	Depreciation for car	1650
				Cash/Bank	2000
			Dec 31	P & L (Loss)	1850
		5500			5500

Working:
Annual instalment of depreciation = 10% x 5500
= $550

» EXERCISE 8.13

Machinery was bought for $6000 on July 5th 20x0 .
Depreciation is calculated using the straight line method @15% p.a. on machinery in use at 31st December .
On 10th October 20x2 the machinery was sold for $1200 cash.
You are required to show:
a) Machinery a/c
b) Provision for depreciation a/c
c) Disposal of machinery a/c
Working:
Annual instalment for depreciation = 15% x 6000
= $ 900

» EXERCISE 8.14

Machinery was bought for $5000 on July 5th 20x0 .
Depreciation is calculated using the straight line method @10% p.a. on machinery in use at 31st December .
On 15th November 20x2 the machinery was sold for $2500 cash. You are required to show:
a) Machinery a/c
b) Provision for depreciation a/c
c) Disposal of machinery a/c

» EXERCISE 8.15

A firm bought two Motor Vehicles for $5000 each paying by cheque on 3rd January 20x1. Their policy was to depreciate their vehicles using the straight line method @ 10% on the basis of 'one month's ownership means one month's depreciation'. On July 1st 20x2 one of the Motor Vehicles was sold for $4500 cash. You are required to show for the period up to December 31 20x2 :
a) The Motor Vehicles A/c
b) The Provision for Depreciation – M.V. a/c
c) The Disposal of Motor Vehicle a/c

Working:
Depreciation at the end of year one = 10 % x 10000
= $1000

Accumulated Depreciation of Vehicle being disposed = 1.5 x 10% x 5000 (The motor vehicle was used for 1.5 years)
= $750

NOTE: Read the question carefully. Most often, depreciation is to be provided in the year of acquisition of an asset and none in the year of disposal. The other method is to provide depreciation on a month-to-month basis from the day the asset is acquired to the day it is disposed of as in the exercise above: Exercise 8.15

PART EXCHANGE

8.11 | What is meant by the term 'Part exchange'?

When a new asset is acquired, it may be acquired in part exchange of a used asset being disposed of.

8.12 | What is the journal entry passed in such a case?

The part exchange value of the asset being disposed of is debited to the Non-current Asset Account and credited to the Disposals Account as the proceeds of disposal.

EXHIBIT

On July 3, 20x2, a Motor vehicle was purchased for $30,000. The cost was settled by a cheque payment of $23,000 and the part exchange of another motor vehicle for the balance. This motor vehicle had cost $22,000 and had accumulated depreciation of $18,000. at July 3, 20x2. Depreciation is charged in the year of purchase but not in the year of disposal.

Solution:

M.V. at cost A/C

20x2		$	20x2		$
Jan 1	Bal b/d	22,000	July 3	M.V disposal a/c	22,000
July 3	Bank	23,000			
	M.V. disposal a/c	7,000			
		30,000			

Provision for Depreciation of M.V. a/c

20x2		$	20x2		$
July 3	M.V. disposal a/c	18,000	Jan 1	Bal b/d	18,000

M.V. Disposal a/c

20x2		$	20x2		$
July 3	M.V. at cost a/c	22,000	July 3	Provision for depr	
Dec 31	P & L a/c (*profit on disposal)	3,000		of M.V. a/c	18,000
				M.V. at cost a/c	7,000
		25,000			25,000

* The profit on disposal is credited in the Profit and Loss Account section of the Income Statement

» EXERCISE 8.16

On May 5, 20x5, a Motor vehicle was purchased for $25,000. The cost was settled by a cheque payment of $19,000 and the part exchange of another motor vehicle, for the balance, which had cost $16,000 and had accumulated depreciation of $11,000 at May 5, 20x5. Depreciation is charged in the year of purchase but not in the year of disposal.

You are required to draw up the following accounts to show all the above transactions:
a) Motor vehicle at cost
b) Provision for depreciation of Motor Vehicle
c) Motor Vehicle disposal

EXERCISE 8.17

A tractor was purchased for $35,000 on Jan 10, 20x4. The cost was settled by a cheque payment of $28,000 and the part exchange of a Motor Vehicle for the balance. The Motor Vehicle had cost $24,000 and had accumulated depreciation of $17,000 at Jan 10, 20x4. Depreciation is charged in the year of purchase and not in the year of disposal.

You are required to draw up the following accounts to show all the above transactions:
a) Tractor at cost
b) Provision for depreciation of Motor Vehicle
c) Motor Vehicle disposal

EXERCISE 8.18

Mallama's transactions in the year ended 31st December 20x5 included the following:

January 1:
Machinery at cost $10,000;
Provision for depreciation of machinery $5,900
August 8:
Sold machine No 2x45 for $ 2,300. This machine had cost $4,500 when purchased in 20x3.
October10:
Purchased Machine No 4x34 which was priced at $2,700. The cost was settled by a cheque payment of $1,900 and the part exchange of Machine No5x34. Machine No 5x34 had cost $1,320 when purchased in 20x2.

Mallama depreciates her machinery at 10% using the straight line method. She provides a full year's depreciation in the year of purchase, but none in the year of disposal.

Required: Prepare the following accounts to show the transactions on August 8 and October 10:

a) Machinery at Cost
b) Provision for Depreciation of Machinery
c) Machinery Disposal

» EXERCISE 8.19
A non-current asset, purchased on 1 June 20x3 at a cost of $34,000, has an estimated scrap value of $4,000 at the end of its 5 year life. It is to be depreciated on the reducing balance basis at the rate of 20% every year.
Required:
Calculate the depreciation charge for the year ended 31 May 20x5.

» Exercise 8.20
Machinery purchased for $450,000 at the start of the year has been incorrectly depreciated for the whole year using the straight line method at 10% instead of 15%.

The Ledger balances after the entries have been posted are as follows:
Machinery at cost $ 450,000
Provision for depreciation $45,000

Required:
a) Prepare a journal entry to correct this error.

8.1| Multiple Choice Questions

i)What happens when the cost of a non-current asset exceeds the accumulated depreciation + the proceeds from it's sale
a) No effect
b) There is a loss on disposal
c) There is a profit on disposal

ii) The following are the balances on Jan 1 20x5 concerning Leasehold premises:

	$
Historic cost	40,000
Provision for depreciation	8,000

The financial year end is 31st December and leasehold premises are to be amortised over the term of the lease of 20 years on a straight-line basis.
What is the provision for depreciation for the year ended December 31 20x5?
a) $1,600
b) $2,000
c) $400
d) $3,200

iii) A Machine was bought for $45,000. It had an expected useful life of 10 years. It is to be depreciated using the reducing balance method at the annual rate of 30%. The machine was sold in the third year for $24,000. What was the profit or loss on disposal?
a) Loss of $1950
b) Profit of $1950
c) Profit of $8565
d) Loss of $8565

iv) A provision for depreciation is made to comply with which of the following concepts?
a) Historic cost
b) Matching
c) Materiality
d) Substance over form

v) The following relates to non-current assets of a business whose financial year ends on 31st December:

	$
Cost at 1st January	6,500
Accumulated depreciation at 1st January	3,500
Non-current assets purchased during the year	9,000

Depreciation is charged at 20% using the reducing balance method. What is the amount debited to the Income Statement for the year for depreciation?

a) $1,800
b) $3,100
c) $2,400
d) $3,600

8.2| You are given the following information:

	$
Net book value of non-current assets on January 1, 20x3	27,900
Net book value of non-current assets on December 31, 20x3	13,500
Net book value of non-current assets disposed of during the year ended December 31, 20x3	9,300
Cost of non-current assets purchased during the year ended December 31, 20x3	7,000

Depreciation is calculated at 10% using the straight line method of depreciation.
What is the amount charged to the income statement for the year ended December 31 20x3 as depreciation?

8.3| On June 1st 20x7, Carol a sole trader purchased machinery on credit from Bunting Machinery company for $15,000. She calculates depreciation on machinery using the straight line method @10% per annum at the end of each financial year. No depreciation is provided for in the year of disposal, but depreciation is provided in the year it is purchased. On 1st September 20x8 , one third of the machinery was sold for $1,000 cash.

Prepare the following accounts in the ledger of Carol for each of the years ended 31st May 20x8 and 31st May 20x9.

a) Machinery account

b) Provision for Depreciation of Machinery Account

c) Disposal of machinery account

8.4| You are given the following information relating to the non-current assets of a business:

	$
Net book value at the start of the year	27,000
Net book value at the end of the year	32,800
Depreciation charge for the year	3,200
Disposals at net book value	1,400

Required:

Calculate the value of non-current assets bought during the year.

8.5| Give three reasons why a provision for depreciation is made.

8.6| Mala, a sole trader, purchased a computer for $6,000 on 1st January 20x4. It was expected to have a useful life of 3 years. It was not expected to have any scrap value at the end of its useful life.

Calculate the depreciation charge for the computer for each of the years ended 31st December 20x4,20x5,20x6, based on:

a) the straight line method

b) the reducing balance method using the rate of 50%

Show your workings

8.7| A company uses the straight line method of depreciation to depreciate its fixed assets. On 1 January 20x3, the company bought a motor van on hire purchase. The cash price was $34,000 and the interest for the year is $1200. The estimated useful life of the motor van is five years with no residual value.

Required:

Calculate the charge for depreciation for the year ended 31 December 20x3.

8.8| The following information is available regarding a business's non-current assets:

	$
Cost at 1 January 20x5	12,300
Accumlated depreciation at 1 January 20x5	3,600
Purchases for the year ended 31 Decemebr 20x5	3,000
Disposals for the year ended 31 December 20x5	800

Depreciation is calculated at 20% per annum on the reducing balance basis.

Required:

Calculate the depreciation charge for the year ended 31 December 20x5.

NOTE: Disposals $800 above, was the cost of the asset.

8.9 A business bought an asset for $50,000. It makes a provision for depreciation using the Straight Line Method @20% per annum, taking into account a residual value of 10%.

Calculate the depreciation charge for Year 1 and Year 2.

8.10 Non-current assets of a company were:

	Start of the year	End of the year
	$	$
At cost	460,000	505,000
Cummulative depreciation	215,000	237,000
NBV	245,000	268,000

During the year assets costing $92,000 were purchased and assets with a NBV of $16,000 were sold.

What was the depreciation charge for the year?

Irrecoverable Debts and Doubtful Debts

9.1 | What are irrecoverable debts?

Irrecoverable Debts are debts that the firm will never be able to collect. They are credited to the customer's (debtor's) account to cancel them and debited to a irrecoverable debts account. They are a normal business expense and must be charged as such when calculating the profit or loss for the period.

EXHIBIT:
On 30 June 20XX, the following debts were written off as irrecoverable: 1) S. Sami $45
                                                                          2) Jules $27
Required: Pass the necessary journal entries.

Solution:

Date	Details	Debit	Credit
20XX		$	$
June 30	1) irrecoverable Debts	45	
	S. Sami		45
	(Debt owing from S. Sami written off as irrecoverable see letter in file no XXX)		
	2) Irrecoverable Debts	27	
	Jules		27
	(Debt owing from Jules written off as irrecoverable see letter in file no XXX)		

» EXERCISE:9.1

Pass the necessary journal entries to record the following:
20XX
(a) May 3   A debt of $35 owing from S Paul was written off as an irrecoverable debt.
(b) May 6   We are owed $65 by M. Salu. He is declared bankrupt and we write off his debt as irrecoverable.
(c) May 19   We are owed $60 by Saleem. He is declared bankrupt and we receive $50 cash in full settlement of the debt.
(d) May 26   A debt owing to us by Jim of $67 is written off as an irrecoverable debt.

9.2 | What is meant by the term 'irrecoverable debts recovered'?

An irrecoverable debt written off in previous years may sometimes be recovered in later years.
When this occurs, the following procedures are taken:

a) Reinstate the debt by making the following entries:
Debit   Debtor's account
Credit   Irrecoverable debts recovered account.
NOTE: This is done in order to have a record of the debtor's account that acts as a guide for granting credit in the future.
b) When the cheque/cash is received in settlement of the account:

Debit	Cash/Bank	
Credit	the Debtor's account.	

EXHIBIT:
December 23, 20x5: An irrecoverable debt of $600 in 20x4 is now recovered in cash from the debtor S. Smith. Pass the required journal entries to record this .
Solution:

Date	Details	Debit	Credit
20x5		$	$
Dec 23	S. Smith	600	
	Irrecoverable debts recovered		600
Dec 23	Cash	600	
	S. Smith		600
	(Irrecoverable debt now recovered)		

√ *Tip: The amount in the Irrecoverable Debt Recovered Account is deducted from the irrecoverable debts account in the Income statement*

» EXERCISE 9.2

Scott had written off Rachael's debt of $450 as **irrecoverable**. At a later date, Rachael had sufficient funds to enable her to pay Scott. On January 3, 20x5 she sent him a cheque for the amount.

Required: Pass the relevant journal entries to record the above transaction in Scott's books.

» EXERCISE 9.3
Sarita had written off Ram's debt of $450 as irrecoverable. At a later date, Ram had sufficient funds to enable him to pay Sarita. On January 3, 20x5 he sent her a cheque for the amount.
» Required: Pass the relevant journal entries to record the above transaction.

9.3 | Why are Provision for Doubtful Debts made?

Provision for DoubtfulDebts are made to achieve the following objectives when drawing up the final accounts:
a)To charge against the profits for that year an amount representing the sales of that year for which the firm will never be paid. This is in accordance with the matching concept.
b)To show as correct a figure as possible the true value of debtors in the statement of financial position at that date. This is in accordance with the Prudence Concept.

9.4 | How can a business avoid irrecoverable debts?

Debts can be avoided by using any of the following methods:
By using a factor.
By sending constant reminders to debtors by way of statements. If this doesn't work, then a warning must be issued threatening legal action.
By offering cash discounts for early and prompt payment.

9.5 | What is the difference between a provision and a liability?

A 'Liability', such as creditors, is an amount that is owing for goods or services supplied and can be determined with substantial accuracy. A 'Provision', on the other hand, is an amount that is an estimate and cannot be determined with substantial accuracy. They are figures that are guessed at, one way or the other and are set aside against a future expense.

9.6 | How many kinds of Provision for Doubtful Debts exist?

There are three kinds of Provision for Doubtful Debts:
1) Specific
2) General
3) Specific and General

9.7 | How does one calculate the amount of a provision for doubtful debts?

It must be remembered that the Provision for Doubtful Debts is only an estimated figure and is arrived at using any of the following methods:
General By making an estimate, using past experience, of what percentage of the total trade receivables will prove to be irrecoverable. The amount is therefore calculated using a percentage of trade receivables.
Specific By examining closely each debt in the Sales Ledger and deciding whether it is going to be irrecoverable. The provision is the total of such debts.
Specific and General The provision is made up as follows: A specific provision is first calculated by examining each debt in the Sales ledger. This amount is deducted from the total debtors' figure before the general provision is calculated.

EXHIBIT
Manoj maintains a specific and general provision for doubtful debts. The general provision is calculated as 5% of debtors after deducting doubtful debts.

For the year ended 31st march	Total Debtors	Doubtful Debts	Provision Specific	General	Total
	$	$	$	$	$
20x1	20,000	3,000	3,000	850	3,850
20x2	21,000	2,000	2,000	950	2,950

» EXERCISE 9.4
Josh maintains a provision for doubtful debts which is made up of a specific provision for doubtful debts and a general provision equal to 4% of the remainder. The following information is available from Josh's books:

At 31 December	Total debtors/ trade receivables	Doubtful debts (included in total debtors)
	$	$
20x2	35,000	2,500
20x3	41,000	7,300
20x4	54,000	4,600
20x5	29,000	8,700

Required:
Calculate the total Provision for Doubtful Debts for each of the above years.

9.8 | What are the accounting entries to record the provision for Doubtful Debts?

The accounting entries for
I) The year in which the provision is **first made** are:
a) Debit the income statement.
b) Credit the Provision for doubtful Debts Account .
II) **In subsequent years,** the amount is either increased or decreased or retained at the same amount

A) If the amount is increased:
a) The Income statement is debited with the increase
b) The Provision for Doubtful Debts Account is credited with the increase.

B) If the amount is decreased:
a) The Provision for Doubtful Debts Account is debited with the decrease.
b) The Income Statement is credited with the increase (this would be an income).

c) If the amount remains the same:
No entries are made.

EXHIBIT
The trade receivables for the year ended 31st August 20x3 amounted to $14,000. $600 of these were written off as irrecoverable. From past experience it is decided that 1% of trade receivables will prove to be irrecoverable.

Required:
Make a provision for these doubtful debts.
Solution:
In the Nominal Ledger:

Provision for Doubtful Debts a/c

20x3	$	20x3	$
		August 31 Inc Statement	134

Working:
Provision for doubtful debts = 1% x (14,000 – 600)
= $134

Income statement (extract)

	$	$
Gross Profit		xxxx
Less expenses : Irrecoverable debts	600	
Provision for doubtful debts	134	
		734

The statement of financial position (extract)

	$	$
Current assets :		
Trade receivables		14,000
Less: Provision for doubtful debts	134	
Irrecoverable debts	600	734
		13,266

» **EXERCISE 9.5:**
Prepare:
a) The provision for doubtful debts account
b) The Income statement extract
c) The statement of financial position extract

To show the effect of each of the following :
i) On 30th June 200X the trade receivables were$24,000. Irrecoverable debts for the year were $3500. Doubtful debts were found to be $1,200. It was decided to make a general provision for doubtful debts at 2%.
ii) On 31st July 200x the trade receivables were $12,000 , irrecoverable debts were $3200. It was decided to provide for doubtful debts at 2.5% of remaining trade receivables.
iii) On 30th June 200X the trade receivables were$20,000. Irrecoverable debts for the year were $1000 and doubtful debts amounted to $500. It was decided to provide for doubtful debts at 1.5% of remaining trade receivables.
iv) On 31st July 200x the trade receivables were $10,000 , irrecoverable debts were $3000 and it was decided to provide for doubtful debts at 2.5% of remaining trade receivables.

WHEN THE AMOUNT OF THE PROVISION IS INCREASED

EXHIBIT:

Leena has the following balances on 1st January 20x1:
Provision for Doubtful Debts $250
On 31st December 20x1 her trade receivables amounted to $3000. She wishes to maintain a provision for doubtful debts at 10% of her trade receivables.

Required at 31st December 20x1:
a) **Provision for Doubtful Debts Account.**
b) **Extract of the income statement.**
c) **Extract of the statement of financial position**

Solution:

Provision for Doubtful Debts

20x1	$	20x1	$
		Jan 1 Bal b/d	250
		Dec 31 Income Statement	50

Working:
Provision at 31st Dec = 10% x 3000
= $300
Increase in Provision = 300 – 250
= $ 50

Income Statement for the year ended 31st December 20x1(extract)

	$
GROSS PROFIT	XXX
Less EXPENSES:	
Increase in provision for Doubtful Debts	50

Statement of financial position as at 31 December 20x1(extract)

CURRENT ASSETS	$	$
Trade receivables	3000	
Less Provision for Doubtful Debts	300	2700

√ Tip: *The amount that goes into the income statement is the increase and the amount that goes into the statement of financial position is the whole provision at the end of the year.*

» EXERCISE 9.6:

Hussein has the following balances
On January 1st 20x2 : Provision for Doubtful Debts $155
On December 31st 20x2 : Trade receivables $4000
He wishes to maintain a Provision for doubtful Debts at 5% of closing trade receivables.

Required:
a)   Provision for Doubtful Debts A/c
b)   Income Statement (extract)
c)   Statement of financial position (extract)

» EXERCISE 9.7

Jason has the following balances:
At 31st December 20x1 : trade receivables $3000
At 31st December 20x2: trade receivables $5000
He maintains a provision for Doubtful Debts at 6% of Closing debtors/trade receivables.
Required as at 31st December 20x2:
a)   Provision for Doubtful Debts A/c
b)   Extract the Income statement
c)   Statement of financial position extract

√ Tip: *The opening balance of the provision = 6% x 3000*
The closing balance of the provision = 6% x 5000

WHEN THE AMOUNT OF PROVISION IS DECREASED

EXHIBIT:
Jose had debtors of $3000 as at 31st January 20x1 and $2000 as at 31st January 20x2. He provides for doubtful debts each year end at 5% of closing debtors.

Show for the year ending 31st January 20x2, the following:
a)   **Provision for Doubtful Debts a/c**
b)   **Extract of the Income statement**
c)   **Extract of statement of financial position.**

a)
Provision for Doubtful Debts A/c

20x2		$	20x1		$
Jan 31	Income Statement	50	Feb 1	Balance b/d	150

Working:

Provision at 31st January 20x1 = 5% x 3000
                                                   = $150
Provision at 31st January 20x2 = 5% x 2000
                                                   = $100
Decrease in Provision   = 150 – 100
                                                = $50

b)Income Statement for the year ended 31st January 20x2 (extract)

	$
GROSS PROFIT	XXX
Add INCOME:	
Decrease in provision for doubtful debts	50

c)
Statement of financial position as at 31 January 20x2 (extract)

	$	$
CURRENT ASSETS:		
Debtors/trade receivables	2000	
Less Provision for doubtful Debts	100	1900

» EXERCISE 9.8:

Mary has debtors amounting to $3000 at 31st December 20x2. Her provision for doubtful debts account has a balance of $400. She wishes to provide for debtors at 10% of closing debtors.

Required:
a)   **Provision for Doubtful Debts a/c**
b)   **Extract of Profit & Loss a/c section of the Income statement**
c)   **Extract of statement of financial position**

» EXERCISE 9.9

A firm starts on 1st January 20x0 and its financial year ends on 31st December annually. Following is a table of Trade Receivables, Irrecoverable debts to be written off and the rate at which a provision is to be made for doubtful debts at the end of the financial year:

Year to 31st December	Trade receivables before irrecoverable debts have been written off	Irrecoverable debts to be written off	Rate at which a provision for doubtful debts is to be made
	$	$	
20x0	3000	300	10%
20x1	4000	500	10%
20x2	2000	100	10%

Required: Double entry accounts and extracts from the financial statements for each of the 3 years.

» EXERCISE 9.10

Joey started business on January 1st 20x0. He adjusted his provision for doubtful debts at the end of each year on a percentage basis, in accordance with the current 'economic climate'. The following details are available for the three years ended 20x0, 20x1 and 20x2:

Year	Debts written off yr. to Dec. 31st	Trade receivables at 31st Dec	% Provision for doubtful debts
20x0	147	4000	6
20x1	300	5000	7
20x2	400	4500	4

Required for each of the three years:
a) **Irrecoverable debts accounts**
b) **Provision for doubtful debts accounts**
c) **Extracts from statements of financial position**

» EXERCISE 9.11

Daisy is a trader dealing in imported goods. The following are the balances taken from her books on 31st December 20x1.

	$
Purchases	73,800
Sales revenue	140,000
General expenses	880
Return inwards	3,900
Air freight charges	6,240
Motor van repairs	7,140
Rent and rates	5,720
Salaries and wages	19,600
Loan interest(Finance costs)	300
Bank Loan (repayment 31st December20x6)	6000
Trade receivables	15,000
Trade payables	6,650
Inventory at 1st January 20x1	8,540
Furniture at 1st January 20x1	6,800
Motor Van at cost	25,400
Drawings	12,200
Capital	34,700
Cash at bank	2,830
Provision for depreciation-Motor van	1,000

You are given the following information:
a) Inventory at 31st December 20x1 was valued at $9,000
b) One half of the Salaries and wages was paid for re-packing the goods for sale.
c) The rent and rates amount includes $600 rent paid for the three months ended 31st January 20x2.
d) Motor vans are to be depreciated by 10%, using the Reducing Balance method.
e) A provision for doubtful debts is to be made as follows: Specific $3,000, General @ 4%
f) Interest on the loan is payable at 10% per annum and has been paid up to 30th June 20x1.
g) Daisy took goods costing $200 for her own use during the year ended 31st December 20x1. No entries had been made in the accounting records.
h) Furniture was valued at $ 6,000 on 31st December 20x1. No furniture was bought or sold during the year ended 31st December 20x1.

Required:
Prepare the Financial statements.

√ *Tip:*
a) For adjustment ' b ' half of $19,600 has to be included in the trading account and the other half in the profit & loss account sections of the Income statements respectively.
b) The rent and rates prepaid will be one third of $600 - adjustment 'c'
c) Interest on the loan for the year is 10% of $6000 = $ 600. Hence interest accrued is $600 - $300(already paid up to June 30th) = $300 ....adjustment 'f'
d) Regarding adjustment 'g', the journal entry that would have to be passed would have been:
Drawings -Debit
Purchases - Credit with the amount of $200. Hence deduct Purchases by $200 and increase Drawings by $200.
e.) Regarding adjustment 'd' – the amount of depreciation will be calculated at 10% of the N.B.V. of the Motor Van at 1st January 20x1 (10% of 25,400-1000)
f) Regarding adjustment 'h' – the depreciation is the difference between the N.B.V on 1st January 20x1 and that at 31st December 20x1. ($ 6,800 - $ 6,000)

Exercise 9.12

Sam is a sole trader. The following trail balance was taken from his books on 31st December, 20x1.

	Dr	Cr
	$	$
Machinery	40,000	
Capital		64,500
Sales revenue		102,000
Salaries	10,000	
Inventory at 1st Jan. 20x1	11,000	
Purchases	58,800	
Carriage inwards	1,000	
Insurance	2,000	
Electricity	1,600	
Irrecoverable debts	500	
Sundry expenses	2,300	
Motor expenses	1,500	
Advertising	1,600	
Discounts received		2,700
Provision for depreciation–Motor Van		500
Furniture at cost	7,000	
Motor Van at cost	10,500	
Cash at bank	2,600	
Trade payables		2,500
Trade receivables	7,000	
Drawings	14,800	
	172,200	172,200

Sam gives you the following information:

1) He purchased goods worth $4500 in November 20x1. The invoice for these goods was not received until 3rd January 20x2. There are no entries in Sam's books regarding this transaction.

2) All purchases are made on credit.

3) Depreciation for the year is as follows: Furniture @ 10% Straight Line; Motor van @ 10% Reducing Balance & Machinery @10% straight line.

4) On 31st December 20x1:
   Insurance prepaid was $300;
   Electricity expenses accrued was $350

5) Inventory at 31st December 20x1 was $12000.

6) A provision for doubtful debts is to be made @ 5% of Trade receivables

Prepare:

a) Sam's Income statement for the year ended 31st December 20x1

b) Sam's statement of financial position as at 31st December 20x1.

√ **Tip:** i) Carriage Inwards is to be included in the Trading Account section of the Income statement. (see format)

ii) For the first adjustment, $4500 will be added to to trade payables and added to purchases. This is because the goods were received.

» EXERCISE 9.13

A trial balance shows:

	$
Provision for doubtful debts	1,400
Trade receivables	20,000

$2,400 of the trade receivables are irrecoverable and are to be written off. The owner wishes to make the provision for doubtful debts equal to 5% of his outstanding trade receivables.

Required:
Calculate the amount credited to the Income statement for the provision for doubtful debts.

9.1   Multiple-choice questions

i) A Trial Balance includes the following: Trade receivables $67,000 and a Provision for Doubtful Debts of $4,500. A provision of 6% is to be made for doubtful debts. What is the amount of Provision for Doubtful Debts in the final accounts?

	The statement of financial position	The Income Statement
A)	$480	$4020
B)	$4020	$480
C)	$8520	$4020
D)	$8520	$480

ii) At December 31 20x3, Kate had debtors amounting to $5,000. Included in this figure was a debt of $100 owing by Mark who has now been declared insolvent. She decided to write off his debt as an irrecoverable debt. On examining her Sales Ledger she found that $200 debts were doubtful. She decided to make a general provision at 2% of the remaining trade receivables. What is her Provision for Doubtful Debts for the year ended December 31, 20x3?

A)	$294
B)	$100
C)	$298
D)	$300

iii) Julie maintains a General Provision for Doubtful Debts of 5%. Her Trial Balance includes the following: Trade receivables $30,000, Provision for Doubtful Debts $3,500. Subsequent to this, it was found that irrecoverable debts amounted to $5,000. There were also some doubtful debts. If the new provision was 2,200 what was the amount of these doubtful debts?

A) $2,300
B) $2,500
C) $1,000
D) $6,000

iv) Marcel increases his General Provision for Doubtful Debts from 3% to 5% in the year ended December 31, 20x1. The following information is available:

	Year ended December 31, 20x0	Year ended December 31, 20x1
	$	$
Debtors /Trade receivables *46,000		30,000
*These included irrecoverable debts		
Irrecoverable Debts	4,500	3,200
Doubtful debts	1,300	2,360

What is the effect on the general provision for doubtful debts in the year ended December 31, 20x1?

A)   The Provision increases by $120
B)   The Provision decreases by $120
C)   The Provision decreases by $16
D   The Provision increases by $16

v) On December 12, Damien received a cheque in respect of a dividend(or part payment) of 20% of Samuel's debt of $2,000. He had previously written off Samuel's debt. Which of the following is the correct treatment of such a transaction?

	Account to be debited	Account to be credited
A)	Bank $400	Samuel $400
B)	Bank$400	Irrecoverable Debts Recovered $400
C)	Bank $800	Samuel $400
		Irrecoverable debts Recovered $400
D)	Irrecoverable Debts $400	Samuel $400

9.2   Explain how the Provision for Doubtful Debts complies with the following concepts:

a)   Prudence
b)   Matching

9.3   Rehmat's trial balance at 31st March 20x1 was as follows:

	Dr	Cr
	$	$
Capital at1st April 20x0		7205
Cash	95	
Purchases	22865	
Sales		41975
Bank overdraft		4355
Inventory at 1st April 20x0	5165	
Sundry expenses	455	
Salaries	8935	
Discounts	1445	935
Carriage outwards	1745	

	Dr	Cr
	$	$
Rent	2165	
Sales returns	815	
Purchases returns		575
Provision for Doubtful debts		665
Trade receivables and payables	11905	6065
Motor Van	2885	
Furniture	2100	
Drawings	1200	
	61775	61775

Adjustments:
1)   Inventory at 31st March 20x1 was $3000
2)   Rent was prepaid 31st March 20x1 $200.
3)   Salaries accrued 31st March 20x1 $ 300
4)   Sundry Expenses owing 31st March 20x1 $40.
5)   Provision for Doubtful Debts is to made as follows: Specific$5,600, General 5% of the remaining trade receivables.
6)   Provide for depreciation : Motor Van $140; Furniture $300.

Required:
a)   The Income Statement for the year ended 31st March 20x1
b)   The statement of financial position as at 31st March 20x1

9.4 | On 1 January 20x7 Salma had a provision for doubtful debts of $ 1,500. On 31 December 20x7 the provision is to be 5% of trade debtors. The balance on the debtors' control account at 31 December 20x7 is $50,600 before writing off a debt of $560. If the business operates a separate irrecoverable debts account, what is the charge to the income statement for the provision for doubtful debts?

9.5 | A trial balance at 31 December 20x1, before making end of year adjustments, showed:

	$
Trade receivables	20,000 (Dr)
Provision for doubtful debts	700 (Cr)

At 31 December 20x1, it was decided to write off a debt of $1,000 and to make a provision for doubtful debts of 2% of trade receivables. During the year an amount of $300 was received from a customer relating to a debt that was written off in the year ended 31 December 20x0.

Required:
Calculate the total irrecoverable and doubtful debts expense for the year ended 31 December 20x1.

Bank Reconciliation Statements

10.1 | What is a Bank Reconciliation Statement?

A Bank reconciliation statement is a Statement that reconciles the closing balance at the bank according to the business cash book and that of the bank statement, when they are different.

10.2 | Why does a bank reconciliation statement become necessary?

A Bank Reconciliation Statement is made due to the fact that the closing balances in the cash book and that of the bank statement differs. The reasons that they differ are:

1) **Transactions recorded by the bank but not by the business:**
a) Bank charges; being the amount the bank has charged us for transactions for the period.
b) Standing orders; being instructions to the bank given by the business to pay a specified amount at given dates.
c) Direct debits; Where the business gives permission for an organisation to collect amounts owing, direct from our account.
d) Bank giro credit; being an amount paid by someone direct into our bank account. This is also known as direct credit or credit transfers.
e) Dishonoured cheques; being cheques not honoured by the bank.i.e. the bank has not paid the amount of the cheque.

2) **Transactions recorded by the business but not by the bank:**
a) Lodgements made but not credited by the bank due to a delay in clearing the cheque at the clearing house. This is known as 'Bank Lodgements not credited'.
b) Cheques written by the business but not presented by the drawee to the bank. These are known as 'Unpresented Cheques'.
c) Cheques written by the business and presented to the bank but not recorded by the bank due to a delay in the clearing of the cheque. These will also be known as 'Unpresented Cheques'.

3) **Errors made :**
a) by the business accountant
b) by the bank

10.3 | What is a bank overdraft?

A bank overdraft is when total withdrawals exceed total deposits in a bank account.

10.4 | Why do items on the debit side of the Cash Book appear on the credit side of the Bank Statement?

When the business deposits money into the bank, its cash at bank increases and hence the bank account in the business's books is debited. However, the bank credits this amount in it's accounts since it owes that sum to the business and hence the business is it's creditor.

NOTE: Steps to reconcile the differences between the closing balances in the Cash Book and the Bank Statement:
1) Mark with a tick the items in both the Cash book and the bank statement that are similar
2) Circle the ones that are not ticked.
   Draw up an updated cash book incorporating the circled items from the bank statement. (Remember, items on the credit side of the Bank Statement will be entered on the debit side of the Cash Book and vice versa).
3) Draw up a Bank Reconciliation Statement using the items circled in the Cash Book.

Exhibit :
Cash book (Bank columns only : after being completed to date)

20x0		$	20x0		$
Jul 1	Bal b/d	2,000	Jul2	C. Murthy	450
" 9	Mike	1,500	" 14	Jessica	150
" 15	Jack	450	" 31	Balance c/d	3,350
		3,950			3,950

Bank Statement:

20x0		Withdrawals $	Deposits $	Balance $
Jul 1	Balance b/d Jun 5			2,000
10987		450		1,550
Jul 11	Deposit		1,500	3,050
Jul 15	2056	150		2,900
Jul 17	Bank Giro credit :			
	Noel		400	3,300
Jul 18	Deposit		450	3,750
Jul 31	Bank charges	200		3,550

Note: All the items in the Cash book have been mentioned in the Bank Statement. However, the following items are missing from the Cash Book :
Bank giro credit : Noel - $ 400 and bank charges - $200.
So we will draw up an Updated Cash Book.

Updated Cash Book (bank columns only).

	$		$
Bal b/d	3,350	Bank charges	200
Cheque from Noel	400	Bal c/d	3,550
	3,750		3,750

√ **Tip:** *The bank reconciliation statement need not be made. The balance in the updated cash book is equal to the balance in the bank statement and this is the balance that will be shown in the statement of financial position as **Cash at Bank** under Current Assets.*

» EXERCISE 10.1

The following are extracts from the cash book and the bank statement of Jason.

You are required to : write up the cash book up to date and state the new balance as on 31st July 20x2.

Cash Book

20x2		$			$
Jul 1	Bal b/d	1400	Jul 4	Gina	100
Jul 4	Lal	470	Jul 12	Viv	160
Jul 7	Neil	430	Jul 20	Samant	150
Jul 20	Bess	140	Jul 31	Bal c/d	2030
		2440			2440

Bank Statement

20x2		Dr	Cr	Balance
Jul 1	Bal b/d			1400
Jul 6	1504	100		1300
Jul 7	Lal		470	1770
Jul 15	Viv	160		1610
Jul 21	Neil		430	2040
Jul 23	Samant	150		1890
Jul 24	Deposit		140	2030
Jul 27	Credit transfer: Penman		200	2230
Jul 31	Bank Charges	50		2180

» EXERCISE 10.2
Draw up a bank reconciliation statement from the following details as at 31st December 20x3:

	$
Cash at bank as per bank column of the cash book	750
Unpresented cheques	250
Cheques paid into the bank but not yet entered in the bank statement	160
Credit transfers entered on the bank statement but not in the cash book	140
Cash at bank as per bank statement	980

» EXERCISE 10.3

The following are extracts from the Bank statement and cash book of M. Ilonga:

INTERNATIONAL BANK
CONFIDENTIAL

Browns Bay
Melsan   STATEMENT OF CURRENT ACCOUNT

ACCOUNT :	ACCOUNT NO:	DATE:
M. ILONGA	1437690	31ST MARCH 20X2

Date 20 x 2	Details	CHQ NO.	DEBITS $	CREDITS $	BALANCE $
March 1	Balance				3450.00
16	Cash and Cheques			2500.00	5950.00
25	Cheque - Hakeem	45	540.00		5410.00

Ilonga's cash book for March 20x2:

Cash Book (Bank columns only)

Date	Details	Amount $	Date	Details	Amount $
March 1 16 24	Bal b/d Cash and chqs Chq. Peter	3450.00 2500.00 340.00	March 23 17	Hakeem Malik & sons Bal c/d	540.00 260.00 5490.00
		6290.00			6290.00

Required:

Prepare a statement reconciling the balances shown in Ilonga's cash book and in the bank statement on 31st March 20x2.

√ **Tip:** *The bank reconciliation statement can start with the balance as per bank statement too. In that case, the unpresented cheques are subtracted and the bank lodgements not entered are added.*

» EXERCISE 10.4

The following Bank Statement was received by Malcolm on July 2, 20x2.

Date	Details	Withdrawals	Deposits	Balance
20x2		$	$	$
June 1	Balance			5000
June 11	Transfer		870	5870
June 18	Kim	2000		3870
June 20	Colin		460	4330
June 25	Returned cheque	460		3870
June 28	Insurance premium	550		3320
June 30	Bank charges	100		3220

His Cash Book (Bank columns only) was as follows:

CASH BOOK

20x2		$	20x2		$
June 1	Balance b/d	5000	June 15	Kim	2000
June 13	Transfer	870	June 25	Cheque returned	460
June 22	Colin	460	June 29	Leslie	400
June 25	Leena	560	June 30	Bal c/d	4030
		6890			6890

Required:
a) Bring the Cash Book up to date.
b) Draw up a Bank Reconciliation Statement reconciling the amended Cash Book balance with the Bank Statement balance.

» EXERCISE 10.5

Larry is a trader. The following is an extract from his Cash Book for July 20x3

Cash Book (Bank columns only)

20x3		$	20x3		$
July 1	Balance b/d	5000	July 5	Insurance	345
13	Cash	2000	8	Electricity	286
25	M. Smiley (debtor)	650	26	Rates	800
			31	Bal c/d	6219
		7650			7650

On 3rd August 20x3 Larry received the following statement from his bank:

20x3 July		Dr $	Cr $	Balance $
" 1	Balance			5000
" 7	Cheque No 340	345		4655
" 13	Cash and cheques		2000	6655
" 10	Cheque No 341	286		6369
" 31	Bank Charges	100		6269

Required
a) Calculate the balance in Larry's Cash Book after the adjustments to bring it up to date have been made.
b) Prepare a statement reconciling the balances shown in Larry's Cash Book (as amended) and in the Bank Statement.

WHEN THERE IS AN OVERDRAFT

√ Tip: *When a firm has an overdraft, then the <u>unpresented cheques are subtracted</u> and the <u>bank lodgements are added</u> to the cash at bank as per the <u>Cash Book.</u>*

Exhibit:
On March 31st 20x2 Edward, a trader had a credit balance in the bank column of her cash book of $1,250. This differed from the balance on the bank statement due to the following reasons:
a. Unpresented cheques amounting to $450
b. Bank lodgement amounting to $500 was not credited to her account in the bank statement.

Required:
A Bank Reconciliation Statement as at 31st March 20x2.

Solution:

Bank Reconciliation Statement as at 31st March 20x2

	$
Cash at bank as per the cash book	1,250
Less Unpresented cheques	450
	800
Add Bank lodgement not credited	500
Overdraft as per the bank statement	1,300

» EXERCISE 10.6

Selma obtained a bank statement from her bank which differed from the bank account closing balance on 31st December 20x1 in her Cash Book. The Cash book balance showed an overdraft of $3,500.
The two balances differed since:
a) Cash paid into the bank amounting to $650 had not yet been credited to her account
b) A cheque of $260 payable to Maitale had not yet been presented for payment.

Required:
A bank reconciliation statement to show the balance which appeared on the bank statement on 31st December 20x1.

NOTE: *The uses of a bank reconciliation statement are:*
- *To arrive at the correct amount of cash at bank.*
- *To therefore ensure that the right bank balance is shown in the statement of financial position.*
- *To act as an instrument of control so that frequent overdrafts are avoided.*
- *To detect errors early*

» EXERISE 10.7

The following are extracts of Kelly's bank statement and Cash book (bank columns) on 30th June 20x3:

Cash Book

20x3		$	20x3		$
June 5	K. Lewis	300	June 1	Bal. B/d	700
" 16	M. Dawson	150	" 6	S. Jewel	200
" 20	I. Jacob	350	" 18	M. Long	270
" 30	Bal c/d	470	" 21	G. Fraser	100
		1,270			1,270

Bank Statement

20x3		Dr	Cr	Balance
		$	$	$
June 1	Balance b/d			700 O/D
" 7	Cheque		300	400 O/D
" 10	Jewel	200		600 O/D
" 22	Fraser	100		700 O/D
" 24	Jacob		350	350 O/D

Required:

A Bank Reconciliation Statement as at 30th June 20x3

» EXERCISE 10.8

The bank statement for Roomey for the month of March 20x1 is :

20x1		Dr	Cr	Balance
March		$	$	$
1	Balance			4370 O/D
6	Tilly	130		4500 O/D
17	Cheque		250	4250 O/D
21	Benny	200		4450 O/D
27	Tom : direct credit		150	4300 O/D
30	MMK : Standing order	50		4350 O/D
31	Bank charges	100		4450 O/D

The Cash book for March 20x1 is:

20x1		$	20x1		$
March15	Jill	250	March 1	Bal. B/d	4370
24	Lucy	350	4	Tilly	130
31	Bal c/d	4400	19	Benny	200
			23	Manny	300
		5000			5000

You are to:

a) Write the cash book up to date. (Remember, what is debited in the Bank Statement is to be credited in the Cash book. This does not change, even though there is an overdraft)

b) Draw up a Bank Reconciliation Statement as on 31st March 20x1.

» EXERCISE 10.9

The Cash Book of Mala showed a balance of $100 at the bank as on December 31, 20x5. On the same date the bank statement balance was $170 (Debit). On comparing the Bank Statement with the Cash Book the following information was revealed:

i) A cheque for $340 lodged with the bank had not been cleared for payment.

ii) A cheque for $300 sent to a creditor had not been presented for payment.

iii) Bank charges of $230 were omitted from the cash book.

Required:

a) Calculate the correct Cash Book Balance at December 31, 20x5.

b) Prepare a bank reconciliation statement at December 31, 20x5.

» EXERCISE 10.10

The Cash Book of Mala showed a balance of $400 at the bank as on March 31, 20x5. On the same date the bank statement balance was $2150 (credit). On comparing the Bank Statement with the Cash Book the following information was revealed:

i. A cheque for $1000 lodged with the bank had not been cleared for payment.

ii. A cheque for $3200 sent to a creditor had not been presented for payment.

iii. Bank charges of $450 were omitted from the cash book.

Required:

c) Calculate the correct Cash Book Balance at March 31, 20x5.

d) Prepare a bank reconciliation statement at March 31, 20x5.

» EXERCISE 10.11

The balance at bank according to the cash book on 31 October 20x9 was $5600. Subsequently, the following discoveries were made:

a) A cheque dated 4 September 20x9 for $130 in favour of Kemp Ltd. has been correctly recorded in the bank statement, but included in the cash book payments as $310.

b) Commission of $135 charged by bank and bank interest of $234 have been included in the bank statement on 20 October 20x9, but not included in the cash book.

c) The latest bank statement shows that a cheque of $101 from Jabba Ltd. credited in the bank statement on 10 October 20x9 has now been dishonoured and debited in the bank statement on 20 October 20x9. The only entry in the cash book for this cheque records its receipt on 9 October 20x9.

d) Cheque for $256 has been recorded twice as a credit in the cash book.

e) $4,560 was recorded in the cash book but not

included in the bank statement. This is a total of amounts received in the last days of October 20x9. These amounts were included in a subsequent bank statement as received on 4 November 20x9.

f) Traders' credits totalling $340 have been credited in the bank statement on 29 October 20x9, but not yet recorded in the cash book.

g) A standing order payment of $35 on 15 October 20x9 has been recorded in the bank statement but is not mentioned in the cash book.

Required:

a) Prepare a computation of the balance at bank to be included in the statement of financial position as at 31

b) October 20x9. Prepare a bank reconciliation statement as at 31 October 20x9.

» EXERCISE 10.12

At 31 December 20x1, a customer's bank statement shows that his bank account is overdrawn by $12,300. Some more information follows:
1) Unpresented cheques amounted to $3450
2) Bank lodgements not entered amounted to $2,560.
3) Bank interest of $250 was not entered in the cash book.

Required:

Calculate the bank balance to be shown in the customer's statement of financial position at 31 December 20x1.

» EXERCISE 10.13

A Bank Reconciliation Statement shows a credit balance of $500 in the Cash Book and a debit balance of $200 in the bank statement. The bank reconciliation statement includes unpresented cheques of $600, in addition to bank lodgements not yet credited by the bank.

Required:

Calculate the total of cheques banked and not yet credited by the bank.

» EXERCISE 10.14

At 31 July Keshav's cash book, bank column, had a balance of $13,000 debit. However, a cheque for $14,500 received from Yadhav and a cheque for $1,350 paid to Madhav appear in the cash book but not on the bank statement. Bank charges of $3,000 have not been entered in the cash book.

Required:

Calculate the balance shown on the bank statement at 31 July. State whether it is a debit or credit balance

10.1| Multiple-choice questions

i) *The bank reconciliation statement is used to:*
A) Ensure that the correct cash balance is shown in the statement of financial position
B) Ensure that the business avoids unintended overdrawing on the bank account
C) Complete double entry for all items entered in the cash book, bank columns
D) Complete double entry for all items entered in the cash book, cash columns

ii) *The balance on a bank statement at 31 March 20x6 was $1,200 credit. The following item had been entered in the cash book in March but did not appear on the bank statements: Amount paid into bank $400*
What was the cash book balance at 31 March 20x6?
A) $ 1,600   B) $800   C) $1,200   D) $2,000

iii) *Manu's bank statement at 31 December 20x7 shows a balance of $1,400. His cash book revealed that a bank lodgement of $350 and a cheque of $400 made out to a supplier were missing from the bank statement. What was his balance in his cash book on that day?*
A) $1,350   B) $ 1,450   C) $2,150   D) $650

iv) *The cash book had a credit balance of $5,600 on July 31,20x8. An examination of the bank statement on that date revealed:*
a) *a cheque for $450 sent to a supplier had not been presented for payment to the bank*
b) *bank charges of $60 was not entered in the cash book*
c) *A cheque for $700 paid into the bank had not been credited in the bank statement.*
What was the balance on the bank statement at July 31, 20x8?
A) $5,910dr   B) $5,410cr   C) $5,910cr
D) $5,410dr

v) *A bank statement showed a balance of $500 at 31 August 20x3. The following was discovered:*
a) *a direct credit of $560, not shown in the cash book was credited twice in the bank statement.*
b) *rent paid by standing order $60 was not entered in the cash book*
c) *amount of $340 received by bank giro was not entered in the cash book*
What was the balance as the cash book?
A) $1,900cr   B) $ 1,900 dr   C) $2,000dr
D) $2,000cr

10.2| The Netherdale Sports Club's Receipts and Payments Account shows the following transactions for the year ended 30 April 20x6.

RECEIPTS	$	PAYMENTS	$
Balance b/d	20,000	National club fees	3,000
Subscriptions	72,000	Restaurant supplies	51,000
Restaurant takings	108,000	Purchase of clubhouse	50,000
		Loan interest	2,200
Annual dance	8,900	Purchase of equipment	14,000
Sale of equipment	6,000		
Loan to purchase clubhouse	20,000	Restaurant wages	22,000
		Repairs and maintenance	12,400
		Annual dance	4,950
		Administration of annual dance	320
		Electricity	11,000
		General wages	60,000
		Balance c/d	4,030
	234,900		234,900
Balance b/d	4,030		

When the club's bank statements for the year ended 30 April 20x6 were studied, the following were discovered.

i) Bank interest of $100 for the year had been credited in the bank statement but no entry appeared in the receipts and payments account.

ii) Electricity was paid by direct debit at $1,000 per month but the entry for January 20x6 had been omitted from the receipts and payments account.

iii) $4,000 had been banked for restaurant takings on 30 April 20x6. This had been entered in the receipts and payments account but did not appear on the bank statement.

iv) A cheque for $2,800 for repairs and maintenance, posted on 29 April 20x6, was included in the receipts and payments account but had not yet been presented to the bank for payment.

Required:
a) Update the Netherdale Sports Club's Receipts and Payments Account.
b) Prepare a bank reconciliation statement at 30 April 20x6 to reconcile the bank statement with the updated receipts and payments balance.
(UCLES, 2006, AS/A level A/c, syllabus 9706/2, May/June)

10.3| Minna's draft statement of financial position shows a bank balance of $2,800. The following information is now available:

	$
Cheques issued but not yet cleared by the bank	140
Bank charges not entered in the cash book	67
Lodgements in the cash book not on the bank statement	320

What will be the amount showing on the Bank Statement?

10.4| Seema's bank statement shows a credit balance of $5,890. A comparison with the cash book reveals the following:

i) Cheques totalling $16,780, sent to suppliers, have not been presented.
ii) Cheques totalling $13,560, received from customers, have not been credited by the bank.
iii) Bank charges of $130 have not been entered in the cash book.
What is the correct cash book balance?

10.5| The following information is available when preparing a bank reconciliation statement:

	$
Balance at bank as per cash book	30,000 (dr)
Uncleared bankings	1,000
Direct debit shown in bank statement but not in cash book	600
Unpresented cheques	1,800

Required:
Calculate the balance as per the bank statement.

Control Accounts

11.1 | What are Control Accounts?

Control Accounts are also called 'total accounts'. This is because they are made up of the (periodic) totals of various appropriate books of prime entry in order to check the arithmetical accuracy of Ledgers in a company that has many ledgers. A control Account for a Sales Ledger is often known as a 'Sales Ledger Control account' or a 'Total Trade Receivables Account'. A control account for a Purchases Ledger is often known as a 'Purchases Ledger control Account' or a 'Total Trade Payables Account'. They are normally kept in the general ledger.

11.2 | What are the uses/ advantages of Control Accounts?

Control Accounts have the following uses:
a) They are used to locate errors in the ledgers that do not balance, thus eliminating the need to check all the books to find the error. For example: The trial balance of Alex reveals a difference in the totals. To locate the error/s control accounts were prepared. The Sales ledger Control account had a difference between the debit side and the credit side of $45. Hence an error has been made in the sales ledger and it would not be necessary to look for an error in the other ledgers.
b) They are used to prevent dishonesty. Control Accounts are under the charge of a responsible official and any transfers made in an effort to disguise fraud will have to pass the scrutiny of this person.
c) Management control is aided since managers often take the balances on the control accounts to equal Trade receivables and Trade payables without waiting for an extraction of individual balances.
d) They are an important system of control on the reliability of ledger accounts.
e) They warn of possible errors in the ledgers they control. If the totals of the balances in those ledgers do not agree with the balances on the control accounts, an error can be suspected.

11.3 | What are the limitations of Control Accounts?

Control Accounts have the following limitations:
a. A control account may itself contain errors.
b. Control accounts cannot guarantee the accuracy of individual ledger accounts e.g. if compensating errors have been made in individual ledger accounts

11.4 | Where is the information for Control Accounts obtained?

A) For the Sales Ledger Control Account :
Opening Trade receivables - from the list of debtors' balances drawn up at the end of the preceding period.
Credit sales - the total of the sales journal.
Return Inwards - the total of the Sales returns journal
Cheques received - the bank column on the debit side of the cash book.
Cash received - the cash column on the debit side of the Cash book.
Closing Trade receivables - the list of debtors' balances drawn up at the end of the current period.

B) For the Purchases Ledger Control Account:
Opening Trade payables - the list of creditors' balances drawn up at the end of the preceding period.
Credit Purchases - the total of the Purchases Journal. **Return Outwards** - the total of the Purchases Returns Journal.
Cheques paid - the bank column on the credit side of the cash book.
Cash paid – the cash column on the credit side of the Cash book.
Closing Trade payables – the list of creditors' balances drawn up at the end of the current period.

NOTE: A trial balance acts as a check on the arithmetical accuracy of *all* the ledgers, whereas a control account acts as a check of the arithmetical accuracy of *one* ledger.

Exhibit :
Prepare a Sales Ledger Control Account from the following for the month of June:

20x0		$
June 1	Sales ledger Balances	3,500
	Totals for June:	
	Sales Journal	30,000
	Returns Inwards Journal	1,000
	Cheques and cash received from customers	20,000
	Discounts allowed	500
	Set-offs against balances in Purchases ledger	200
	Unrecoverable debts	50
	Dishonoured cheques	500
June 30	Sales ledger balances (dr)	?
	Sales ledger balances (cr)	50

Solution:

Sales Ledger Control Account

20x0		$	20x0		$
June 1	Balances b/d	3,500	June 30	Return Inwards	1,000
June 30	Sales	30,000		Cash and Bank	20,000
	Bank:				
	Dishonoured Cheques	500		Discounts allowed	500
				Set- off	200
	Bal c/d	50		Unrecoverable debts	50
				Bal c/d	12,300
		34,050			34,050

√ Tip:

1) Set-offs are amounts of inter-indebtedness between two firms that are both suppliers and customers for each other. The amount will be written on the credit side of a Sales Ledger Control Account and on the debit side of a Purchases Ledger Control Account.

2) There are two closing balances : a credit balance and a debit balance. This happens when, for instance, a customer returns goods after paying in full his account. Keep the following in mind:

Opening Balances: i.e. on the first day of the period.- Balance b/d	A credit balance	A debit balance
	On the credit side of the account	On the debit side of the account
Closing balance i.e. on the last day of the period – Balance c/d	A credit balance	A debit balance
	On the debit side of the account	On the credit side of the account

3) Remember: Whatever lowers Debtors /Trade receivables will appear on the credit side of the Sales Ledger Control Account and whatever increases Debtors /Trade receivables will appear on the debit side.

4) Remember: Whatever lowers Creditors /Trade payables will appear on the debit side of the Purchases Ledger Control Account and whatever increases Creditors /Trade payables will appear on the credit side.

Exhibit :
Prepare a Purchases Ledger Control Account from the following for the month of July:

20x1		$
July 1	Purchases Ledger – debit balances	500
	Purchases Ledger – Credit balances	5,500
July 31	Totals for July:	
	Purchases Journal	25,000
	Return outwards journal	500
	Cheques paid to creditors /trade payables	15,000
	Discounts received	300
	Interest charged by suppliers	50
	Purchases ledger – debit balances	5,000
	Purchases ledger – credit balances	?

Solution:

Purchases Ledger Control Account

20x1		$	20x1		$
July 1	Balances b/d	500	July 1	Balances b/d	5,500
July 31	Return outwards	500	July 31	Purchases	25,000
	Bank	15,000		Interest charged	50
	Discounts received	300		Balances c/d	5,000
	Balances c/d	19,250			
		35,550			35,550

» EXERCISE 11.1

Prepare a Sales Ledger Control Account from the following for the month of August:

20x2		$
August 1	Sales ledger balances	5,000
	Totals for August:	
	Sales Journal	20,000
	Return inwards	2,400
	Discounts allowed	450
	Unrecoverable Debts	600
	Cash received from customers	5,000
	Cheques received from customers	10,000
August 31	Sales ledger balances	?

EXERCISE 11.2

Prepare a Purchases Ledger Control Account from the following information for the month of March:

20x1		$
March 1	Purchases Ledger balances	4,500
" 31	Totals for March:	
	Purchases journal	13,600
	Return outwards	550
	Discounts received	650
	Cash paid to suppliers	5,400
	Cheques paid to suppliers	10,200
	Purchases ledger balances	?

» EXERCISE 11.3

During the month of June 20x0, the following were the entries in the sales ledger control account:

	$
Balances b/f	34,500
Credit sales	23,500
Return inwards	2,400
Cash and cheques	35,600
Discounts allowed	1,000
Increase in provision for doubtful debts	60

Required:
Prepare the Sales Ledger Control account for the month of June 20x0.

√ *Tip: The increase in the provision for doubtful debts will **not** be included in the Control account.*

» EXERCISE 11.4

The following figures are taken from the books of Tom:

20x0		$
October 1	Balances brought down in the	
	Purchases ledger: Debit	50
	Credit	4,500
31	Totals for the month:	
	Purchases journal	5,600
	Purchases returns journal	1,000
	Cheques paid to suppliers	6,500
	Discounts received	200
	Cash refunded by suppliers	30
	Purchases ledger balances (dr)	40

Required:
Prepare Tom's Purchases Ledger Control Account for the month of October 20x0

NOTE: Debit and credit balances should never be netted. In Exercise 11.4, above, the closing debit balance ($40) will be shown under current assets as trade receivables and a credit balance as trade payables under current liabilities in the statement of financial position.

» EXERCISE 11.5

From the following prepare the Purchases Ledger Control account and the Sales Ledger Control account for the month of March 20x3 .

20x3		$
March 1	Purchases ledger balances	3,400(cr)
		20(dr)
	Sales ledger balances	5,200(dr)
		26 (cr)
	Totals for the month:	
	Purchases journal	34,700
	Sales journal	14,500
	Return inwards journal	1,250
	Return outwards journal	2,500
	Cheques paid to suppliers	20,000
	Cheques and cash received	
	from customers	10,000
	Discounts received	500
	Discounts allowed	300
	Balances on the sales ledger set off against	
	balances in the purchases ledger	1,200
	Decrease in provision for doubtful debts	30
March 31	Debit balances on purchases	
	ledger accounts	400
	Credit balances on sales ledger	
	accounts	120

RECONCILIATION OF CONTROL ACCOUNTS WITH LEDGERS

11.5 | What is meant by the term ' Reconciling the Control Accounts'?

When the balance on a Control Account and the total of the balances in the ledger it controls differ, the cause or causes must be found and the necessary corrections made. This is known as 'Reconciling the Control Accounts'.

11.6 | What happens when an item is incorrectly posted from a book of prime entry to a personal account in the sales or purchases ledger?

The control Account is not affected. However, a reconciliation, as mentioned above, should be made as the balances of the control account and the totals of the balances in the ledger it controls will differ. The control account will reveal the error.
NOTE: It is customary to treat control accounts as part of double entry and to regard the accounts in the sales and purchases ledgers as memorandum records or else the records will be duplicated.

Exhibit :
A credit sale of $467 to Sam is correctly entered in the Sales journal but is posted to Sam's account in the Sales ledger as $764. The sales ledger balances totalled $45,000.
Required:
Calculate the revised Sales Ledger Balance

Solution:
The difference = 764-467 = $297
The total of the Sales ledger balance is overstated by $297
The revised sales ledger balance will now be: 45,000 – 297
= $44,703

11.7 | What happens when a page of a book of prime entry has been wrongly totalled ?

The Control Account will be incorrect but the ledger it controls will not be affected. The control account will reveal the error.

Exhibit :
The Sales Journal total for January has been overstated by $ 3,000. At 31 January the credit sales as per control account are: $23,000
Required:
Calculate the total of the balances as per the Sales Ledger at 31 January

Solution:
The correct balance as per the control account should be: $23,000 – 3,000 = $20,000. This will then match the total of the balances as per the Sales Ledger.
Hence the total of the balances as per the Sales Ledger at 31 January is $20,000.

11.8 | What happens when a transaction is entered incorrectly in a book of prime entry?

When this happens, the error is repeated in the Control Account as well as in the personal account in the corresponding ledger. The Control Account will not reveal this error

Exhibit :
A supplier's invoice for $650 has been entered in the purchases journal as $560. The total trade payables as per the purchases ledger was $7,800.
Required:
a) Calculate the revised figure for total trade payables
b) By how much would the control account be affected?

Solution:
a) The difference = 650-560 = $90
The revised total trade payables will now be $7,800 + 90 = $7,890.
b) The control account balance will also have to be increased by $90.

11.9 | What happens when a transaction is omitted from a book of prime entry?

The transaction will be omitted from the personal account in the appropriate ledger and from the control account. The control account will not reveal the error.

Exhibit :
A sales invoice for $600 has been omitted from the sales journal. The total trade receivables as per the control account is $2,300.
Required:
a) Calculate the revised figure for total trade receivables
b) By how much would the control account be affected?
Solution:
a. The total trade receivables will now be $2,300 + $600 = $2,900
b. The Sales ledger control account balance will also have to be increased by $600.

» EXERCISE 11.6
The following errors have been discovered:
a. A credit note for $50 has been entered as an invoice.
b. Purchases of $359 have been entered on the wrong side of a supplier's account in the Purchases ledger.
c. No entry has been made to record an agreement to contra an amount owed to Mac of $780 against an amount owed by Mac of $380.
d. An invoice for $769 has been entered in the purchases journal as $697.
e. A cash discount of $50 from a trade payables (creditor) had been completely omitted from the accounting records.

Required:
Fill in the following table showing the numerical effect of correcting each of these items on the total trade payables Account.

Item	Decrease	Increase	No effect

» EXERCISE 11.7

The following balances have been extracted from the books of Madonna at 31 December 20x7.

	$
Total of purchases ledger balances(cr)	3,980
Total of sales ledger balances (dr)	8,885
Total of sales ledger balances (cr)	79
Balance on total trade receivables' account(dr)	9,836
Balance on total trade payables' account(cr)	5,000

The following errors have been discovered:
1) A debit balance in the sales ledger $45 has been extracted as a credit balance in the list of sales ledger balances.
2) A purchases invoice of $140 has been omitted from the purchases day book.
3) Discounts received in December amounting to $340 have been credited to the Total trade payables' Account.
4) The Sales day book has been overcast by $600.
5) A balance of $340 on a customer's account in the sales ledger has been set against the amount owing to her in the purchases ledger but no entries have been made for this in the total trade receivables' and total trade payables' accounts.
6) A supplier's invoice for $760 has been entered in the purchases journal as $670

Required:
1) Prepare the amended Sales Ledger and Purchases ledger control accounts
2) Calculate the following as at 31 December 20x7:
a)   The revised sales ledger balances
b)   The revised purchases ledger balances.

11.1| Multiple-choice questions

i) The following information has been obtained from the books of Chenny Ltd.

	$
At Jan 1 20x5 the purchases ledger balances b/f (cr)	8,000
(dr)	25
In the month of January 20x5:	
Total invoices received from suppliers	45,000
Goods returned to suppliers	546
Discounts received	2,000
Cheques sent to suppliers	28,000
Cash paid to suppliers	1,200
At January 31 20x5 the purchases ledger balances c/f (dr)	300

What is the credit balance in the purchases ledger at January 31, 20x5?
A) $20,929   B) $22,729   C) $21,529
D) $ 22,429

ii) Which of the following items do not appear on the debit side of the Sales Ledger Control account?
A) Dishonoured cheques   B) Credit sales   C) Cash Sales
D) Irrecoverable debts recovered

iii) The following information is given to you:

	$
Total of sales ledger balances at 31 December 20x9 (debit)	23,000
Total of sales ledger balances at 31 December 20x9 (credit)	150

The following errors have been discovered:
1)   A credit sale of $560 has been omitted from the journal
2)   A page of the sales journal has been overstated by $2,000
What is the correct sales ledger debit balance?
A) $ 22,850   B) $ 23,560   C) $21,560   D) $21,410

iv) The balance on the Purchases Ledger Control Account is $45,000 (cr) at 31 March 20x5. The following errors have been discovered:
1)   A balance of $300 on a customer's account in the sales ledger has been set against the amount owing to him in the purchases ledger but no entry has been made for this in the Sales or Purchases ledger control accounts.
2)   A supplier's invoice for $790 has been entered as $970 in the purchases journal.
What is the amended balance in the Purchases Ledger Control account after the above errors have been corrected?
A) $44,700   B) $44,520   C) $44,320   D) $44,820

v) A Sales Ledger Control account has been reconciled with the Sales Ledger Balances as shown.

	$
Balance as per Control Account	*81,000*
Total of Sales Journal for one month not included in the control account	*2,000*
Cash received from customers not included in the control account	*1,400*
Total of balances in the Sales Ledger	*81,600*

What is the correct figure for trade receivables to be shown in the statement of financial position?

A) $81,000   B) $83,000   C) $83,600   D) $82,400

11.2 | The books of Mary Rose gave the following information for the month ended 31 May 2003. All sales and purchases were on credit.

	$000
Sales ledger balance at 1 May 2003	5,627
Purchases ledger balance at 1 May 2003	4,388
Sales for the year	100,384
Purchases for the year	64,987
Sales returns	1,997
Purchases returns	864
Payments received from customers (all banked)	92,760
Payments made to suppliers	63,520
Debtor's dishonoured cheque	109
Discount allowed	4,082
Discount received	3,241
Irrecoverable written off	1,884
Debit balances transferred to purchases ledger control account	208

The total of Mary Rose's sales ledger balances is $9,387, which differs from the closing balance in the sales ledger control account.

REQUIRED:

a) Extract the relevant information from the above and prepare the sales ledger control account for the month ended 31 May 2003.

The following errors have been discovered since the sales ledger control account was prepared.

i)   A sales invoice for $2001 had been completely omitted from the books.

ii)   A page of the sales day book with entries totalling $7820 had been omitted from the total sales but the individual entries had been posted to the debtors' accounts.

iii) A debit balance of $4020 had been omitted from the list of debtors.

iv) A sales ledger account has been understated by $220

v)   A purchases ledger account had been overstated by $350.

vi) Discount allowed had been overstated by $620.

vii) Discount received had been understated by $450.

viii) An entry for $1620 in the sales day book had been omitted from the customer's account.

ix)   A contra entry had been made in the purchases ledger for a debit balance of $1412 in the sales ledger, but no entry had been made in the control accounts.

x)   A receipt of $1210 was debited to bank but not posted to the customer's account.

xi)   A credit note for $720, sent to a customer, had been entered in the sales day book and posted as a sale to both accounts.

xii) A customer owing $1820 was declared bankrupt during May 2003. The debt was written off in the control account but no entry had been made in the customer's account.

REQUIRED

b.

1) Prepare an amended sales ledger control account, extracting the relevant information from the list of errors given above.

2) Prepare a statement altering the total of the sales ledger balance to agree with the new sales ledger control account balance.

[UCLES, 2004, AS/A Level Accounting, Syllabus 9706/2, Oct/Nov]

11.3 | a) Outline three reasons for keeping control accounts

The following information was extracted from the books of William Noel for the year ended 30 April 2001.

	$
Purchases ledger balance at 1 May 2000	43,120
Credit purchases for the year	824,140
Credit purchase returns	12,400
Cheques paid to suppliers	745,980
Cash purchases	8,940
Discount received on credit purchases	31,400
Credit balances transferred to sales ledger accounts	5,210

b) REQUIRED

Draw up the purchases ledger control account for the year ended 30 April 2001.

The total of the balances in William Noel's purchases ledger amounts to $67,660, which does not agree with the closing balance in the control account.

The following errors were then discovered:

1)   Discount received had been overstated by $ 1,000.

2)   A credit purchases invoice for $2,040 had been completely omitted from the books.

3)   A purchases ledger account had been understated by $100.

4)   A credit balance of $850 in the purchases ledger had been set off against a contra entry in the Sales Ledger but no entry had been made in either control account.

5) A payment of $1,450 had been debited to the supplier's account but was omitted from the bank account.
6) A credit balance of $3,210 had been omitted from the list of suppliers.

REQUIRED

i) Extract the necessary information from the above list and draw up an amended purchases ledger control account for the year ended 30 April 2001.

ii) Beginning with the given total of $67,660, show the changes to be made in the purchases ledger to reconcile it with the new control account balance.
[UCLES,2001,AS/A Level Accounting, Syllabus 8706/2, October/November.]

11.4 | The closing balance on a Purchases Ledger Control Account is $ 143,000. The Purchases Journal has been undercast by $2,500. What is the correct closing balance on the Purchases Ledger Control Account?

11.5 | The balance on a sales ledger control account is $50,000. The following items are then discovered:
i) The total of the sales journal is understated by $400
ii) Discounts allowed $1,400 has not been entered in the sales ledger control account
iii) Irrecoverable debts written off $300 have not been recorded in the sales ledger control account.
iv) A provision for doubtful debts of $3,000.
What is the total of the balances in the sales ledger?

11.6 | At 1 Janaury 20x1 a business has a provision for doubtful debts of $3,100. At 31 December the provision is to be 5% of trade receivables. The balance on the Trade Receivables Control account at 31 December 20x1 is $48,900 before writing off an irrecoverable debt of $450. The business operates a separate irrecoverable debts account.

Required:
Calculate the entry in the income statement for the provision for doubtful debts, stating whether it is a debit or credit entry.

11.7 In a control account prepared by a business, trade receivable was $ 15,000. A customer, who owes the business $500, is also a supplier to whom the business owes $300 for inventory supplied.
What is the accurate trade receivables control account balance?

11.8 The following information is given at 31 Dec 20x5

		$
Total of sales ledger balances	debit	15,055
	credit	300
Total of purchases ledger balance	debit	500
	credit	30,000
Balance on sales ledger control a/c	debit	15,000
Balance on purchases ledger control a/c	credit	30,540

The following errors were discovered:
1. Discounts received $400 was credited to the purchases ledger control a/c
2. A supplier who had a debit balance of $500 on 31 Dec had a purchases return of $120 credited to his account in the purchases ledger during the year.
3. A credit balance of $55 in the sales ledger had been extracted as a debit balance in the list of sales ledger balances.

The profit for the year ended 31 December 20x5 was $47,000. A provision for doubtful debts of 5% is to be made.

REQUIRED:
a. Calculate the following at 31 December 20x5:
  i. the revised purchases ledger balances
  ii. the revised sales ledger balances
b. Prepare the amended purchases ledger control account.
c. Prepare a statement of revised profit for the year ended 31 December 20x5
d. Prepare an extract from the statement of financial position at 31 December 20x5 to show trade receivables and trade payables.

Suspense Accounts

12.1 | When is a suspense account opened?

A suspense account is opened when the two sides of the trial balance differ and the cause for this difference is not immediately apparent. It is opened with the difference between the totals in the trial balance.

12.2 | When is a suspense account closed?

When the errors are subsequently discovered, they are corrected, using a journal entry. If all the errors are discovered, the suspense account will close when this journal entry is passed. E.g The sales account was undercast by $50.

> Debit   the suspense account with $50
> Credit   the sales account with $50.

√ **Tip:** When the error has resulted in an imbalance of the trial balance, the suspense account is involved.

12.3 | How can errors be classified?

Errors can be broadly classified as:
I.Errors that affect the trial balance.
II.Errors that do not affect the trial balance

12.4 | Explain: Errors that affect the Trial Balance.

These are predominantly of three types and are shown up by differing totals in the trial balance. These would be the result of **errors in additions, using one figure for the debit entry and another figure for the credit entry,** entering only **one aspect of a transaction,** and so on.

12.5 | Name the errors that do not affect the trial balance agreement.

Errors that do not affect the trial balance agreement are:
> Errors of omission
> Errors of commission
> Errors of principle
> Errors of original entry

Errors caused by the complete reversal of entries
Compensating errors
Errors of transposition.
(Go back to chapter 3 to see a full explanation of these errors.)

12.6 | How will an item posted to the wrong side of an account be corrected?

This error will be corrected by an adjustment equal to twice the amount of the original error: once to cancel the error and once to place the item on the correct side of the account.

12.7 | How will errors that do not affect the double entry be corrected?

Such errors do not need to be corrected by debit and credit entries. E.g. a balance on a purchases ledger account was copied incorrectly onto a summary of balances for inclusion in the trial balance. The summary of balances should be amended and a one-sided entry in the journal prepared to correct the suspense account.

Exhibit :
The bookkeeper extracted a trial balance on 30th June 20x3 which failed to agree by $440, a shortage on the credit side of the trial balance. A suspense account was opened for the difference.
In the first week of July 20x3, the following errors made in the previous financial year were found:
a)   Sales of $380 to Manuel had been debited in error to Mason's account.
b)   Sales journal had been undercast by $780.
c)   Rent account had been undercast by $300.
d)   Purchases journal undercast by $90.
e)   The sale of a machinery $1,500 had been credited in error to Sales account.
f)   A credit balance of $50 in the purchases ledger had been omitted from the list of balances extracted from the ledger. The total of the list had been included in the trial balance.

You are required to:

1) Show the journal entries necessary to correct the errors(Narratives are required).
2) Draw up the suspense account after the errors described have been corrected.
3) If profit had been calculated at $4500 for the year ended 30 June 20XX, show the calculations of the corrected profit for the year.

SOLUTION

1) Journal Entries

		$	$
a)	Manuel's account	380	
	Mason's account		380
	(Error of commission, now corrected)		
b)	Suspense account	780	
	Sales account		780
	(Correction of an undercast in the Sales account)		
c)	Rent account	300	
	Suspense account		300
	(Correction of an undercast in the Rent account)		
d)	Purchases account	90	
	Suspense account		90
	(Correction of an undercast in the Purchases account)		
e)	Sales account	1, 500	
	Machinery account		1,500
	(Error of principle, now corrected)		

f)NOTE *This is not a double-entry error. Nevertheless, it has affected the trial balance. The list of balances must be corrected and a one-sided entry in the Suspense account is required:*

	Dr
Suspense account	50

2) Suspense Account

	$		$
Sales	780	Difference on trial balance	440
Correction of trade payables	50	Purchases	90
		Rent	300
	830		830

NOTE: *A suspense account enables a business to prepare its draft financial statements quickly even though the trial balance did not balance.*

3) Calculation of corrected profit for the year ended 30 June 20xx

	(+)	(-)	
	$	$	$
Profit before corrections			4,500
a) No effect on profit			
b) Increase in sales	780		
c) Increase in rent		300	
d) Increase in purchases		90	
e) Decrease in sales		1,500	
f)No effect on profit			
	780	(1890)	(1,110)
Revised profit for the year			3,390

√ *Tip:* *If the error has a name then the Suspense account is not involved: example b, above is an error of commission, hence the Suspense account is neither debited nor credited.*

» Exercise 12.1

A bookkeeper extracted a trial balance on 30th June 20x4 which failed to agree by $70, a shortage on the credit side of the trial balance. A suspense account was opened for the difference. In the first week of July 20x4, the following errors made in the previous financial year were found:

a) Purchases journal was undercast by $30.
b) Sales of $350 to Himanshu had been debited in error to Gogia's account.
c) Sales journal had been undercast by $900.
d) Rent account had been undercast by $800.
e) The sale of a furniture $4,500 had been credited in error to sales account.

You are required to :

1) Show the journal entries necessary to correct the errors (the first one is done for you).
2) Draw up the suspense account after the errors described have been corrected.
3) If profit for the year had been calculated at $5600 for the year ended 30 June 20XX, show the calculations of the corrected profit for the year.

Solution:
1)

Date	Details	Debit $	Credit $
a	Purchases Suspense (Purchases book undercast last year, now corrected)	30	30
b			
c			
d			
e			

2)

Date	Details	Debit	Credit	Balance
20XX	**Suspense a/c**	$	$	$
July 1	Diff in trial bal totals		70	70 (cr)
July 7	Purchases (a)			
"	(c)			800 (dr)
"	Rent (d)			

3)

Statement of corrected profit for the year for the year ended 30th June 20XX

	$	$
Profit for the year per the accounts		5600
Add: Sales undercast (c)		
Less: Purchases undercast (a)		
Rent Undercast (d)		
Sales overcast (e)		
Corrected profit for the year for the year		

» EXERCISE 12.2
Study the following and answer the questions below:

The trial balance of Sally as at 31 July 20x6 showed a difference that was posted to a suspense account. Draft final accounts for the year ended 31 July 20x6 were prepared showing a profit for the year of $5000. The following errors were subsequently discovered:

1) Sales $580 to Sushma had been debited to Shashi's account
2) A payment of $570 for rent had been entered on the debit side of the Rent account as $560.
3) The Sales journal had been undercast by $80.
4) Repairs to Motor Van $78 had been charged to Motor van account.
5) A cheque for $700 being rent received from Josh, had only been entered in the cash book.
6) A purchase of furniture $690 had been entered in the purchases account.
7) A cheque for $95 received from a debtor had been correctly entered in the cash book but posted to the customer's account as $99.

Questions:
a) Give the journal entries necessary to correct the above errors.
b) Prepare Sally's suspense account, showing clearly the difference on the trial balance at 31 July 20x6 as the first entry and the entries required to adjust the errors.

c) Show the effect of each of these adjustments on the profit for the year in the draft accounts and the correct profit for the year ended 31 July 20x6.

» EXERCISE 12.3
Study the following and answer the questions below:

The trial balance of Helen as at 31 December 20x9 showed a difference that was posted to a suspense account. Draft final accounts for the year ended 31 December 20x9 were prepared showing a profit for the year of $8900. The following errors were subsequently discovered:
1) Sales $670 to Merci had been debited to Mern's account
2) A payment of $560 for rent had been entered on the debit side of the Rent account as $650.
3) The Sales journal had been overcast by $370.
4) Repairs to Motor Van $56 had been charged to Motor van account.
5) A cheque for $500 being rent received from Mala, had only been entered in the cash book.
6) A purchase of Machinery $5000 had been entered in the Purchases account.
7) A cheque for $69 received from a debtor had been correctly entered in the cash book but posted to the customer's account as $70.

Questions:
a) Give the journal entries necessary to correct the above errors.
b) Prepare the Suspense Account in Helen's Ledger showing clearly the difference on the Trial Balance at 31 December 20x9 as the first entry and the entries required to adjust the errors.
c) Show the effect of each of these adjustments on the profit for the year in the draft accounts and the correct profit for the year ended 31 December 20x9.

» EXERCISE 12.4
Show how each of the following errors would affect the agreement in the totals of a trial balance:
a) A sale of goods to Malcolm $480 was correctly entered in the sales book but was entered in Malcolm's account as $840.
b) $95 taken for personal use was credited to the capital account.
c) Stock at close was overvalued by $1,000.
d) $75 discounts received was debited to the discounts allowed account.
e) $80 rent received was debited to the sales account.
f) Cheque from Jenny $900 was credited to Jenna's account.
g) Cash received from the sale of a motor van $4,000 was credited to the sales account and debited to cash account.

Solution:

Transaction	No effect	Debit side will exceed the credit side by amount shown	Credit side will exceed the debit side by the amount shown
a			
b			
c			
d			
e			
f			
g			

» EXERCISE 12. 5

Show how each of the following errors would affect the agreement in the totals of a trial balance:

a) A sale of goods to Manoj $870 was correctly entered in the sales book but was entered in Manoj's account as $780.

b) $65 discounts allowed was credited to the discounts received account.

c) $56 taken for personal use was credited to the capital account.

d) Stock at close was overvalued by $1200.

e) $45 sales were debited to the purchases account.

f) Cheque from Jenny $980 was debited to Jemma's account.

g) $95 Cash received from the sale of Furniture was credited to the sales account and debited to cash account.

Solution:

Transaction	No effect	Debit side will exceed the credit side by amount shown	Credit side will exceed the debit side by the amount shown
a			
b			
c			
d			
e			
f			
g			

If the working capital before the errors were found was $2,400, find the revised working capital.

Calculation of revised working capital

	Decrease	Increase	
	$	$	$
Unrevised working capital			2,400
Manoj's account undercast		90	
Closing inventory overvalued	1,200	___	
	1,200	90	(1,110)
Revised working capital			1,290

» EXERCISE 12.6

The following is a trial balance incorrectly drawn up:

	$	$
Purchases		3500
Returns inwards	450	
Inventory 1st January 20x9		350
Sales revenue	3850	
Inventory 31st December 20x9		1000
Trade payables	1200	
Discounts received	450	
Telephone		50
Premises		3000
Trade receivables	350	
Discounts allowed		50
Furniture and fixtures		400
Capital	6000	
Suspense		3950
	12300	12300

a) Required:

A corrected version of the trial balance dated 31st December 20x9 based on the above information, but with an amended figure for the suspense account.

b) The following errors were found after the corrected version of the trial balance, above, was prepared.

i) The total of the sales journal was understated by $300.

ii) A payment of $3800 to a supplier has not been posted from the cash book to the purchases ledger.

iii) A cheque for $450 received from a debtor has been correctly entered in the cash book but has been entered in the debtor's personal account as $300.

iv) A purchase of furniture $600 had been included in the purchases account.

v) A sale of motor van for $600 cash has been completely omitted from the books of account.

Required:

1) Journal entries to correct each of these errors (narratives not required).

2) The suspense account, using the amount arrived at in the corrected version of the trial balance from (a), above.

» EXERCISE 12.7

Manana's trial balance does not balance and she has opened a Suspense Account with the difference in the totals. The following errors have now been discovered.

1) Rent paid $450, had been credited to the Rent Receivable account.

2) Goods returned to Kala had been credited to Kala's account and debited to the Purchases Returns account. The goods had cost $690.

3) Discounts received, $70 had been posted to the debit of the Discounts Allowed account in error.

4) A debit balance of $60 in the sales ledger had been completely omitted from the list of balances extracted from the ledger. The total of the list had been included in the trial balance as trade receivables.
5) The debit side of the Telephone Charges account had been understated by$100.

Required

a) Prepare Journal entries to correct the errors. (Narratives are required.)
b) Prepare the suspense account showing the opening balance and the correcting entries.
c) The draft financial statements showed a profit for the year of $6,890 and working capital of $2,000. Calculate the revised profit for the year and working capital for the year.

» EXERCISE 12.8

When Manish extracted a trial balance at July 31 20x5, it failed to agree and he placed the difference in a Suspense account. He then discovers the following errors:

1) A credit balance in the Sales Ledger of $78 had been extracted as a debit balance. Manish does not maintain Control accounts.
2) A cheque paid to a supplier of $65 had been credited to her account as $56.
3) The total in the sales journal for one month is $56,000. It has been entered in the Sales account as $65,000.
4) A credit balance in the sum of $45 has been omitted from the list of balances extracted from the Sales ledger.
5) Wages paid $980 was entered correctly in the cash book but was debited to the wages account as $890.

Required

a) Prepare journal entries to correct the above errors. (Narratives are not required.)
b) Prepare a suspense account showing clearly the difference on the trial balance totals at July 31, 20x5 as the first entry and the entries required to correct the errors.
c) Manish's draft Income statement showed a profit for the year of $18,670 for the year ended July 31, 20x5. Calculate the corrected profit for the year at July 31, 20x5.

» EXERCISE 12.9

The following errors in the accounting records of a business have been detected and corrected:

a) A purchase invoice for $300 was omitted from the books of accounts.
b) A sale for $250 to M was debited to the account of N.
c) The sales journal was over-stated by $150.
The gross profit for the year before the errors were corrected was $56,900.

Required:
Calculate the correct Gross Profit for the year.

» EXERCISE 12.10

A trial balance does not balance. The difference has been entered in a suspense account. Subsequent to that, the following errors were discovered:

1) The provision for depreciation had been overcast by $1,000
2) The credit balance on the purchases ledger control account of $43,000 has been included as a debit balance.
3) A payment in cash of $450 for heating and lighting has been credited in the cash book and debited to the Irrecoverable debts account.

Required:
Prepare the requisite credit entry to the suspense account.

» EXERCISE 12.11

A company omitted discounts allowed of $500 from its trial balance. During the year a Motor van had been sold for cash of $700 but the only accounting entry made was a debit in the Bank account.

Required:
Calculate the balance on the Suspense Account stating whether it is a debit or credit balance.

» EXERCISE 12.12

A trial balance does not balance and a Suspense Account is opened.
Subsequently the following errors are found and the Suspense Account is cleared:

1) The purchase day book was undercast by $2,000.
2) A sales invoice for $1,500 had been omitted from the books.
3) Rent paid of $1,900 was entered correctly in the cash book but incorrectly as $9,100 in the Rent account.

Required:
Calculate the original balance on the Suspense Account. State whether it was a credit or debit balance.

12.1 | Multiple-choice questions

i) The balance of closing stock $7,600 had been entered on the debit side of the Trial Balance as $6,700. What is the effect on the trial balance?

	Debit total	Credit total
A)	none	none
B)	Overstated by $6,700	none
C)	Overstated by $900	none
D)	none	Overstated by $900

ii.) Repairs to Machinery $930 had been posted to the Machinery at Cost account as $390 in error. Which of the following entries are required to correct this error?

	Debit	Credit
A)	Machinery at cost account with $390 Suspense account with $540	Repairs to Machinery account with $930
B)	Repairs to Machinery account with $930	Machinery at cost account with $390 Suspense account with $540
C)	Machinery at cost account with $540	Repairs to Machinery account with $540
D)	Repairs to Machinery account with $540	Machinery at Cost account with $540

iii) A debt of $70 in the sales ledger had been written off as bad but no entry had been made in the Irrecoverable debts account. What is the effect on the Trial Balance?
A) The credit side is overstated by $70.
B) The credit side is understated by $70.
C) The debit side is overstated by $70.
D) The debit side is understated by $70.

iv) A cheque for $23 from Chenai, a customer, had been credited to his account as $32. Which of the following entries will correct this error?

	Debit	Credit
A)	Chenai's account with $9	Suspense account with $9
B)	Suspense account with $9	Chenai's account with $9
C)	Chenai's account with $23	Suspense account with $23
D)	Suspense account with $23	Chenai's account with $23

v) An invoice for $135 for the purchase of inventory from Nancy had been completely omitted from the books. What is the effect on the Trial Balance?
A) The credit side is understated by $135.
B) The debit side is understated by $135.
C) The credit side is overstated by $135.
D) No effect.

12.2 | The Trial Balance as at 30 June, 20x6 drawn up by Melissa does not balance. She has opened a suspense account with the difference in the totals of the Trail Balance. The draft Income statement showed a profit of $5,600 for the year ended 30 June, 20x6 and the statement of financial position at that date showed working capital of $4,560. The following errors were then discovered.

i) $300 stock was taken for personal use without paying for them.
ii) Repairs to machine $35 was debited to Machinery account.
iii) A cheque $45 received from Ali was debited to Ali's account and credited to Bank account.
iv) $566 goods purchased from Fatima were entered in the books as $560.
v) Sales on credit to Kyle $350 were entered in the account of Wyle.
vi) The sales account was undercast by $45 and the Discounts received account was overcast by $45.

Required
a) Pass Journal entries to correct these errors. (Narratives are not required.)
b) Calculate the revised working capital at 30 June, 20x6.
c) Calculate the revised profit for the year ended 30 June, 20x6.

12.3 | Madeline Jones has discovered the following :

1) A machine was purchased from Jones &Co. for $4,600 but no entry has been made in Madeline's books.
2) $350 paid for Motor van has been wrongly debited to Purchases account as $530.
3) A cheque for $2,600 received from Sami has been debited to Sami's account and entered on the credit side of the cash book, in error.
4) A purchase of office stationery $ 350 had been debited to the purchases account as $530 in error.
5) Goods have been sold to Harry on credit for $2,500 less 25% trade discount. Correct entries have been made in the sales journal but $2,000 has been posted to Harry's ledger account.

Required:
a) Prepare entries required in Madeline's Journal regarding each of the above matters. Narratives are required.
b) Prepare a suspense account starting with the difference on the trial balance.

12.4 | Which of the following errors in the general ledger would cause the debits to exceed the credits in a Trial Balance:

i) A contra between the sales and purchases ledgers has been entered on the credit side of both control accounts.

ii) A rental receipt has been entered twice in the rent receivable account.

iii) The closing inventory at the end of the previous period has not been entered in the inventory account.

iv) The opening electricity accrual has been brought forward on the wrong side of the ledger account.

12.5 | A cheque for payment of wages of $214 has been debited to the purchases account as $241. What are the correcting entries?

12.6 On 1st January Harry had prepaid rent of $65. During the year, four rent payments of $100 each were made. On 31st December, Harry owes $35. Harry has only charged the rent payments made during the year in in his Income Account. What is the effect on profit for the year?

12.7 Rent accrued $670 was treated as a prepayment when preparing the Income Statement of Hyung Ho's sole trader business. What was the effect on profit?

Incomplete Records

13.1 | What are incomplete records?

Any method other than that of double entry used to maintain books of accounts will produce incomplete records. Very small businesses may often maintain only a cash book or records of debtors and creditors. In such a case, only one aspect of a transaction is recorded and this is termed Single-entry Bookkeeping. If a business does not maintain any books of accounts but retains source documents such as invoices, notes, cheque counterfoils and bank statements, then the final accounts cannot be prepared in the normal way and this is an incomplete record situation.

13.2 | What is a 'Statement of Affairs'?

A 'Statement of Affairs is a statement from which the capital of the owner is deducted. It resembles a statement of financial position, but is missing some information. It contains the Assets, Liabilities and Capital of the owner.

13.3 | How can profit for the year of the owner be calculated without the aid of double entry records?

The capital shown in the Opening Statement of affairs is compared to that in the Closing Statement of Affairs. Drawings and capital introduced by the owner is taken into consideration too. The equation to be used is:
Profit for the year = Closing capital − Opening capital + Drawings − Capital introduced (if any).

Exhibit :
M. Mosambi started business on 1st January 20x1. He introduced $40,000 cash into the business and a Motor Van valued at $5,000.
At 31st December 20x1 he has trade receivables of $3,500, a bank balance of $36,000, Cash in hand $4,400, inventory $2,000 and trade payables $ 5,900. The motor van is to be depreciated by $ 500. His drawings were $5,000.

Required:
Statements to show the profit or loss for the year ended 31st December 20x1.
Solution:

M. Mosambi
Statement of Affairs as at 1st Jan. 20x1

	$
Motor Van	5000
Cash	40,000
	45,000
Capital:	45,000

M. Mosambi
Statement of Affairs as at 31st Dec. 20x1

	$	$
Motor van	5,000	
Less Depreciation	500	4,500
Inventory	2,000	
Trade receivables	3,500	
Cash at bank	46,000	
Cash in hand	4,400	55,900
		60,400
Capital:		
Balance at 1st Jan. 20x1:	45,000	
Add Profit for the year*	14,500	59,500
Less Drawings:		5,000
		54,500
Trade payables		5,900
		60,400

*Profit for the year = Total assets − Opening Capital + Drawings - trade payables
= 60,400 − 45,000 + 5000 - 5,900 = $ 14,500

» EXERCISE 13.1:

Kenneth does not keep a complete accounting system, but the following information is available from his records:

	At 31st Dec. 20x1	At 31st Dec. 20x2
	$	$
Cash	4,500	4,900
Trade receivables	3,500	2,090
Trade payables	1,370	1,000
Computers	3,400	3,100
Inventory	4,750	5,140

Kenneth has drawn $90 per week from the business for personal expenses.

Required:

Kenneth's profit for the year ended 31st December 20x2

» EXERCISE 13.2

Hemant does not keep a complete accounting system, but the following information is available from his records:

	At 31st Dec. 20x4	At 31st Dec. 20x5
	$	$
Inventory	4,500	3,600
Trade receivables	2,500	1,500
Trade payables	900	200
Shop fittings	10,000	8,500
Cash at bank	4,500	5,600

Hemant has drawn $100 per week from the business for personal expenses.

Required:

Hemant's Profit for the year ended 31st December 20x2

» EXERCISE 13.3

Bertha is a sole trader who does not keep full accounting records. She is able to provide the following information:

	At 31st August 20x2	At 31st August 20x3
Non-current Assets at cost	$50,000	$ 46,000
Current Assets	$18000	$ 21,000
Current liabilities	$6, 000	$ 5,000

Bertha's drawings for the year ended 31st August 20x3 were $400 per month.

Required:

a) Bertha's Statement of Affairs as at 31st August 20x2
b) Kelly's Statement of Affairs as at 31st August 20x3
c) Kelly's profit/loss for the year ended 31st August20x3

13.4 | What are the advantages & disadvantages of maintaining full financial records?

Advantages:

- Financial statements can be prepared quickly.
- They help guard against errors and fraud.
- There may be a legal requirement to prepare them.

Disadvantages:

- They take time
- They are expensive
- The owner may not have enough knowledge of double entry.

» EXERCISE 13.4

Hema does not keep a complete accounting system, but the following information is available from her records:

	At 31st Dec. 20x1	At 31st Dec. 20x2
	$	$
Inventory	3,200	3,000
Trade receivables	2,470	4,490
Trade payables	640	200
Shop fittings	7,400	7,000
Cash at bank	4,000	12,000

Drawings for the year ended 31st December 20x2 were $1,500

Required:

Hema's Profit for the year ended 31st December 20x2

» EXERCISE 13.5

Karmi is a sole trader who does not keep full accounting records. She is able to provide the following information:

	At 31st August 20x2	At 31st August 20x3
Non-current Assets at cost	$ 30,000	$ 36,000
Current Assets	$ 12,000	$ 34,000
Current liabilities	$ 3,000	$ 1,000

It is decided that the non-current assets held at 31st August 20x3 should be depreciated by 5% on cost. Kami's drawings for the year ended 31st August 20x3 was $2,000

Required:

a) Kami's Statement of Affairs as at 31st August 20x2
b) Kami's Statement of Affairs as at 31st August 20x3
c) Kami's profit or loss for the year ended 31st August 20x3

13.5 | How are sales and purchases calculated using incomplete records?

A total trade receivables account (you did this in chapter 11 on control accounts) is used to calculate total credit sales and the total trade payables account is used to calculate total credit purchases.

Exhibit:

A & Sons Traders had the following figures for the years ended:

	31st December 20x3	31st December 20x4
	$	$
Trade receivables	34,500	53,600

For the year ended 31st December 20x4: Cash sales :$1,500
Cash receipts from debtors: $1060
Discounts allowed: $45
Irrecoverable debts: $56

Required:
Calculate the sales for the year ended 31st December 20x4
Solution:

Total trade receivables account

20x4		$	20x4		$
Jan 1	Balance b/d	34,500	-	Discounts allowed	45
-	Credit sales	20,261	-	Cash received from customers	1060
			-	Irrecoverable debt	56
			Dec 31	Balance c/d	53,600
		54,761			54,761
20x5					
January 1	Balance b/d	53,600			

Total sales for the year	= Credit sales + Cash sales
	=20,261+1,500
	= $21,761

» EXERCISE 13.6

ABC Traders had the following figures for the Years ended:

	31st December 20x1	31st December 20x2
	$	$
Trade receivables	14,500	13,600

Cash sales :$2,500
Cash receipts from trade receivables: $560
Receipts by cheque from trade receivables: $ 360
Discounts allowed : $50
Irrecoverable debt: $70

Required:
Calculate the sales for the year ended 31st December 20x2

Exhibit :
Calculate the total purchases for the year ended 31st December 20x3 from the following information:

Trade payables at 1st Jan 20x3 : $ 2,450
Trade payables at Dec 31st 20x3 :$1,200
Payments to creditors during the year : Cash $3,609
Cheque $2,870
Cash purchases for the year : $1,000
Discounts received: $35

Solution:

Total Trade payables account

20x2		$	20x2		$
-	Cash	3,609	January 1	Balance b/d	2,450
-	Bank	2,870	-	Credit purchases	5,264
-	Discounts received	35			
Dec 31	Balance c/d	1,200			
		7,714			7,714
			20x3		
			January 1	Balance b/d	1,200

Total purchases for the year = 5,264+1,000 = $ 6,264

» EXERCISE 13.7

Calculate the total purchases for the year ended 31st December 20x3 from the following information:

Trade payables at 1st Jan 20x3 : $ 4,500
Trade payables at Dec 31st 20x3 :$3,600
Payments to trade payables during the year :
Cash $3,500; Cheque $3,800
Discounts received $47

NOTE: Using the Total sales and purchases figure, it is possible to prepare the Trading Account.

» EXERCISE 13.8

Mason is a trader buying and selling entirely on credit terms. He does not keep complete accounting records but is able to provide the following information for the year ended 31st December 20x3:

	At 1st January 20x3	At 31st December 20x3
	$	$
Inventory of goods	4,000	3,000
Trade payables	1,500	2,000
Trade receivables	3,700	5,600

During the year cheques received from customers amounted to $3,700 and cheques paid to suppliers amounted to $2,500.

Required: Prepare Mason's Trading account for the year ended 31st Dec. 20x3.

» EXERCISE 13.9

Kelly owns a trading business and does not keep full accounting records. However, she supplies the following information for the year ended 31st March 20x4:

	At 31st March 20x3	At 31st March 20x4
	$	$
Inventory	4,670	3,680
Trade receivables	1,200	4,500
Trade payables	2,000	1,500

Other information:		$
Receipts from Debtors :	Cash	5,000
	Cheque	2,000
Payments to creditors	Cheque	1,400
Cash sales		2,000

Required:
a) Calculate the sales and purchases for the year
b) Calculate Kelly's Gross Profit for the year.

MARK UP AND MARGIN

$$\text{Mark} - \text{up} = \frac{\text{Gross profit}}{\text{Cost of sales}} \times 100$$

$$\text{Margin} = \frac{\text{Gross profit}}{\text{Sales}} \times 100$$

√ Tips:

1) If the mark – up is known, the margin can be found out:
   Take the same numerator to be the numerator of the margin;
   the denominator is the total of the mark- up's numerator and
   denominator.
   e.g. if Mark – up is 25% (¼) then the Margin is 1/5

2) If the margin is known, the mark – up can be found out:
   Take the same numerator of the margin; the denominator is the
   difference of the denominator and the numerator of the Margin
   e.g. If the Margin is 20% (1/5) then the Mark-up is 1/4

Exhibit :

Tom provides the following information for the year ended
31st December 20x3:

	$
Margin = 25%	
Sales	20,000
Inventory at 1st January 20x3	4,500
Inventory at 31st December 20x3	4,800

Prepare a Trading Account to show the calculation of the
purchases for the year.

Solution:

Tom's Trading Account for the year ended 31st Dec., 20x3

	$	$
Sales		20,000
Less Cost of sales		
Inventory at 1st Jan., 20x3	4,500	
Add Purchases	*15,300	
	19,800	
Less Inventory at 31st Dec. 20x3	4,800	15,000
**Gross Profit		5,000

Working:

** Margin = $\frac{\text{Gross Profit}}{\text{Sales}}$ x 100

25 = $\frac{\text{Gross profit}}{20,000}$ x 100

$\frac{25 \times 20,000}{100}$ = Gross Profit

$ 5,000 = Gross Profit

* Sales – (Opening Inventory + Purchases – Closing Inventory)
= Gross Profit

20,000 – (4,500 + Purchases – 4,800) = 5000

20,000 + 300 – Purchases = 5000

20,300 – 5,000 = Purchases

$ 15,300 = Purchases

» EXERCISE 13.10

The sales of a business were $40,000. The cost of goods sold
was $ 25,000. Calculate:

a)   The Mark – up
b)   The Margin

NOTE: If mark-up is: The margin is:

1/2	1/3
1/3	1/4
2/3	2/5
2/5	2/7

To convert a fraction to a percentage multiply by 100 e.g. 2/5 = 40%

» EXERCISE 13.11

A trader bought goods for $1,000 and sold them for $ 1,500.

What is :

a)   **The mark – up**
b)   **The margin ?**

» EXERCISE 13.12

Malati's restaurant caught fire on 10th June 20x3. All the
inventory was destroyed. On 1st January her inventory was
valued at $800. From 1st January to 10th June 20x3, her
sales were $ 5,000 and her purchases were $3,000. Her profit
margin was 50%.

**Calculate the cost of the inventory destroyed. Show your
answer in the form of a Trading Account.**

» EXERCISE 13.13

The following are the figures for 20x2:

	$
Inventory 1st January 20x2	500
Inventory 31st Dec. 20x2	700
Purchases	5,000

A uniform rate of mark –up of 25% is applied.

Find the Gross Profit and Sales figures.

Exhibit :

The following is a summary of Trevor's bank account for the
year ended 31st December 20x4:

	$		$
Balance 1st Jan. 20x3	1,000	Payment to suppliers	34,000
Receipts from customers	48,000	Rent	1,000
Balance 31st Dec. 20x3	7,225	Insurance	500
		Office expenses	275
		Drawings	20,450
	56,225		56,225

All of the business takings have been paid into the bank with
the exception of $9,000. Out of this, Trevor paid wages of
$6,200, drawings of $1,100 and purchase of inventory $1,700.
Additional information available:

	As at 31st December 20x3	As at 31st December 20x4
	$	$
Inventory	14,000	16,000
Trade payables	5,500	6,600
Trade receivables	10,000	9,650
Rent prepaid	150	200
Insurance owing	50	100
Machinery at valuation	3,500	3,250

Required:

Draw up a set of Financial Statements for the year ended 31st
December 20x4.

Solution:

Trevor's Income Statement for the year ended 31st Dec,20x4

	$	$
Sales		56,650
Less Cost of goods sold:		
Inventory at 1st January 20x4	14,000	
Add Purchases	36,800	
	50,800	
less inventory at 31st Dec. 20x4	16,000	34,800
Gross Profit		21,850
Less Expenses:		
Rent (1,000+ 150 – 200)	950	
Insurance (500 –50 + 100)	550	
Office expenses	275	
Wages	6,200	
Depreciation (3,500 – 3,250)	250	8,225
Profit for the year		13,625

Trevor's statement of financial position as at 31st Dec. 20x4

Assets:	$	$	$
Non-current Assets:	Cost	Depreciation	N.B.V .
Machinery	3,500	250	3,250
Current assets:			
Inventory		16,000	
Trade receivables		9,650	
Other receivables		200	25,850
Total assets			29,100
Capital and liabilities:			
Capital:			
Balance at 1st Jan. 20x4		* 23,100	
Add profit for the year		13,625	36,725
Less Drawings (20.450 + 1,100)			21, 550
			15,175
Trade payables		6,600	
Other payables		100	
Overdraft		7,225	13,925
Total capital and liabilities			29,100

Working:

1.Capital at 1stJan. 20x4 = Assets – liabilities
= (1,000+ 14,000+ 10,000+ 150 + 3,500) – (5,500 + 50)
= *$ 23,100

√ *Tips:*

Always calculate the opening capital (using all the opening balances including the opening bank balance), the sales and purchases for the year before writing up the financial statements.

You may have to prepare a receipts and payments account (like a bank account) in order to calculate either opening or closing bank balances.

EXERCISE 13.14

Tom does not keep a complete accounting system, but he provides the following information:

	At 31st March 20x1	At 31st March 20x2
	$	$
Inventory	2,000	4,000
Trade payables	2,400	3,700
Trade receivables	3,500	3,900
Shop fittings	6,000	5,500
Balance at bank	2,100	2,800

Additional information:

a) Cheques received from trade debtors $36,000.
b) Cash sales banked $4,700.
c) Cheques paid to trade creditors $16,700.
d) Toms drawings for the year were $550 per month.

From the above information above, calculate:

1. Purchases and sales
2. Capital at 31st March 20x1 and at 31st March 20x2.
3. Profit for the year ended 31st March 20x2.

» EXERCISE 13.15

Jeswant owns a retail business but he does not keep accounting records.

The table below shows his assets and liabilities at 31st December 20x2 and 20x3:

	At 31st December 20x2	At 31st December 20x3
	$	$
Inventory of goods	6,500	6,000
Trade receivables	2,500	3,000
Trade payables	1,500	2,100
Electricity accrued	150	170
Rent prepaid	1,400	1,700
Motor vans	3,500	4,600

All takings were banked and all payments were made by cheque. The receipts and payments for the year ended 31st December 20x3 were as follows:

	Receipts		Payments
	$		$
Takings from cash sales	28,000	Paid to suppliers	20,000
Received from customers	12,000	Electricity	600
		Rent	2,500
		Insurance	150
		Office expenses	550
		Drawings	10,000
		Motor Van	1,500

Required:

a) Prepare Jeswant's Income statement for the year ended 31st December 20x3

» EXERCISE 13.16

The following is a summary of Max's bank account for the year ended 31st December 20x4:

	$		$
Balance 1st Jan. 20x3	5,000	Payment to creditors	20,000
Receipts from debtors	35,000	Rent	12,000
Balance			
31st Dec. 20x3	6,220	Insurance	400
		Office expenses	270
		Drawings	13,550
	46,220		46,220

All of the business takings have been paid into the bank with the exception of $5,600. Out of this, Max paid wages of $2,500, drawings of $600 and purchase of goods $2,500. Additional information available:

	As at 31st December 20x3	As at 31st December 20x4
	$	$
Inventory	22,000	17,000
Trade payables	5,300	5,000
Trade receivables	12,000	19,000
Rent prepaid	0	50
Insurance owing	150	200
Machinery at valuation	4,700	4,350

Required:
Draw up a set of Financial Statements for the year ended 31st December 20x4.

» EXERCISE 13.17

Moby does not keep a complete accounting system, but he provides the following information:

	At 31st March 20x1	At 31st March 20x2
	$	$
Inventory	4,000	6,000
Trade payables	2,000	3,500
Trade receivables	2,500	5,000
Shop fittings	6,560	6,000
Balance at bank	2,010	3,000

Additional information:
a)   Cheques received from trade debtors $25,000.
b)   Cash sales banked $3,000.
c)   Cheques paid to trade creditors $10,000.

Moby's drawings for the year were $1550 .

From the above information, calculate Moby's
A i)   Purchases and sales
   ii) Capital at 31st March 20x1 and 31st March 20x2.
   iii) Profit for the year ended 31st March 20x2.
B Draw up Moby's statement of financial position as at 31 March 20x2

» EXERCISE 13.18

Fred Sinatra set up business on 1 April 2003 selling watches from a market stall.

Fred has asked you to calculate his profit for the year ended 31 March 2004 using the following information.
(i)   All sales were made for cash. Payments were made by cheque unless otherwise stated.
(ii)   Opening capital was $17,600 which was paid into a bank account opened on 1 April 2003.
(iii)   The bank balance on 31 March 2004 was $2120 Dr.
(iv)   Fred's purchases for the year totalled $33,120, but on analysing this figure it was found to include $2000 paid for secure display cabinets and $800 for petrol for Fred's motor car. The remainder was for the purchase of watches for resale.
(v)   Fred bought a motor car to be used in the business for $5750.
(vi)   Rent of $60 per month had been paid from cash sales.
(vii)   Drawings of $100 per week were taken from cash sales.
(viii)   Motor car expenses for the year cost $515.
(ix)   Fred kept a petty cash float of $100.
(x)   Fred's pricing policy was cost plus 75%.
(xi)   The motor car and display units are both to be depreciated over five years on a straight line basis, with no residual value. A full year's depreciation is applied in the year of purchase.

Required
(a)   Prepare Fred's bank account for the year ended 31 March 2004.
(b)   Calculate Fred's total sales for the year ended 31 March 2004.
(c)   Calculate Fred's inventory at 31 March 2004.
(d)   Prepare Fred's Income statement for the year ended 31 March 2004.

[UCLES, 2004, AS/A Level Accounting, Syllabus 9706/2, Oct/Nov]

» EXERCISE 13.19

A business does not keep proper accounting records. The following information is available at the start of the year:
1)   Machinery valued at $8,000
2)   Inventory which cost $5,600 with a sale value of $8,000
3)   Bank overdraft of $300
4)   A loan to a friend from the business bank account $2,000

What was the capital account balance at the start of the year?

» EXERCISE 13.20

A sole trader provides the following information:

	$
Opening Trade payables	25,000
Cash paid to Trade payables	100,000
Purchases on credit	125,000
Balances set-off against sales ledger	3,000
Discount received	4,500

Required:
a. Calculate the closing trade payables balance.

13.1 | Multiple-choice questions.

i.) A 1June 20x6 Kusum's trade receivables amounted to $13,000. In the year to 31 May 20x7 she received $78,000 from trade receivables and allowed them settlement discounts of $2,560. At 31 May 20x7 her trade receivables were $15,600. What were Kusum's sales for the year?

A) $83,160   B) $80,600   C) $77,960   D) $75,400

ii) Melanie's mark up on inventory is 25% to arrive at the selling price. All of her inventory was stolen on 5 July 20x3. Her inventory at 31 December 20x2 was $15,000. From 1 January to 5 July 20x3 sales totaled $36,000 and purchases were $18,000. What was the cost of the stolen inventory?

A) $18,000   B) $ 9,000   C) $4,200   D) $3,000

iii) At 1 January 20x8 Dudley's business assets were: Motor van $35,000 (cost $40,000), Furniture $1,500, inventory $500, trade receivables 3,500 (of which $550 were known to be irrecoverable), cash at bank $1,400. His Trade payables totaled $2,300. At 31 December 20x8 his assets were: Premises which had cost $1,00,000 and on which a mortgage of $80,000 was still outstanding, motor van $31,000, Furniture $1,100, inventory $350, trade receivables $2,000, cash $2,900.
His trade payables amounted to $5,600 and he had a bank overdraft of $60. During the year Dudley's drawings amounted to $300 a month.
What was his profit for the year?

A)$8,940   B)$13,940   C) $12,640   D) $16,240

iv) Kacey's records showed the following: Opening inventory $5,600, Closing inventory $3,400 and Sales for the year $45,000. Kacey sells her goods to produce a gross margin of 25%. What were Kacey's purchases?

A) $ 31,550   B) $33,800   C) $42,800   D) $47,200

v) Mildred commenced business with $12,000 she had received as a gift from her grandmother and $5,000 she had received as a loan from her father. She used some of this money to purchase a Motor van for $8,000. She obtained a mortgage for $50,000 to purchase a workshop. What was her capital?

A) $15,000   B) $12,000   C) $17,000   D) $67,000

13.2 | On the night of 4 September 20x3, Bailey's warehouse was burned down and most of the inventory destroyed. The inventory salvaged was valued at cost in the sum of $3,400. Bailey claimed for compensation from his insurance company. Additional information:

Statement of financial position as at
31 December 20x2 (extract)

	$
Inventory	27,000
Trade receivables	13,450
Trade payables	10,980

Further information for the
period 1 Jan 20x3 – 4 September 20x3:

	$
Receipts from trade receivables	37,800
Cash sales	14,500
Payments to trade payables	30,700
At 4 September 20x3:	
Trade receivables	20,560
Trade payables	18,730

Bailey achieves a margin of 30% on all sales.

Required:

Using the information, calculate the amount of the claim.

13.3 | Nick commenced business on 1 January 20x4 when he paid $23,000 into the bank in addition to a loan of $ 10,000 he had received from his aunt. At 31 December 20x4, his assets and liabilities were as follows:

	$
Motor vehicle	12,000
Furniture and fixtures	8,000
Machinery	5,000
Inventory	2,000
Trade receivables	1,340
Bank balance	5,780
Trade payables	5,000
Loan from aunt	8,000

Nick's drawings were $200 a month. In addition, he had paid his personal insurance of $450 from the business bank account and had $600 owing for rent of premises.

Required:

a) Prepare Nick's statements of affairs at
   (i) 1 January 20x4 and (ii) 31 December 20x4.

b) Calculate Nick's profit or loss for the year
   ended 31 December 20x4.

13.4 | A Sole Trader does not keep double-entry records. At the beginning of the financial period he owed his suppliers $34,890. He made cheque payments to his suppliers during the period of $ 145,700. At the end of the period he owed his suppliers $23,500. What are his total purchases for the period?

13.5 | Manish suspects a loss of cash has occurred. He provides the following data:
i) Cash balance at the start of the month $500.
ii) Cash balance at the end of the month $200.
iii) Cash banked $20,600.
iv) Cash sales for the month $ 30,000.
How much cash has been lost?

13.6 | John has not kept proper records for his business. Between 31 December 20x5 and 31 December 20x6 his net assets had increased by $35,000. On 1 January 20x6, John brought his private car which had cost $15,000, into the business. This car now has a re-sale value of $9,000. Drawings for the year ended 31 December 20x6 were $10,000. What was John's profit for the year ended 31 December 20x6?

13.7 | A trader suspects that there has been a loss of cash. She provides the following data:

	$
Cash balance at 1 January 20x2	240
Cash balance at 31 January 20x2	90
Cash banked	8,900
Cash sales per till records	9,200

Required:
Calculate the amount of cash that has been lost.

13.8 | Menaksi and company provide the following information:

	$
Trade receivables at 1 January 20x2	200,000
Cash received from customers during the year	560,000
Discounts allowed during the year	10,000
Irrecoverable debts written off during the year	8,500
Trade receivables at 31 December 20x2	234,000

Required:
Calculate the sales during the year.

13.9 | A trader, whose records are incomplete, makes all his purchases on credit. He furnishes the following information:

	$
Opening trade payables	34,500
Payments to suppliers during the year	138,000
Closing trade payables	30,500
Discount received for the year	1,400

Required:
Calculate the credit purchases for the year.

13.10 David Qin started a business 2 years ago and has a capital of $220,000 at the end of year 2.
Over that period, his profits have been $33,000 and his drawings $9,000. In year 1 he introduced a motor van with market value of $12,000. It had cost $50,000 when he bought it. In year 2 David took out of the business, for his own use, a computer with a net book value of $ 800.
How much capital did he start the business with?

13.11 At the end of a financial year the following information is available:

	$
Sales	250,000
Opening inventory	10,000
Closing inventory	13,000

The business makes a standard mark-up of 20%.
Required:
Calculate the purchases.

Valuation Of Inventory

14.1 | How is Inventory to be valued?

Inventory should be valued at Cost or Net Realisable Value. Cost is what was paid for the goods or Historic Cost. The Accounting principle of Prudence is being followed when this is done. IAS 2 requires inventory to be valued at the lower of cost and Net Realisable Value.

Net Realisable Value = Selling price less expenses that are to be incurred to get the goods into a saleable condition. These costs could include completion of goods if they are being manufactured and selling and distribution costs.

Tip√ *If you increase the value of closing Inventory you will increase profit.*
If you decrease the value of closing Inventory you will decrease profit.
If you increase the value of opening Inventory you will decrease profit.
If you decrease the value of opening Inventory you will increase profit.

EXHIBIT
A warehouse-full of goods was flooded and this resulted in damage to these goods which had cost $5,000. These goods can now be sold for $2,000 after they are repaired and cleaned at a cost of $200.

What is the Net Realisable Value of these goods?
Solution:
Net Realisable value = Selling price – expenses incurred to get goods in saleable condition
$$= 2000 - 200$$
$$= \$1,800.$$

» EXERCISE 14.1
Goods which were bought for $2,300 were damaged by fire and can now be sold for $2,400 after repair costing $300.
a)   What is the Net Realisable Value of these goods?
b)   What is the value of these goods.

» EXERCISE 14.2
Details as in 14.1 but the goods after repair can now be sold for $3,000.
a)   What is the Net Realisable Value of these goods?
b)   What is the value of these goods.

14.2 | How are groups of similar items of inventory valued?

Each item in the group should be considered separately when deciding whether they should be valued at cost or Net Realisable Value. This is to ensure that there are no 'hidden' losses.

EXHIBIT
Mally sells five different grades of products. The following are the costs and Net Realisable value of these grades:

	Cost	NRV	Value to be used for inventory valuation
	$	$	$
Grade 1	400	350	350
Grade 2	1,000	980	980
Grade 3	600	640	600
Grade 4	570	600	570
Grade 5	1,500	2,000	1,500
	4,070	4,570	4,000

» EXERCISE 14.3
Celina sells five different grades of products. The following are the costs and Net Realisable value of these grades. Fill in the blank spaces:

	Cost	NRV	Value to be used for inventory valuation
	$	$	$
Grade 1	600	670	…….
Grade 2	1,500	1,080	…….
Grade 3	900	940	…….
Grade 4	870	900	…….
Grade 5	1,900	2,000	…….
	5,770	5,590	…….

14.3 | How is closing inventory to be valued in the case of manufactured goods?

If it is the policy of the manufacturer to add factory profit to the cost of production, then closing inventory will be overvalued. It is necessary to deduct this factory profit in order to arrive at a correct valuation of closing inventory. This is in accordance to the Realisation and Matching principles. As no sale has taken place, profit was not realised and should not be included.

14.4 | How is work in progress valued?

IAS 2 dictates how work in progress is to be valued. Work in progress is to be valued at prime cost plus an appropriate proportion of manufacturing overheads.

14.5 | What is meant by replacement cost?

Replacement cost is the price that will have to be paid to replace goods used or sold. It is not acceptable as a basis of valuing inventory under IAS 2. However, replacement costs are used to cost jobs and for budgets.

14.6 | How are heterogeneous goods different from homogenous goods?

Heterogeneous goods are goods that are not similar and can be told apart. Examples of such goods are: designer chairs, antique furniture etc. Such goods pose no problem to cost as they can be easily costed at historic cost. However, goods that are bought or manufactured in bulk and cannot be told apart, are difficult to cost at historic cost. Examples of such goods are: tubes of toothpaste, wheat etc. They may have been bought at different times at differing prices. In order to value these goods it will be necessary to assume that stock movements occur in a particular pattern even if this is not actually the case. This is often called convention.

14.7 | How is homogenous Inventory valued?

The principle of consistency should be followed. Either one of the following three methods should be used:
First In First Out (FIFO), where the assumption is made that inventory is sold or used in the same order in which it is received.

Last In First Out (LIFO), where the assumption is made that the latest delivery of inventory is used or sold before inventory received earlier.
Average Cost or Weighted Average Cost (AVCO), which involves calculating the weighted average cost of inventory-on-hand after every delivery.

Tip √ When the purchase prices are rising over the period under review:
FIFO reveals the highest profits.
LIFO reveals the lowest profits.
AVCO gives a profit figure between the two extremes.

14.8 | Does the method of inventory valuation affect the profits over the whole life of a business?

No, the profit made over the whole life of a business is not affected by the choice of method of valuing inventory

14.9 | What are the advantages and disadvantages of using FIFO?

The advantages are:
1) It is comparatively simple to use.
2) As materials are normally used in the FIFO order, and goods sold in that order, too, it is a realistic method.
3) It will be found that closing inventory is valued at current price levels.
4) FIFO is acceptable as a method of stock valuation for the purposes of the Companies Act 1985 and International Accounting Standards (IAS2).
5) Prices used in valuing inventory are ones that have actually been paid for materials and inventory.

The disadvantages are:
1) Closing inventory will be priced at the latest high levels in times of rising prices. This results in increasing Gross Profit, which goes against the accounting principle of prudence.
2) To arrive at realistic selling prices, Manufacturers may prefer to use LIFO or AVCO rather than FIFO. They might, however, use FIFO for their financial accounts, to value inventory.
3) Quotations for jobs when raw materials are valued on the basis of FIFO may be unreliable as job X may be charged for raw materials at a different price from job Y, for instance, though the jobs are similar.

14.10 | What are the advantages and disadvantages of using LIFO?

The advantages of using LIFO are:
1) Raw materials are issued at the most recent prices.
2) It is comparatively simple to use.
3) Prices used to value inventory have actually been paid.

The disadvantages are:
1) Quotations for jobs when raw materials are valued on the basis of LIFO may be unreliable as job X may be charged for raw materials at a different price from job Y, for instance, though the jobs are similar.
2) As Inventory are not normally used in the LIFO order or sold in that order, this method is not realistic.
3) LIFO is not acceptable by the Companies Act 1985 or IAS 2 as a basis for valuing inventory.
4) Closing inventory is not valued at the current price levels. Hence, in times of rising prices closing inventory may be valued at prices lower than the current prices. This would result in Gross Profit being understated. Accounting standards warn against profits being artificially understated.

NOTE: Detailed calculations of LIFO is not in the syllabus.

14.11 | What are the advantages and disadvantages of using AVCO?

The advantages are:
1) AVCO is acceptable by the Companies Act 1985 and IAS 2 as a basis of valuing inventory.
2) Prices used to value closing inventory are fairly close to the current prices.
3) This method smoothes variations in production costs and comparisons between different periods become more reliable.
4) Homogenous inventory have almost identical values, though purchased at different times.
5) Costing of different jobs using the same raw materials is now more reliable and equal.

The disadvantages are:
1) It is not as simple to use as FIFO and LIFO as it entails re-calculation of the average prices every time a purchase is made.
2) The average price arrived at may not represent any price actually paid for inventory.

EXHIBIT

At 31 December 20x5, inventory of a certain raw material consisted of 50 Kgs which had cost $0.40/kg. The receipts and issues of the material in January were as follows:

Date	Receipts (Kgs)	Price per Kg	Issues (Kgs)
January 1 b/f	50	0.40	
4	70	0.60	
6			60
12	100	0.80	
16			80
20	50	1.00	
26			70

Required

Calculate the value of stock at 31 January 20x5 using
a) FIFO
b) LIFO
c.) AVCO

Solution

a) FIFO

January		1	4	12	20	Cl. Inv.
Price per kg		0.40	0.60	0.80	1.00	
Inventory (kg)		50				
	Receipts (kg)		70	100	50	
6	Issued	(50)	(10)			
		-	60			$36
16	Issued		(60)	(20)		
			-	80		$64
26	Issued			(70)		
	Closing Inventory			10	50	
	Valuation at cost			$8	$50	
						Total $58

b) LIFO

January		1	4	12	20	Cl Inv
Price per kg		0.40	0.60	0.80	1.00	
Inventory (kg)		50				
	Receipts (kg)		70	100	50	
6	Issued		(60)			
			10			$26
16	Issued			(80)		
				20		$42
26	Issued			(20)	(50)	
	Closing inventory	50	10		-	
	Valuation at cost	$20	$6			
						Total $26

c) AVCO

January		kgs	Price ($)	Weighted average cost($)	Balance($)
1	b/f	50	0.40	0.40	20.00
4	Received	70	0.60		42.00
	Balance	120		*0.52	62.00
6	Issued	(60)			**(31.20)
	Balance	60			30.80
12	Received	100	0.80		80.00
	Balance	160		0.69	110.80
16	Issued	(80)			(55.20)
	Balance	80			55.60
20	Received	50	1.00		50.00
	Balance	130		0.81	105.60
26	Issued	(70)			(56.70)
	Balance	60			48.90

Value of Closing inventory = $49 (rounded off)

Working :

*Average cost = $\frac{(20+42)}{120}$ = $0.52

**Cost of issue = 60 x 0.52 = $ 31.20

√ **Tip:** *The value of inventory based on AVCO lies between the values based on LIFO and FIFO*

» EXERCISE 14.4

At 30 June 20x3, inventory of a certain product consisted of 200 units which had cost $2.40/unit. The receipts and sales of the product in July were as follows:

Date	Receipts (Units)	Price per Unit ($)	Issues (Units)
July 1 b/f	200	2.40	
5	40	1.60	
10			160
15	100	1.80	
19			120
23	150	2.00	
29			60

Required
Calculate the value of inventory at 31 July 20x3 using
a) FIFO
b) AVCO

» EXERCISE 14.5

A company uses the Weighted Average Cost (AVCO) method of inventory valuation. During the month of February the following transactions took place:

February		Total ($)
1	Opening inventory 150 units @ $2.00 per unit	300
10	Received 200 units$2.10 per unit	420
16	Issued 150 units	-
25	Received 50 units $2.20 per unit	110

Required:
Calculate the value of inventory at 28 February.

14.12 | What is meant by the term Stock Inventory?

A Stock Inventory is a record of goods received by and issued or sold by a business.

14.13 | What is meant by the term Perpetual Inventory?

A Perpetual Inventory is a record of a running balance of stock-on-hand after each transaction. The methods used above are examples of Perpetual Inventory.

14.14 | What is meant by the term Periodic Inventory?

A periodic inventory shows the value of stock-on-hand only at the end of a period of say a month. The total issues are deducted from the total receipts to arrive at the balance of items in stock. The 'quick' method below of calculating closing inventory using FIFO is an example of a Periodic Inventory.

'Quick' Method of calculating closing inventory using FIFO and the figures in the exhibit:
Units received = 50+70+100+50 = 270
Units issued = 60+80+70 = 210
Balance of units = 60
Valuation: 50 Units at latest price of $1 = $50
10 Units at previous price $0.80 = $8 = $58

» EXERCISE 14.6

A company has two items in inventory requiring repairs before resale. The following information is available:

	Item 1	Item 2
Cost	$4,500	$3,450
Selling price	$6,700	$3,500
Repair cost	$1,000	$ 600

What is the total inventory value of these items?

» EXERCISE 14.7

A business ends its financial year on 31 December. Inventory was not counted until 7 January when it was found to be $110,000. The following transactions took place from 1 to 7 January concerning inventory:

1) Inventory purchased $20,000
2) Inventory sold at a mark up of 20% $12,000.

Required

Calculate the value of the inventory at 31 December.

» EXERCISE 14.8

A business started operations on 1 January 20x1. The purchases and sales of inventory for January were as follows:

Date	Purchases	Sales
4 January	2@$250	-
10 Janaury	-	1 @ $450
18 January	4@$300	-
25 January	-	2@ $500

The business uses the First In First Out (FIFO) method of inventory valuation.

Required:

Calculate the gross profit for January.

» EXERCISE 14.9

Mollie undertook her annual stock-take on January 5th 20x5 instead of at the end of her financial year on 31st December 20x4. At January 5th 20x5 stock was valued at cost at $1,500. The following information is available:

Mollie had a uniform mark-up of 25% on all goods she sells. In the period 1January 20x5 to 5th January 20x5 the following transactions took place:

1. Purchases of goods for resale $1,560.
2. Sales of stock on credit amounted to $3,000.
3. Cash sales amounted to $350.
4. Sales returns were $50.
5. Purchases returns were $35.

Required:

Calculate Mollie's closing inventory(stock) at 31st December 20x4.

» EXERCISE 14.10

Archie Pelago buys and sells a single product. His first three months of trading showed the following purchases and sales.

2005	Purchases	Sales
February	300 @ $25	150 @ 35
March	120 @ $27	210 @ 38
April	240 @ $29	205 @ 41

For the following requirement either perpetual or periodic inventory may be used. Calculations should be taken to a maximum of two decimal places.

Required

(a) Calculate Archie's closing inventory at 30 April 2005 using the FIFO (first in first out) method of inventory valuation.

(b) Calculate Archie's closing inventory at 30 April 2005 using the AVCO (weighted average cost) method of inventory valuation.

(c) Calculate Archie's gross profit using each of the above methods of inventory valuation.

(UCLES, 2007, AS/A level Accounting, Syllabus 9607/2, May/June)

EXERCISE 14.11

A company has the following costs for an item of inventory:

Storage cost	$ 8,000
Conversion costs	$12,000
Carriage inwards	$3,000
Purchase costs	$23,000

Required:

Calculate the value of this item of inventory.

14.1 | MULTIPLE CHOICE QUESTIONS.

i) A manufacturing company has made the following purchases and issues for the month of June

	Purchases	Issues
June 1	30kgs @$10	
4	20kgs@ $15	
15		15
23	10kgs@$18	
29		40

What is the value of the inventory at 30 June based on FIFO?

A. $90   B. $50   C. $75   D. $95

ii) A company sells four different grades of cement. The following are the cost to the company and the Net Realisable Value (NRV):

	Cost	NRV
	$	$
Grade 1	24,000	20,000
Grade 2	15,700	16,000
Grade 3	10,900	11,000
Grade 4	10,000	9,800

What is the value of the inventory of cement?

A. $60,600   B. $56,800   C. $56,400   D. $61,000

iii) You are given the following information:

Cost	Replacement Cost	NRV	Selling Price
$	$	$	$
3,000	2,700	3,500	3,700

What is the value of inventory for statement of financial position purposes?

A. $3,000   B. $2,700   C. $3,500   D. $3,700

iv) The following are the values of opening and closing inventory using LIFO and FIFO:

	FIFO	LIFO
	$	$
Opening inventory	14,000	13,600
Closing inventory	10,000	9,700

What is the effect on the company's profits if they change from LIFO to FIFO due to SSAP9?

	Gross Profit	Profit for the year
A.	Decrease of $4,000	Decrease of $4,000
B.	Decrease of $ 100	Decrease of $100
C.	Increase of $100	Increase of $100
D.	Increase of $$4,000	Increase of $4,000

v) Ace & Co had a inventory of 30 items at 30 June. The following is the activity for the month of June:

	Purchases	Sales
June 4	120@$4	
June 10	50 @ $3	
June 15		100@ $5
June 20	20 @ $3.50	
June 28		60@ $5.40

What is the value of Ace & Co's closing inventory using AVCO?

A. $110   B. $ 162   C. $105   D. $120

14.2 | A trader buys inventory costing $5,000. She is entitled to trade discount at 10% and cash discount of 5%. On the same day she discovers that she can only sell the inventory for $4,000. What amount should she record as the purchase price of the inventory?

14.3 | Mariam's first 6 months of trading showed the following purchases and sales of inventory:

20x4	Purchases	Sales
January	300 @ $40	
March	100 @ $45	150 @ $55
April		100 @ $60
May	50 @ $ 48	
June		100 @ 58

Calculate Mariam's Gross Profit for the six months ended 30 June 20x4 using the following methods of inventory valuation:
a)   FIFO
b)   AVCO

14.4 | A company's inventory has been damaged by water. The inventory cost $3,000. It could have been sold for $ 4,500 in perfect condition. It can be sold for $3,500 if repairs are undertaken at a cost of $400. To replace the inventory would cost $2,000.

At what value should the damaged inventory be shown in the financial statements?

14.5 | The table below shows data about three products:

Product	A	B	C
Cost	$16	$18	$21
NRV	$12	$24	$21
Selling expenses	$3	$6	$9

1. What is the value of the inventory?

Partnership Accounts

15.1 | What is a partnership?

A Partnership is formed to overcome the disadvantages of a Sole Trader-ship. It enjoys the advantages of multiple ownership. Normally, there can be a minimum of two partners and a maximum of twenty. It is formed under the Partnership Act of 1890 (n the U.K.) The partners have unlimited liability.

15.2 | What are the advantages of a Partnership type of business organisation?

The advantages are:
a)   More capital is available to the business.
b)   The new partner/s will have skills that will be beneficial to a business and this can increase its customer base. e.g. a solicitor who perhaps was an expert in civil law now acquires a partner who is an expert in criminal law.
c)   The management of the firm is shared and this makes the firm more efficient, in that there are more ideas and the burden of running the firm does not rest on the shoulders of one person alone as in a sole tradership.
d)   Losses can be shared.

15.3 | What are the disadvantages of a Partnership type of business organisation?

The disadvantages are:
a)   The profit has to be shared.
b)   Since every partner is involved in decision making, the decision making process will take longer; not a good thing when time is money.
c)   All partners must abide by the decisions made, even if they were not in favour of them.
d)   All partners are personally responsible for the debts of the business. They have unlimited liability.
e)   Disagreements may occur.

15.4 | What is a Partnership Deed?

A Partnership Deed is also known as a Partnership Agreement. It is a written agreement drawn up in order to avoid future disagreements. Though it is not a legal requirement, it eliminates problems between partners. The usual accounting contents are:
a)   The amount of Capital to be invested by each partner.
b)   The rate of interest, if any, to be paid on capital. Interest on capital is paid if the work done by each partner is of equal value but the capital contributed is unequal. Interest is a form of compensation to the partners concerned for the money they have invested in the business that they could have invested elsewhere.
c)   The ratio in which profits or losses are to be shared between the partners.
d)   The rate of interest, if any, to be charged on partners' drawings. Interest is charged on drawings as a 'penalty' to deter partners from making excessive drawings.
e)   If a salary is to be paid to any of the partners, and, if so, the amount. Salary is paid to a partner as a reward for taking on more responsibility than the other partners or for doing more tasks.
f)   The rate of interest, if any, to be paid on partners' loans. It must be remembered that a loan is not to be regarded as capital and a separate loan account is opened. The interest on such a loan is treated as an expense with any other loan interest, in the income statement.
g)   The upper limit, if any, to be placed on partners' drawings. It is evident that a business benefits if it has good liquidity to finance expansion or to take advantage of bargains or cash discounts given by suppliers for prompt payments of debts. Hence, if drawings were restricted, the firm would benefit from the additional liquidity.
h)   Arrangements for the admission of new partners.

15.5 | What happens if there is no Partnership Deed?

In the U.K., where no partnership deed exists, the Partnership act of 1890 governs the situation. The act states:
a) Profits and losses should be shared equally.
b) No interest on capital is to be charged.
c) No interest on drawings is to be charged.
d) There are to be no salaries paid to partners.
e) A rate of 5% per annum is given to partners who contribute a sum of money to the firm in excess of the capital he has agreed to subscribe.

15.6 | What is the difference between Fixed Capital and Fluctuating Capital Accounts?

When the Capital Account of each partner remains at the figure of capital contributed by the partner year after year and does not change due to profits or interest earned or drawings made, for example, then such an account is called a Fixed Capital Account. A Current account is required to be maintained in addition to a Fixed Capital Account. Profits and losses, drawings and interest are recorded in this current account. On the other hand, if the Capital Account is used to record drawings, interest and profits or losses in addition to the capital contributed, the account is a Fluctuating Capital Account. The balance on the Capital Account will then change each year.

15.7 | Which of the two: Fixed or Fluctuating Capital Account is preferred? Why?

The maintaining of a Fixed Capital Account in addition to a Current Account is preferred. This is due to the fact that when partners withdraw from the firm more than they have earned by way of profits, salary or interest, then they will have a debit balance on their current accounts and this can act as a warning.

15.8 | What is meant by a Profit and Loss Appropriation Account?

This is an account drawn up after the preparation of an Income Statement at the end of a financial year. The appropriation account shows how the profit for the year is shared out between the partners.

15.9 | Name three items that would appear in a partnership's appropriation account.

The three items that would appear are:
a) Salaries to partners, if any
b) Interest on drawings of partners
c) Interest on partners' capital

15.10 | Name three items that would appear in a partner's current account.

Three items that would appear are:
a) Drawings made by the partner.
b) Interest on these drawings.
c) The partner's share of profit.

The Appropriation Account

Exhibit:
Sally and June are in partnership and share profits and losses in the ratio of 1:3. Sally has contributed a capital of $5,000 and June, $3,700 on which they are entitled to an interest of 10%. Sally's drawings are $1,800 and June's, $3000. They are to be charged an interest of 5% on drawings. June is to have a salary of $1,000. The profit for the year, before appropriation is $9,000 for the year ended 31st December 20x5. Balances on their current accounts are : Sally $60, June $300

Required :
a) Profit and Loss appropriation account for the year ended 31st December 20x5.
b) The partners' current accounts for the year ended 31st December 20x5.
c.) The statement of financial position extract as at 31st December 20x5.

Sally & June's Profit and Loss Appropriation A/c
For the year ended 31st December 20x5.

	$	$	$
Profit for the year			9,000
Add Interest on drawings:			
June (5% x 3000)		150	
Sally (5% x 1,800)		90	240
			8,760
Less			
Salary : June		1,000	
Interest on capital:			
Sally (10% x 5000)	500		
June (10% x 3700)	370	870	1,870
Balance of profits to be shared:			6,890
Sally (1/4 x 6000)		1,773	
June (3/4 x 6000)		5,117	6,890

Sally & June Current accounts

Date 20x5	Details	Sally $	June $	Date 20x5	Details	Sally $	June $
Dec. 31	Drawings	1800	3000	Jan 1	Balances b/d	60	300
"	Int. on drawings	90	150	Dec 31	Int. on capital	500	370
"	Balance c/d	443	3637	"	Salary		1000
				"	Profit share	1,773	5117
		2333	6787			2,333	6787

Sally and June
Statement of financial position as at 31st December
20x5 (extract)

		$	$	$
Capital as at 1st January 20x5 :				
	Sally		5,000	
	June		3,700	8,700

Current Accounts	Sally	June
Balance at 1st Jan., 20x5	60	300
Interest on capital	500	370
Share of profits	1,773	5,117
Salary	_____	1000
	2,333	6,787
Less:		
Drawings	(1,800)	(3,000)
Interest on drawings	(90)	(150)
	1,773	5,117

	6,890
	15,590

» EXERCISE 15.1

Saleem and Sulaiman own a grocery store. The following balances were taken from their books at 31st December 20x9 :

	Saleem	Sulaiman
Capital	$ 45,000	$ 30,000
Partnership salaries	$ 4,000	$ 2,000
Drawings	$ 1,200	$ 4,000

Additional information:
a) Interest on capital is to be allowed at 10% per annum.
b) The firm's profit for the year was $ 62,000.
c) Profits and losses are to be shared: Saleem 2/3 and Sulaiman 1/3.
d) Balances on current accounts at 1st January 20x9 : Saleem $ 450(dr) Sulaiman $ 300 (cr)

Required:
i) Prepare a Profit & Loss Appropriation Account for the year ended 31st December 20x9.
ii) Prepare the partners' current accounts.
iii) Their statement of financial position extract as at 31st December 20x9

» EXERCISE 15.2

Wilma and Brenda decided to carry on business in a partnership. They agreed that they would be allowed interest on their capitals @ 10% and that Wilma would receive a salary of $ 4,000 a year. The profit/ loss would be shared Wilma ¼ and Brenda ¾. In their first year ended 31st March 20x4 the business made a profit of $ 40,000. Interest on capitals was as follows : Wilma $ 1,800 and Brenda $700. The partners' drawings were as follows: Wilma $5,500 and Brenda $ 3,000.

a) Prepare the partnership's Profit and Loss Appropriation Account for the year ended 31st March 20x4.
b) Write up the partners' current Accounts for the year ended 31st March 20x4.
c) Prepare an extract of the statement of financial position as at 31st March 20x4 showing the capital and current accounts.

» EXERCISE 15.3

Ferris and Bueller are partners sharing profits and losses in the ratio 1:2. Bueller receives an annual salary of $ 10,000. For the year ended 31st August 20x6, the partnership's profit was $60,000. Calculate the amount credited to Bueller's Current Account on 31st August 20x6. Show your workings.

Solution:

Ferris & Bueller
Profit and Loss Appropriation a/c for the year ended 31st August 20x6

	$	$
Profit for the year		60,000
Less:		
Salary: Bueller		....
Balance of profit to be shared:		50,000
Ferris (1/3)	....	
Bueller (2/3)	....	....

Amount to be credited to Bueller's Current Account
= Salary + profit share
= .... + ...
= $ ....

» EXERCISE 15.4

Melissa and Amy are partners sharing profits and losses in the ratio 1:2. Amy receives an annual salary of $ 10,000. For the year ended 31st August 20x6, the partnership's profit for the year was $50,000.
Calculate the amount credited to Amy's Current Account on 31st August 20x6. Show your workings.

» EXERCISE 15.5

Linda and Nikita are in partnership sharing profits in the ratio 1:4. The following was the trial balance as at 31st July 20x7:

	Dr.	Cr.
	$	$
Capital accounts:		
Linda		30,000
Nikita		15,000
Current accounts at 1st August 20x6:		
Linda		1,300
Nikita		1,200
Office equipment at cost	8,000	
Motor van at cost	9,500	
Provision for depreciation 1st August 20x6:		
Motor van		2,550
Office equipment		1,000
Trade receivables and payables	21,000	6,600
Inventory at 1st August 20x6	24,930	
Cash in hand	1055	
Cash in bank	600	
Purchases and sales revenue	71,600	100,000
Salaries	8,400	
Rent	1,400	
Drawings:		
Linda	5,165	
Nikita	5,000	
	157,650	157,650

Required:

Draw up a set of financial statements for the year ended 31st July 20x7 for the partnership. The following notes are applicable at 31st July 20x7:

a) Inventory at 31st July 20x7 was $ 12,000
b) Rent owing $ 150 .
c) Provide for depreciation using the reducing balance method : Motor van 20%, Office equipment 15%.
d) Interest on capitals is to be allowed at 10%.
e) Interest on drawings is to be charged : Linda $300, Nikita $310

Solution:

Linda & Nikita
Income Statement Account for the year ended 31st July 20x7

	$	$	$
Sales revenue:			....
Less cost of sales			
Inventory at 1st August 20x6		....	
Add Purchases of ordinary goods		....	
		....	
Less Inventory at 31st July 20x7		....	....
Gross Profit			....
Less Expenses:			
Depreciation :			
Motor van		....	
Office equipment	....	....	
Salaries		....	
Rent (............. + 150)		....	....
Profit for the year			....
Add Interest on drawings:			
Linda	300		
Nikita	....	....	
			....
Less:			
Interest on capital:			
Linda (10% x 30,000)	....		
Nikita (10% x 15,000)	....	....	
Balance of profits to be shared:			....
Linda:1/5	....		
Nikita: 4/5	....	....	

Linda & Nikita
Statement of financial position as at 31st July 20x7

	$	$	$
Non-current Assets:	Cost	Depreciation	N. B.V
Office equipment	8,000	*...............	....
Motor Van	9,500	....	....
	....	....	....
Current assets:			
Inventory at 31st July 20x7		....	
Trade receivables		....	
Cash at bank		....	
Cash in hand		....	....
Total assets			....

Working:

*Depreciation: On

office equipment = For the year + to date
= 15% x (8,000 – 1000) + 1000
= $..........................

On motor van = for the year + to date
= 20% x (9,500 – 2550) + 2550
= $..........................

	Linda	Nikita	
	$	$	$
Capital			
Balance at 1st			
August 20x6	30,000	15,000	45,000
Current accounts:			
Balance at 1st			
August 20x6(a)	....	....	
Add interest on			
capital (b)	....	....	
Add share of			
profits(c)	....	....	
	....	....	
Less:			
Drawings(d)	(...........)	(...........)	
Interest on drawings(e)	(300)	(310)	
(a) + (b) + (c) –(d) – (e)	....	....	....
			....
Current liabilities:			
Trade payables		....	
Other payables: rent owing		150	....
Total Liabilities			.... -

15.11 | How is Interest on partners' loan treated in the books of a partnership?

Interest on partners' loan is treated as an expense in the income statement of the business and should not be an appropriation of profit. Hence, it does not appear in the profit and loss appropriation account.

» EXERCISE 15.6

(No partnership agreement regarding interest, partners' salaries or sharing of profits/losses)

Michelle and Jane are partners in a business that they started on 1 January 20x5. On that date Michelle introduced $20,000 cash as capital and Jane contributed $35,000. On 1 July 20x5, Michelle lent $10,000 to the business. The partnership trial balance at 31 December 20x5 was as follows:

	Dr	Cr
	$	$
Sales revenue		14,000
Purchases of ordinary goods	7,000	
Rent	1,000	
Sundry expenses	800	
Staff wages	5,000	
Premises at cost	25,000	
Trade receivables	12,000	
Trade payables		6,700
Bank	21,500	
Capital accounts:		
Michelle		20,000
Jane		35,000
Loan from Michelle		10,000
Drawings: Michelle	7,800	
Jane	5,600	
	85,700	85,700

Further information
1) Inventory at 31 December 20x5 was $1,400.
2) Depreciation on premises : 5% per annum on cost.
3) The partners had not drawn up a partnership deed regarding interest on capital and drawings, salaries or sharing of profits.

Required:
a) Prepare the Income Statement and Appropriation Account for the year ended 31 December 20x5.
b) Prepare the partners' Current Accounts at 31 December 20x5.
c) Prepare the Statement of financial position at 31 December 20x5

» EXERCISE 15.7

Mason and Darling are partners in a business and share profits and losses in the ratio of 2:1. Their profit is $50,000. Interest on capitals are: Mason $4,000, Darling $3,000. Interest on drawings are: Mason $900, Darling $1,000.
How will the residual profit for the year be shared?

» EXERCISE 15.8

Sharon and Mercy commenced partnership on 1 January 20x5. There was no partnership agreement concerning the division of interest on the loan or of profits. The capital contributions were as follows: Sharon $6,000, Mercy $7,000. Mercy had loaned the partnership $2,000. At the year end, 31 December 20x5, profit for the year before loan interest was $5,600. What would be Mercy's share of the profit?

15.1 | MULTIPLE CHOICE QUESTIONS

i) A and B are in partnership. Which item should appear in the partnership appropriation account?
A. *salary due to A*
B. *drawings made by A and B*
C. *Loan given to partnership by A*
D. *salary paid to B's son*

ii) A and B are in partnership sharing profit and losses in the ratio of 3:2. A is entitled to a salary of $1,000 per month and 10% interest per annum on the loan she has made to the partnership of $30,000. The partnership has made a net loss of $15,000. What is A's share of the loss?

A. $9,000   B. $7,500   C. $8,600   D. $2,800

iii) The partnership Act 1890 does not include this:
A. That profits and losses are to be shared equally
B. The partners are entitled to interest on loans they make to the partnership @5% per annum
C. The partners are entitled to interest on capital they introduce into the business @ 5% per annum
D. All partners are entitled to contribute equally to the capital of the partnership.

15.2 | Tom and Gill Kayumba are in partnership. Their financial year ends on 31 March.

The income statement for the year ended 31 March 2013 showed a profit for the year of $22 500.
The following errors were then discovered.

1 No entry had been made for stationery, $260, purchased on credit.

2 The income statement includes $1800 for an advertising campaign covering 18 months to 30 September 2013.

3 No entry had been made for goods, $1000, taken by Gill Kayumba for her own use.

4 No adjustment had been made for motor vehicle expenses, $320, accrued on 1 April 2012.

(a) Prepare a statement of corrected profit for the year ended 31 March 2013.

Tom and Gill Kayumba supplied the following information.

1 Capitals at 1 April 2012 –

Tom Kayumba $60 000   Gill Kayumba $40 000

On 1 October 2012 Tom Kayumba invested a further $20 000.
Interest on capital is allowed at the rate of 5% per annum.

2 Gill Kayumba was entitled to an annual partnership salary of $10 000. This was increased to $14 000 per annum on 1 October 2012.

3 For the year ended 31 March 2013 interest on drawings was charged –
Tom Kayumba $1040   Gill Kayumba $1300

4 Tom Kayumba is entitled to the first $2000 of the profit after interest and partnership salary and the remainder of the profit is shared equally.

(b) Using the corrected profit for the year calculated in (a), prepare the profit and loss appropriation account of Tom and Gill Kayumba for the year ended 31 March 2013.
(c) (i) State one reason why the partners receive interest on capital.
(ii) State one reason why the partners are charged interest on drawings.
Adapted from UCLES, 2013, IGCSE Accounting, Syllabus 0452/21/M/J

15.3 | Jeswant and Selwyn are in partnership. Their financial year ends on 31 December. On 1 January 20x6 the credit balances on their capital accounts were as follows:

Jeswant $18,000; Selwyn $15,000
On 1 July 20x6 Jeswant transferred the $2,000 debit balance on his current account to his capital account.
On 1 December 20x6 Selwyn paid an amount of cash into the business so that his capital was equal to that of Jeswant's.
Required:
Write up the partners' capital accounts as they would appear in the ledger for the year ended 31 December 20x6.

Partnership Changes

16.1 | What is a partnership change?

A partnership is said to have changed when :
1. partners agree to change the profit and loss sharing ratios
2. a new partner joins a firm
3. an existing partner retires.

16.2 | What happens when the profit and loss sharing ratio changes?

The partners may decide to change the profit and loss sharing ratio at any date. All the profits and losses must be shared in the old profit/loss sharing ratio before and up to that date. However, subsequent to that date, the new ratio should be applied. Both realised and unrealised profits/losses should be shared.

16.3 | What is meant by the term realised profits/losses?

Realised profits and losses are those that are revealed by the income statement.

16.4 | What is meant by the term unrealised profits/losses?

Unrealised profits/losses are those that arise from the revaluation of assets and liabilities when the partnership change has been instituted. These will result in adjustments to the partners' capitals. Goodwill is another example of an unrealised profit.

16.5 | When is a revaluation account opened?

A Revaluation account is opened when assets and liabilities are revalued at the time of a change in a partnership. The profit/loss on revaluation is then transferred to the capital accounts of the partners in the old profit sharing ratio.

EXHIBIT

Malcolm and Peter are in partnership sharing profits and losses in the ratio of 1:2. Their financial year ends on 31 December. On 1 July 20x3 they decide to change their profit sharing ratio to 2:3. Their statement of financial position at 31 December 20x2 was as follows:

	$	$
Non-current assets at NBV:		
Property		80,000
Motor Vehicles		12,000
Furniture and Fixtures		9,000
		101,000
Current Assets:		
Inventory	18,000	
Trade receivables	8,000	
Cash at bank	10,000	36,000
Total assets		137,000
Capitals:		
Malcolm		50,000
Peter		78,000
		128,000
Current liabilities:		
Trade payables		9,000
Capital and liabilities		137,000

The partners decide to revalue their assets at 30 June 20x3 as follows:

	$
Property	100,000
Motor Vehicles	10,000
Furniture and Fixtures	8,000
Inventory	20,000
Trade receivables	7,000

Required:
a) Prepare the journal entries to record the revaluation of assets
b) Prepare a redrafted Statement of financial position at 30 June 20x3 after the revaluation of assets.

Solution:

a)

	DR $	CR $
The Journal		
Property	20,000	
Inventory	2,000	
Furniture and Fixtures		1,000
Motor Vehicles		2,000
Trade receivables		1,000
Revaluation account		18,000

(Being revaluation of assets at 30 June 20x3)

	DR $	CR $
Revaluation account	18,000	
Capital Accounts:		
Malcolm		6,000
Peter		12,000

(Profit on revaluation of assets credited to the partners' capital accounts in their old profit sharing ratios)

b)   Malcolm's and Peter's Statement of financial
                      position at 30 June 20x3

	$	$
Non-current Assets at NBV:		
Property		100,000
Motor Vehicles		10,000
Furniture & Fixtures		8,000
		118,000
Current Assets:		
Inventory	20,000	
Trade receivables	7,000	
Cash at bank	10,000	37,000
Total Assets		155,000
Capitals:		
Malcolm (50,000+ 6,000)		56,000
Peter (78,000 + 12,000)		90,000
		146,000
Current liabilities: Trade payables		(9,000)
Capitals and liabilities		155,000

» EXERCISE 16.1

Mary and Noeman are in partnership sharing profits and losses in the ratio of 3:2. Their financial year ends on 31 December. On 1 July 20x2 they decide to share profits and losses equally.

Their statement of financial position at 30th June 20x2 was as follows:

	$	$
Non-current assets at NBV:		
Premises		60,000
Plant and machinery		29,000
Furniture and Fixtures		7,000
		96,000
Current Assets:		
Inventory	15,000	
Trade receivables	10,000	
Cash at bank	8,000	33,000
Total assets		129,000
Capitals:		
Mary		65,000
Neoman		57,000
		122,000
Current liabilities:		
Trade payables		7,000
Capitals and liabilities		129,000

The partners decide to revalue their assets at 30 June 20x2 as follows:

	$
Premises	100,000
Plant and machinery	25,000
Furniture and Fixtures	4,000
Inventory	12,000
Trade receivables	7,000

Required:

a.   Prepare the journal entries to record the revaluation of assets

b.   Prepare a redrafted Statement of financial position at 30 June 20x2 after the revaluation of assets.

Goodwill

16.6 | What is meant by Goodwill?

Goodwill is an intangible non-current asset. It is the difference between the purchase price and value of identifiable net assets. Goodwill = Purchase price – value of identifiable net assets.

16.7 | Why is Goodwill paid?

People who are investing in an existing business that has any or all of the following advantages pay goodwill:

a)   The business has a good reputation.
b)   The business has a large number of loyal customers.
c)   The business is situated in a good location.

d) The workforce is very efficient.
e) The business has a good network of reliable suppliers.
f) The business is in possession of valuable trademarks and well known brand names.

16.8 | Name two other intangible non-current assets.

Two other intangible non-current assets are:
a) trademarks
b) brand names.

16.9 | When is goodwill calculated? Why?

Goodwill is calculated when there is a change in the profit/loss sharing ratios or a change to the membership of the Partnership. e. g. the admission of a new partner. The benefit due to Goodwill is to be shared in the old profit sharing ratio since Goodwill was earned during that time, prior to any change.

16.10 | Where is goodwill shown in the final accounts of a business?

Goodwill is shown as an intangible non-current asset, and is listed before the tangible non-current assets in the statement of financial position of a business at the end of the financial year. However, most businesses write off goodwill, in accordance with the concept of Prudence. In such a case, Goodwill will not be shown.

Journal entries to be passed if:

a) The firm decides to maintain a Goodwill Account in the books of Account-

	Dr.	Cr
Goodwill a/c	xxxxx	.
Capital accounts of old partners in the old profit sharing ratio		xxxxx

NOTE: The Goodwill Account will remain open and goodwill will appear in the statement of financial position as an Intangible asset.

b) The firm decides not to maintain a Goodwill Account in the books of Account

	Dr	Cr.
1) Goodwill a/c	xxxxx	
Capital accounts of old partners in the old profit sharing ratio		xxxxx

	DR	CR
2) Capital accounts of new partners in the new profit sharing ratio	xxxxx	
Goodwill a/c		xxxxxx

NOTE: The Goodwill Account is opened and immediately closed. Goodwill will not appear in the Financial statements.

Exhibit:

A, B and C are in partnership. They share profits in the ratio 2:1:2. It was decided to admit X as a partner. Goodwill was valued at $10,000. X will bring $5000 cash as Capital. The new profit sharing ratio is A-3:B-2:C-4:X-1.

The statement of financial position before X was admitted was as follows:

	$
Assets (other than in cash)	12,000
Cash	3,000
	15,000
Capitals: A	4,000
B	2,000
C	4,000
Trade payables	5,000
	15,000

Required:
1) Assume that Goodwill is to be kept in the books of account
a) The entries in the capital accounts of A,B,C and X
b) The entries in the Goodwill Account
c) The statement of financial position after X has been admitted.
2) Assume that Goodwill is not to be kept in the books of accounts.
A) The entries in the Capital accounts of A,B,C and X
B) The entries in the Goodwill Account.
C) The statement of financial position after X has been admitted

Solution:
1. Goodwill is to be kept in the books of accounts:

Goodwill Account

	$		$
Capital – A	4,000	Balance c/d	10,000
B	2,000		
C	4,000		
	10,000		10,000
Balance b/d	10,000		

Capital Accounts

	A	B	C	X		A	B	C	X
	$	$	$	$		$	$	$	$
Balances c/d	8,000	4,000	8,000	5000	Balances b/d	4,000	2,000	4,000	
					Goodwill	4,000	2,000	4,000	
					Cash				5,000
	8,000	4,000	8,000	5,000		8,000	4,000	8,000	5,000
					Balances b/d	8,000	4,000	8,000	5,000

	$
Intangible Assets :Goodwill	10,000
Assets (other than in cash)	12,000
Cash (3,000 + 5,000)	8,000
	30,000
Capitals: A	8,000
B	4,000
C	8,000
X	5,000
Trade payables	5,000
	30,000

2. Goodwill is not to be kept in the books of accounts:

Goodwill Account

	$		$
Capital: A	4,000	Capital : A	3,000
B	2,000	B	2,000
C	4,000	C	4,000
		X	1,000
	10,000		10,000

Capital Accounts

	A	B	C	X		A	B	C	X
	$	$	$	$		$	$	$	$
*Goodwill	3,000	2,000	4,000	1,000	Balances b/d	4,000	2,000	4,000	
Balances c/d	5,000	2,000	4,000	4,000	**Goodwill	4,000	2,000	4,000	
					Cash				5,000
	8,000	4,000	8,000	5,000		8,000	4,000	8,000	5,000
					Balances b/d	5,000	2,000	4,000	4,000

* Goodwill to be shared in the new profit sharing ratio

** Goodwill to be shared in the old profit sharing ratio

Statement of financial position as at ....

	$
Assets (other than in cash)	12,000
Cash (3,000 + 5,000)	8,000
	20,000
Capitals: A	5,000
B	2,000
C	4,000
X	4,000
Trade payables	5,000
	20,000

» EXERCISE 16.2

S and T are in partnership sharing profits and losses equally. On 1st March 20x4 they decide to admit M into the partnership and that profits and losses would now be shared in the ratio – S:4, T:3, M:3.

At that date S's Capital was $ 20,000 and T's capital was $ 15,000. Goodwill was valued at $ 10,000. It was agreed that a Goodwill Account will not be maintained in the books of accounts.

M introduced $ 14,000 into the business bank account.

Required:

Journal entries with narratives to show:

    a) The admission of M

    b) Adjustments to Goodwill.

Solution:

		Debit	Credit
		$	$

a)

20x4

1st March	Bank a/c	14,000	
	M's Capital a/c		....

(Being the amount introduced by M as capital contribution)

b) 20x4

		Dr.	Cr.
		$	$
1st March	Goodwill	....	
	S's Capital a/c		5,000
	T's Capital a/c		5,000

(Being Goodwill introduced - in the old profit sharing ratio)

		Dr.	Cr.
		$	$
1st March	S's Capital a/c	4,000	
	T's Capital a/c	....	
	M's Capital	3,000	
	Goodwill		....

(Being Goodwill written off in the new profit sharing ratio)

» EXERCISE 16.3

The partners have always shared profits in the ratio Ann 2: Basil 3. It is decided to admit Cecil. Goodwill was valued at $15,000, but it is not to be brought into the business records. Cecil will bring $6,000 cash into the business as Capital. The new profit sharing ratio is to be Ann2: Basil2: Cecil1. The statement of financial poisition before Cecil was admitted was as follows:

	$
Total Assets (not including Goodwill)	26,000
Capitals: Ann	16,000
Basil	10,000

Show

a) The entries in the Capital accounts of Ann, Basil and Cecil in columnar form.

b) The statement of financial position after Cecil has been admitted.

» EXERCISE 16.4

X, Y and Z are in partnership. They share profits in the ratio 1:1:2. It was decided to admit A as a partner. Goodwill was valued at $12,000. A will bring $6000 cash as Capital. The new profit sharing ratio is X-2;Y-2;Z-1;A-1. The statement of financial position before A was admitted was as follows:

	$
Assets (other than in cash)	20,000
Cash	5,000
	25,000
Capitals: X	10,000
Y	6,000
Z	8,000
Trade payables	1,000
	25,000

Required

1) Assume that Goodwill is to be kept in the books of account
   a) The entries in the capital accounts of X,Y,Z and A
   b) The entries in the Goodwill Account
   c) The statement of financial position after A has been admitted.
2) Assume that Goodwill is not to be kept in the books of accounts.
   a) The entries in the Capital accounts of X,Y,Z and A
   b) The entries in the Goodwill Account.
   c) The statement of financial position after A has been admitted.

EXERCISE 16.5

M and N are in partnership sharing profits and losses equally. On 1st March 20x4 they decide to admit C into the partnership and that profits and losses would now be shared in the ratio – M-2:N-2:C-1.
At that date M's Capital was $ 25,000 and N's capital was $ 10,000. Goodwill was valued at $ 15,000. It was agreed that a Goodwill Account will not be maintained in the books of accounts. C introduced $ 24,000 into the business bank account.

Required :

Journal entries with narratives to show:

a) The admission of C
b) Adjustments to Goodwill.

APPORTIONMENT OF PROFIT WHEN CHANGES TAKE PLACE DURING THE FINANCIAL YEAR

EXHIBIT

Merrick and Danny are partners sharing profits and losses in the ratio of 1:2. Their financial year ends on 31 December. On 1 January 20x4 their capital and current accounts were as follows:

	Merrick	Danny
Capital accounts	$20,000	$15,000
Current accounts	$ 5,500	$ 3,000

On 1 July 20x4 the partners decided to adopt the following changes in their partnership deed:
1) Danny to receive a salary of $4,000 per annum
2) Profits and losses to be shared equally.

3) Danny to transfer $5,000 from his capital account into a loan account on which he will earn 10% interest per annum.

Further information for the year ended 31 December 20x4:

	$
Sales (spread evenly throughout the year)	180,000
Cost of sales	78,000
Wages	10,000
Heating and lighting	8,000
General expenses	12,000

Of the general expenses, $2,000 was incurred in the six months to 30 June 2ox4.
All sales produce a uniform rate of Gross Profit.

Required:

a) Prepare the Income Statement and appropriation accounts for the year ended 31 December 20x4.
b) Prepare the partners' current accounts for the year ended 31 December 20x4.

Solution:
a)

Merrick and Danny
Income Statement and Appropriation Account for the year ended 31 December 20x4

	$
Sales revenue	180,000
Less Cost of sales	78,000
Gross Profit	102,000

	6 months to 30 June 20x4		6 months to 31 December 20x4		Year to 31 December 20x4	
	$	$	$	$	$	$
Gross profit b/f		51,000		51,000		102,000
Less Expenses:						
Wages	5,000		5,000		10,000	
Heating & Lighting	4,000		4,000		8,000	
General expenses	2,000		10,000		12,000	
Interest on loan		(11,000)	250	(19250)	250	(30,250)
Profit for the year		40,000		31,750		71,750
Less Salary:						
Danny		_____	(2,000)		(2,000)	
		40,000		29,750		69,750
Share of profit:						
Merrick	13,333		14,875		28,208	
Danny	26,667	40,000	14,875	29,750	41,542	69,750

20x4	Merick $	Danu $	20x4	Merick $	Danu $
Dec 31 Balances c/d	33,708	46,542	January 1 Balances b/d	2,500	3,000
			December 31 Salary		2,000
			December 31 Share of profit	28,208	41,542
	33,708	46,542		33,708	46,542
			January 1 Balances b/d	33,708	46,542

16.11 What happens when a partner retires?

The balance on her current account is transferred to the capital account. If there is goodwill, the partner is given her share of goodwill. The capital account is then closed after the balances, if any, are paid to the retiring partner.

16.12 Sometimes a partner leaves a part of his capital as a loan to a business. How is this treated?

The loan amount is taken out of the proceeds paid to the retiring partner and transferred from his capital account to a loan account.

EXHIBIT

Pam, Sam and Tammy are partners sharing profits and losses equally. Tammy decides to retire on 31 December 20x4. After the appropriation account was drawn up, the share of profits were as follows:

Pam $35,000

Sam $45,000

Tammy $20,000

The capital and current account balances at 1 January 20x4 were as follows:

	Capital	Current
Pam	$30,000	$4,000(cr)
Sam	$25,000	$1,000(cr)
Tammy	$40,000	$2,500(cr)

Drawings for the year were: Pam $12,000, Sam $6,000, Tammy $15,000.

Tammy left $15,000 of her capital as a loan with interest at 8% pa.

The partners decided not to revalue assets but valued goodwill at $15,000. Goodwill was not to be kept in the books.

Required

a. Partner's current accounts at 31 December 20x4

b. Partner's capital accounts at 31 December 20x4.

Solution:

Partners' current accounts

20x4	Pam $	Sam $	Tammy $	20x4	Pam $	Sam $	Tammy $
Dec 31 Drawings	12000	6000	15000	Jan 1 Bal b/	4000	1000	2500
Dec 31 Tammy capital a/c			7500	Dec 31 Share of profit	35000	45000	20000
Dec 31 Balances c/d	27000	40000					
	39000	46000	22500		39000	46000	22500
				Jan 1 Balances b/d	27000	40000	

Partners capital accounts

20x4	Pam $	Sam $	Tammy $	20x4	Pam $	Sam $	Tammy $
Dec 31 Goodwill	7500	7500		Jan 1 Balances b/d	30000	25000	40000
Dec 31 Tammy loan a/c			15000	Dec 31 Goodwill	5000	5000	5000
Dec 31 Bank			37500	Dec 31 Tammy's current a/c			7500
Dec 31 Balances c/d	27500	22500					
	35000	30000	52500		35000	30000	52500
				20x5 Jan 1 Balances b/d	27500	22500	

16.13 How is the dissolution of a partnership treated?

When a partnership is dissolved (ceases to exist), one of the following two methods is used:

- All the business assets and liabilities are sold to a new business. Some of the assets may be taken over by one or more of the partners. Some of the liabilities may be paid off. A realisation account is opened to record all this.

- Alternatively, the assets may be sold to many different people and the money used to pay off the liabilities. The partners then retire and the balance in the bank account is transferred to them. The partnership is dissolved.

16.14 List the steps taken upon dissolution of a partnership.

The steps are as follows:

1.   Open a realisation account to record the sale of assets. The following entries are to be made:

	Debit	Credit
a. All assets to be sold:	Realisation (at NBV)	Assets
b. Proceeds of sale of assets	Bank	Realisation
c. Assets taken over by partners (at valuation)	Capital accounts of partners' concerned	Realisation
d. Costs of dissolution	Realisation account	Bank (cash)
e. Discounts received from creditors	Trade payables	Realisation
f. Irrecoverable debts and discounts allowed	Realisation a/c	Trade receivables
g. Debit balance on realisation account	Partners' capital	Realisation
h. Credit balance on realisation account	Realisation	Partners capital

2. The balance of cash is used to pay creditors (Trade payables) and expenses of dissolution.

	Debit	Credit
a. Payment of creditors	Trade payables a/c	Bank (cash)
b. Cash received from debtors	Bank (cash)	Trade receivables
c. Repayment of partner's loan to firm	Partner's loan a/c	Bank

3. Finally, the balance of cash is used to repay the partners for the balances on their capital accounts.

	Debit	Credit
a. Repayment of partners' capital accounts	Partners' capital accounts	Bank
b. Debit balance on partners' capital accounts	Bank	Partners' capital accounts

4. All the accounts should now be closed.

16.15 Why are closing entries necessary, even though the business will no longer be in existence?

The reasons for making closing entries are:
1. To ensure that all debts are collected.
2. To ensure that all creditors are paid.
3. To record disposal of assets with subsequent profits and losses on disposal calculated and transferred to the partners' capital accounts.
4. After steps 1-3 above have been completed, the amounts due to or from partners on their capital accounts cannot be correctly ascertained.

Exhibit:

Errol, Leslie and Max are partners sharing profits and losses in the ratio 2:2:1. Their statement of financial position at 31 March 20x0 follows:

	Cost	Depreciation	N.B.V
	$	$	$
Non-current assets			
Property	21,000	16,000	5,000
Motor vehicles	7,000	5,000	2,000
Furniture & fixtures	3,000	1,000	2,000
	31,000	22,000	9,000

Current assets: Inventory	12,000	
Trade receivables	3,400	15,400
Total assets		24,400
Capitals: Errol	5,000	
Leslie	2,000	
Max	2,000	9,000
Current liabilities:		
Trade payables	3,900	
Bank overdraft	900	4,800
Loan from Stella		3,000
Current accounts: Errol	3,400	
Leslie	2,500	
Max	1,700	7,600
Capitals and liabilities		24,400

On 31 March 20x0, the partners decided to dissolve the partnership. Errol took over one of the motor vehicles valued at $2,500 with a N.B.V. of $1,000. Max took over inventory with a valuation of $6,000.

The inventory had cost $6,500. The property, furniture & fixtures and remaining motor vehicles were sold for $11,500. Trade receivables realised $3,225. The trade payables were paid in full. Errol, Leslie and Max either received the monies due to them on their capital accounts or paid what was due to the business on their capital accounts.

Required:

Entries to record the above events in:
a.   The realisation account
b.   The firm's bank account
c.   The partners' capital accounts

Solution:

a.   Errol, Leslie and Max Realisation account

20x0		$	20x0		$
Mar 31	Property	5,000	Mar 31 Errol: capital		2,500
	Motor vehicles	2,000		Leslie: capital	6,000
	Furniture and Fixtures	2,000		Bank	11,500
	Inventory	12,000		Capitals:	
	Trade receivables- diff	175		Errol	470
				Leslie	470
				Max	235
		21,175			21,175

b.   Bank account

20x0		$	20x0		$
Mar 31	Realisation	11,500	Mar 31 Bal b/f		900
	Trade receivables	3,225		Trade payables	3,900
	Max – capital	2,535		Loan – Stella	3,000
				Errol – capital	5,430
				Leslie – capital	4,030
		17,260			17,260

Capital accounts

	Errol	Leslie	Max		Errol	Leslie	Max
	$	$	$		$	$	$
Realisation a/c				Balances b/f	5,000	2,000	2,000
-M. vehicles	2,500			Current a/c	3,400	2,500	1,700
-Inventory			6,000	Bank			2,535
-loss on realisation	470	470	235				
Bank	5,430	4,030					
	8,400	4,500	6,235		8,400	4,500	6,235

Exercise 16.6

Ernie, Bernie and Mernie are partners sharing profits and losses in the ratio 3:2:1. The statement of financial position at 30 June 20x5 follows:

	Cost	Depreciation	Net book value
Non-current assets	$	$	$
Property, plant & equipment	25,000	13,000	12,000
Delivery vans	18,000	15,000	3,000
Furniture and fixtures	3,000	2,400	600
	46,000	30,400	15,600
Current assets:			
Inventory		21,000	
Trade receivables		6,400	
Bank		3,800	31,200
Total assets			46,800
Capitals: Ernie		20,000	
Bernie		10,000	
Mernie		2,000	32,000
Current accounts: Ernie		4,000	
Bernie		5,000	
Mernie		(1,900)	7,100
			39,100
Current liabilities:			
Trade payables			2,700
Long term liabilities: Loan from Sternie			5,000
Total capitals and liabilities			46,800

On 30 June 20x5, the partners decided to dissolve the partnership. Mernie took over one of the delivery van valued at $1,000.

The property, plant & equipment, furniture & fixtures and remaining delivery vans realised $15,400.

Trade receivables realised $6,200. Inventory was sold for $24,000.

The trade payables were paid in full and discounts received amounted to $74.

Dissolution expenses were $800. (The loan was from Ernie, not Sternie)

Required:
Entries to record the above events in:
a.   Journal entries to close asset accounts (narratives not required)
b.   The realisation account
c.   The firm's bank account
d.   The partners' capital accounts

» EXERCISE 16.7

James and Lewis have been in partnership for some years sharing profits and losses equally. They had no partnership agreement. Their statement of financial position at 30 September 20x5 showed the following information.

	$
Non-current assets	230 000
Net current assets	60 000
	290 000
Capital accounts	
James	200 000
Lewis	70 000
	270 000
Current accounts	

	James	Lewis	
	$	$	
Opening balance	31 000	17 000	
Share of profit	15 000	15 000	
Drawings	(21 000)	(37 000)	
Closing balance	25 000	(5 000)	20,000
			290 000

Additional information

On 1 October 2015 Ahmed joined the partnership. A partnership agreement was drawn up. The terms set out in the agreement were:

1 Profits and losses are to be shared equally.

2 Interest is to be charged at 5% on drawings.

3 Interest is to be allowed at 10% on capital.

The following also took place:

1 Ahmed introduced capital of $80 000, which he paid into the business bank account.

2 Goodwill was valued at $60 000 but no goodwill account is to be maintained in the books of account.

3 Non-current assets were revalued at $270 000.

4 The inventory value was to be reduced by $4000.

Required:
a. The revaluation account
b. The capital accounts to record the admission of Ahmed.

Adapted from UCLES, 2016, AS/A Level Accounting, Syllabus 9706/22,/F/M/16

» EXERCISE 16.8

A and B are sole traders. On 1 July 20x4 they agreed to form a partnership which would take over the assets of the separate businesses.

At 30 June 20x4 the following information was available:

	A	B
	$	$
Goodwill	12,000	10,000
Motor Vans	18,500	16,700
Inventory	3,000	1,900
Trade receivables	4,000	3,000
Cash at bank/(overdraft)	8,000	(3,000)

Required:

Calculate the total of the tangible assets taken over by the newly formed partnership

16.1 | MULTIPLE CHOICE QUESTIONS

i) M and N are partners sharing profits and losses in the ratio of 1:2. As per their partnership deed, they are allowed interest on capital and loans at 8% per annum. N is to get a salary of $5,000 per annum. M's capital was $30,000 and N's capital was 20,000. N loaned $40,000 to the partnership 6 months into the financial year. The partnership made a profit of $45,000 for the year. What is N's share of the profit?

A. $24,000

B. $25,600

C. $ 29,000

D. $30,600

ii) Nelly and Furtado are partners sharing profits and losses equally. They admit Beryl to the partnership on 1 June 20x1. On that date they revalued their net assets and realised a profit of $21,000. The new profit sharing ratio is Nelly 1/6 Furtado 2/6 Beryl 3/6. How will the revaluation of net assets be recorded in the partners' capital accounts?

	Nelly's capital a/c	Furtado's capital a/c	Beryl's capital a/c
A)	Credit $10,500	Credit $10,500	
B)	Credit $ 3,500	Credit $7,000	
C)	Credit $10,500	Credit $10,500	Credit$10,500
D)	Credit $7,000	Credit $7,000	Credit $ 7,000

iii) On 31 Dec 20x4, Meenakshi and Manish decide to dissolve their partnership. Their balances on 1 January 20x4 were: Capital accounts : Meenakshi $40,000 Manish; $50,000 and Current accounts Meenakshi $ 15,000 (cr); Manish $10,000 (cr). Loss on disposal of net assets was $4,000. On dissolution how much money would Meenakshi receive if the profit and losses were shared equally?

A) $ 55,000 B) $53,000 C) $60,000 D) $58,000

iv) P, Q and R are in partnership.Their assets and liabilities are: Land and buildings $500 000; Furniture $350 000; Trade receivables$30,000; Closing inventory $ 15,000; Cash and cash equivalents $400 The partnership was dissolved on the following terms.
R took the land and buildings and half the furniture at a valuation of$450,000. The inventory was sold for $12,000 and the remaining furniture for $100,000. Cost of dissolution was $1,500. The trade receivables realised $20,000. What was the profit/loss on dissolution?

A) Loss $876,500 B) Profit $876,500 C) Profit $314,500   D) Loss $ 314,500

v) Eileen and Menaka are in partnership and share profits and losses in the ratio 2:1. They decide to admit Monica to the partnership and revise the profit-sharing ratio to Eileen2/5, Menaka 2/5, Monica 1/5. Goodwill is to be valued at $30,000 but not to be shown in the books. Which of the following entries will be made in the capital accounts?

	Eileen's capital a/c	Menaka's capital a/c	Monica's capital a/c
A)	Credit $8,000	Debit $2000	Debit $6000
B)	Debit $8,000	Credit $2,000	Credit $6,000
C)	Credit $ 12,000	Credit $12,000	Credit $6,000
D)	Debit $12,000	Debit $12,000	Debit $6,000

16.2 Amit and Binu were in partnership sharing profits and losses in the ratio 3:2 resp. At 31 December 20x6, their total assets were $121,700 and current liabilities, including a bank overdraft were $20,100. Capital accounts at that date were: Amit $30,000; Binu $20,000 and current accounts: Amit $ 33,200; Binu $18,400.

The partnership was dissolved on that date and the following resulted: Trade receivables of $13,100 realised $12,600. Trade payables were settled in full for $9,800. Inventory of $18,600 were sold for $15,000. Machinery was sold at a loss of $3,000.

Amit took over premises valued at $40,000 for $30,000. Motor vehicles valued at $18,000. Binu took over one of them at an agreed valuation of $6,500 and the remaining were sold for $12,000. Dissolution costs were $6,300.

Required:

a. The Realisation account
b. A statement showing how much Binu will receive when the partnership bank account is closed.

Adapted from UCLES, 2017, AS/A Level Accounting, Syllabus 9706/21/M/J/17

16.3| A and B are in partnership sharing profits and losses equally. No goodwill account is maintained in the books. C is admitted into the partnership and pays $25,000 cash for his share of the Goodwill. Profits are to be shared equally between A, B and C.
Required:
Pass the requisite journal entries to record the admission of C into the partnership.

16.4| Malini, Mahesh and Sonal are in partnership sharing profits and loses in the ratio 2:2:1. Interest is charged on drawings at 5% per annum, and interest is credited on capital at 6% per annum. On 31st May 20x8, the statement of financial position of the partnership was as follows:

	$	$	$
Non-current Assets:			
Freehold property			180,000
Machinery			60,000
Office equipment			15,000
Motor Vehicles			35,000
			290,000
Current Assets:			
Inventory		34,000	
Trade receivables		41,000	
		75,000	
Current Liabilities:			
Trade payables	45,000		
Bank	10,000	55,000	20,000
			310,000
Capital Accounts:			
Malini		140,000	
Mahesh		100,000	
Sonal		70,000	310,000

The partners have now realised that their capital account balances do not reflect the following matters:
i) Interest has not been charged on the following drawings:

Date	Malini	Mahesh	Sonal
20x7	$	$	$
June 1	6,000	15,000	10,000
December 1	9,000	-	5,000

ii) Interest on partners' capital at 6% per annum has not been credite
Partners' capital, **for the purpose of interest calculation,** is taken as:

	$
Malini	70,000
Mahesh	50,000
Sonal	30,000

These amounts were unchanged throughout the year.
Sonal decided to retire on 1 June 20x8, on the following terms:
1) She would receive $8,000 payable by cheque immediately.

2) The freehold property is to be revalued at $250,000.
3) Goodwill is to be valued at 100,000.
4) Sonal will take ownership of the partnership vehicle at its statement of financial position value of $9,000.
5) The balance of Sonal's capital will be left on loan in the partnership.

It was decided to open a goodwill account in the partnership books.

Required:
a) Prepare the capital accounts of the three partners, showing in detail all the adjustments necessary, and the revised balances both at (i) 31st May 20x8 and (ii) after Sonal's retirement on 1st June 20x8.
b) Prepare the statement of financial position of the partnership of Malini and Mahesh as at 1st June 20x8.
c) Give two reasons why the partnership should charge interest at only 5% per annum on partners' drawings when it is having to pay 14% per annum to the partnership's bank in respect of its overdraft.

16.5 Hyung Ho and Sun Min are in partnership, sharing residual profits and losses equally after the payments mentioned below are made.
  a. 2% interest on drawings
  b. Salary of $8,000 per annum to Sun Min

The drawings were:

Hyung Ho $ 10,000
Sun   Min $ 7,000
The profit for the year is $50,000

Required:
How much will each partner receive in share of residual profits?

16.6 A, B and C are in partnership sharing profits and losses equally. You are given the following information:

Total drawings for the year	$60,000
Partnership salary for B	$30,000
Net assets at end of the year	$600,000
Capital account balances at start of the year	$320,000
Current account balances at start of the year	$100,000 (cr)

Required:
Calculate B's share of profit for the year.

Accounts Of Limited Companies-An Introduction

17.1 | What is a limited company?

A limited company, unlike other forms of legal business structures, is a separate legal entity. The shareholders (owners) of a limited company enjoy limited liability which means that they do not stand to lose more than the sum invested in the company, in the event of a bankruptcy or liquidation.

17.2 | What are the two main characteristics of a limited company as opposed to other forms of business organisations?

The two main characteristics are:
1) If the company is declared insolvent, it is the creditors who lose as they can only be paid to the extent of the issued capital of the business. If they are owed more than that sum, they risk not being paid.
2) Ownership and management are divorced, in that shareholders are not entitled to help manage the company. It is the directors that manage the company for them.

17.3 | What are the two documents that are required, by the Companies Act of 1985, to be filed with the Registrar of Companies?

The two documents are:
1. The Memorandum of Association: This document contains information regarding the relationship of the company with the rest of the world. The following information is to be contained:
a) The name of the company which must be followed by the suffix plc, if it is a public limited company, or Ltd. if it is a private limited company.
b) A statement that the liability of the company is limited.
c) The amount of authorised capital.

2. The Articles of Association: This document defines the rights and duties of the company's shareholders and directors. Regulations for meetings, forfeiture of shares, voting rights, and directors' qualifications are also contained in this important document.

17.4 | What is the difference between a private and public limited company?

A private limited company cannot sell its shares to the general public. Therefore, its shares cannot be sold on the stock exchange. They may have authorised capitals of less than fifty thousand pounds. Their names should be followed by the suffix Ltd. which stands for 'Limited'.
A public limited company may offer their shares to the general public and its shares can be traded on the stock exchange. Their authorised share capital should be at least fifty thousand pounds of which one quarter must have been paid by shareholders. The whole of any premium on shares must have also been paid.

17.5 | What is meant by the term 'directors' qualifications'?

This stands for the number of shares a director must hold in the company.

17.6 Define:
a) Dividend
b) Interim dividend
c) Final dividend

Dividend is defined as the share of profits that is distributed to each shareholder. Dividends are paid out of distributable profits. Dividends are expressed as cents per share or as a percentage of the nominal value of the shares.
Interim dividend may be paid to shareholders during a company's financial year if the directors feel that the profits and cash resources are sufficient for the purpose. These dividends are debited in the company's income statement for the year to which they relate.
Final dividends are proposed by the directors of the company but must be approved by shareholders at the Annual General Meeting before they can be paid. They are paid after the end of the financial year. Hence they are not recorded in the year-end financial statements but are shown as a note.

17.7 | How are partnerships different from limited companies with reference to the number of owners?

In a partnership, the minimum number of partners is two and the maximum is twenty (except in certain professional firms e.g. lawyers' and accountants'). In a company the minimum number of shareholders should be two and the maximum number is decided on by the number of shares permitted by the authorised share capital.

17.8 | How are partnerships different from limited companies with reference to the liability of the owners?

Partners have unlimited liability (except for limited partners in a limited partnership), whereas shareholders in a limited company have limited liability.

17.9 | How do partnerships differ from limited companies with reference to the management of the business?

All partners, except those with limited liability, may manage the affairs of a partnership. However, the management of a company is left entirely to the directors by the shareholders.

17.10 | How are partnerships different from limited companies as far as taxation is concerned?

Partnerships are not required by law to pay tax on their profits. Partners pay individual tax on the income they make from the profits of the partnership. Companies are liable to pay tax on their profits. The tax paid is treated as an appropriation of profit.

17.11 | How are partnerships different from limited companies as far as distribution of profit is concerned?

Partners share profits and losses as per their partnership deed or equally if there is no partnership deed. Companies distribute their profits to their shareholders in the form of dividend. They may not distribute all the profits made and any undistributed profit is retained in the company as a reserve.

17.12 | What is the difference between liabilities, provisions and reserves?

Liabilities are defined as that which the company owes. They are determined with substantial accuracy. They are created by carrying down credit balances on personal or expense accounts.

Provisions are created by the company to provide for liabilities that are known to exist but cannot be determined with substantial accuracy. They are created by debiting the approximate amount of the known liability to the income statement and crediting it to provision accounts. E.g. Provision for depreciation of non-current assets.

Reserves are amounts set aside apart from the ones mentioned above. They are an appropriation of profits and are created by debiting the Appropriation Account and crediting the Reserve accounts. They may also be created by premiums paid on ordinary or preference shares or by revaluing non-current assets.

17.13 | What are the different types of reserves?

There are two classes of reserves: revenue reserves or capital reserves.

Revenue reserves are created by transferring profit from the appropriation section of the income statement to the reserve. Hence the creation of such reserves (usually termed a general reserve) reduces the amount of profit available to pay dividends.

Capital reserves are not normally created by transferring profit from the income statement. They generally represent gains that have not been realised. Capital reserves may never be credited back to the income statement and can never be used to pay cash dividends.

17.14 | What are the different types of revenue reserves?

If revenue reserves are created for a specific purpose such as a replacement of a non-current asset or for the planned expansion of the business, then they are named accordingly. However, if they are just retained profits to strengthen the financial position of the company, then they are known as general reserves. Retained profit is also a revenue reserve.

17.15 | What are the different types of Capital reserves?

The following are the more common types of Capital reserves:
1) Share Premium Account.
2) Capital Redemption Reserve
3) Revaluation reserve

17.16 | Write a short note on 'Share Premium Account'.

When shares are issued at a price above their face (nominal) value they are said to be issued at a premium. The premium on each share is credited to a special account called the Share Premium Account. The Companies Act 1985 permits the Share Premium Account to be used only for the following purposes:
1) To write off preliminary expenses incurred by the company in its formation.
2) To provide for any premium payable on the redemption of debentures.
3) To provide any commission payable on the redemption of shares and debentures.
4) To write off expenses incurred in the issue of shares or debentures including any commission payable on the issue of shares.
5) To pay up bonus shares.

EXHIBIT
The directors of Ace & Co issued 100,000 Ordinary shares of $1 at $1.20 a share. All the shares were subscribed for and issued.
Required:
Prepare Journal Entries to record the issue of the shares.

SOLUTION:

	DR	CR
	$	$
Bank	120,000	
Ordinary Share capital		100,000
Share Premium Account		20,000

(Issue of 1,00,000 ordinary shares of $1 at $1.20 a share)

» **EXERCISE 17.1**
Belling and Co. issued 50,000 ordinary shares of a nominal value of $1 for $1.30 a share.

Required:
Pass Journal entries to record the issue of these shares.

» **EXERCISE 17.2**
Anacin and Co. issued 40,000 preference shares of $1 at a premium of $0.25 a share.

Required:
Prepare journal entries to record the issue of these preference shares.

17.17 | Write a short note on 'Capital Redemption Reserve'.

This reserve is created by transferring profit from the income statement when a company redeems any of its shares otherwise than out of the proceeds of a new issue of shares. This reserve can be used to pay up bonus shares.

17.18 | Write a short note on 'Revaluation Reserve'.

This reserve is created with the gain on revaluation of non-current assets that the company may undertake from time to time. This is unrealised profit and may not be credited to the income statement. However, this reserve may be used to issue bonus shares.

EXHIBIT
An extract from Malini Ltd's **statement of financial position** is as follows:

	$
Premises at cost	50,000
Provision for depreciation	12,000
Net book value	38,000

The Premises have been professionally revalued at $80,000. A decision has been made to revalue the premises in the books of the company.
Required:
Prepare journal entries to revalue the premises in the company's books.

SOLUTION

	DR	CR
	$	$
Premises at cost	30,000	
Prov for depreciation	12,000	
Premises revaluation reserve		42,000

An extract from Tosca and Company's statement of financial position is as follows:

	$
Property at cost	100,000
Provision for depreciation	42,000
Net book value	58,000

The property has been professionally revalued at $180,000. A decision has been made to revalue the property in the books of the company.

Required:

Prepare journal entries to revalue the property in the company's books.

» EXERCISE 17.4

An extract from Gemini and Company's statement of financial position is as follows:

		$
Premises at cost	90,000	
Provision for depreciation		34,000
Net book value		56,000

The Premises have been professionally revalued at $120,000. A decision has been made to revalue the premises in the books of the company.

Required:

Prepare journal entries to revalue the premises in the company's books.

17.19 | Write a short note on 'Issued Capital'.

This is made up of the total nominal value of shares issued to shareholders. It is always less than the authorised capital.

17.20 | Write a short note on ' Called-up capital'.

A company may require its shareholders to pay only part of the amount due on their shares until further sums are required. That part of the shares that the shareholders are required to pay immediately is called 'called up capital'. For instance if a share has a nominal value of $1, and the company's immediate requirement is for them to pay only 25 cents, then the called-up capital is 25 c. If there are 100,000 shareholders, then the called-up capital is $25,000.

17.21 | Write a short note on 'uncalled capital'.

That portion of the nominal value of the share that has not been called up is uncalled share capital.

17.22 | What are forfeited shares?

If shareholders do not pay their calls then their shares are forfeited and may be re-issued to other shareholders. These are forfeited shares.

17.23 | What is meant by the term 'paid-up capital'?

This is the total money received from shareholders on the called-up capital. It may not be equal to called-up capital as some shareholders may pay their calls late or not at all.

17.24 | What is meant by the term 'calls in advance'?

This is money received from shareholders who have paid their calls before they are due.

17.25 | What is meant by the term 'calls in arrears'?

The is money due from shareholders who are late in paying their calls.

17.26 | What are the different types of shares?

There are two types of shares: Ordinary shares and Preference shares.

17.27 | What are ordinary shares?

Ordinary shares form what is known as the equity of a company. Ordinary shareholders are entitled to vote at annual general meetings. They are however, paid dividend out of the remaining profit left after the dividend of the preference shareholders has been paid. All the reserves also go up to make up the ordinary shareholders' fund and belong to ordinary shareholders. When a company is wound up the assets remaining after all the creditors, debenture holders and preference shareholders are paid, belong to the ordinary shareholders. Hence the ordinary shareholders may receive more or less than their original investment in the company.

SHARES ISSUED AT A PREMIUM

All shares have a nominal or face (par) value. If the directors issue shares of nominal value $1 for a price of $1.30 because they believe that it will attract subscribers, the shares are said to be issued at a premium. The premium on each share should be credited to a special account called the share premium account.

17.28 | What are Preference shares?

Preference shares entitle their holders to certain rights which ordinary shareholders do not enjoy. Preference shareholders receive a dividend at a fixed rate which is expressed as a percentage of the nominal value of the share. This percentage is mentioned when the share is described. These dividends are paid before the ordinary shareholders get paid their dividend. In the event of a company being wound up, preference shareholders are entitled to have their capital repaid before ordinary shareholders receive their capital.

17.29 | What are the different types of Preference Shares?

The different types of Preference Shares are:
1) Cumulative Preference shares
2) Non-cumulative Preference Shares
3) Redeemable Preference Shares
4) Non Redeemable Preference Shares
5) Secured Preference Shares
6) Non-secured preference shares.
7) Participating preference shares.

17.30 | What is the difference between cumulative and non-cumulative preference shares?

Cumulative preference shares are entitled to have arrears of their dividend carried forward in the event of there being insufficient profit in the current year. Non-cumulative preference shares, however are not entitled to have any arrears of dividend carried forward to future years if the profit of the current year is insufficient to pay their dividend.

EXHIBIT

The Magic Company Ltd. have the following share capital break-up:
20,000 10% preference shares of $1 each
50,000 ordinary shares of $1 each.
The profits available for dividend were as follows:

	$
20x1	2000
20x2	1900
20x3	3,000
20x4	1,000
20x5	900
20x6	6,000

Required:
Calculate the dividends paid to the preference shareholders and the rate of dividend available to their Ordinary shareholders from the balance of profits if the preference shares were:
a) Non – Cumulative
b) Cumulative

a) SOLUTION:

In the case of Non – Cumulative Preference Shares

	20X1	20X2	20X3	20X4	20X5	20X6
	$	$	$	$	$	$
Profit	2,000	1,900	3,000	1,000	900	6,000
Preference dividend paid	2,000	1,900	2,000	1,000	900	2,000
Profit left for ordinary Shareholders	nil	nil	1,000	nil	nil	4,000
Maximum ordinary dividend paid	nil	nil	2%	nil	nil	8%

b. SOLUTION:

In the case of Cumulative Preference Shares

	20X1	20X2	20X3	20X4	20X5	20X6
	$	$	$	$	$	$
Profit	2,000	1,900	3,000	1,000	900	6,000
Preference dividend paid	2,000	1,900	2,000	1,000	900	2,000
Arrears of dividend brought forward			100	1,000		2,100
Profit left for ordinary Shareholders	nil	nil	900	nil	nil	1,900
Maximum ordinary dividend paid	nil	nil	1.8%	nil	nil	3.8%

» EXERCISE 17.5

Marlebee & Co.'s share capital consists of 100,000 ordinary shares of $1 each and 40,000 8% preference shares of $1 each. Profits for six years were as follows:

	$
20x1	3,200
20x2	3,000
20x3	2,000
20x4	8,000
20x5	2,900
20x6	7,000

Required:
Calculate the dividends paid to the preference shareholders and the rate of dividend available to their ordinary shareholders from the balance of profits if the preference shares were:
a) Non – Cumulative
b) Cumulative

» EXERCISE 17.6

Shareef & Co.'s share capital consists of 1,00,000 ordinary shares of $1 each and 50,000 10% preference shares of $1 each. Profits for six years were as follows:

	$
20x1	3,200
20x2	6,000
20x3	2,000
20x4	6,000
20x5	2,900
20x6	10,000

Required:

Calculate the dividends paid to the preference shareholders and the rate of dividend available to their ordinary shareholders from the balance of profits if the preference shares were:

a)   Non – Cumulative
b)   Cumulative

17.31 | How can one calculate the value of one ordinary share?

It must be remembered that all the reserves of the company belong to the ordinary shareholders. Hence the value of one

$$\text{ordinary share} = \frac{\text{Sum of ordinary share capital and reserves}}{\text{Number of ordinary shares}}$$

EXHIBIT

What follows is a summarised statement of financial position of Bangle & Co.

	$	$
Total non-current assets		120,000
Total current assets	45,000	
Total current liabilities	(23,000)	22,000
		142,000
Non-current liabilities		(50,000)
		92,000
Share capital and reserves:		
80,000 ordinary shares of $0.50		40,000
30,000 5% preference shares of $1		30,000
Share premium account		10,000
General reserve		10,000
Retained profit		2,000
		92,000

Required:

Calculate the statement of financial position value of one ordinary share.

SOLUTION:

Value of one ordinary share = $\dfrac{\text{sum of ordinary share capital and reserves}}{\text{number of ordinary shares}}$

$$= \frac{92,000 - 30,000}{80,000}$$

$$= \$ 0.775$$

» EXERCISE 17.7

The following is a summarised statement of financial position of Samir & Co.

	$	$
Total non-current assets		140,000
Total current assets	40,000	
Total current liabilities	(13,000)	27000
		167,000
Non-current liabilities		(37,000)
		130,000
Share capital and reserves:		
100,000 ordinary shares of $0.50		50,000
40,000 5% preference shares of $1		40,000
Share premium account		25,000
General reserve		20,000
Retained profit		(5,000)
		130,000

Required:

Calculate the statement of financial position value of one ordinary share.

» EXERCISE 17.8

The following is an extract from the statement of financial position of Valueadded Ltd

	$
Share capital and reserves:	
120,000 ordinary shares of $1 each	120,000
100,000 10% preference shares of $1 each	100,000
Share premium account	40,000
General reserve	56,000
Capital redemption reserve	44,000
	360,000

Required:

Calculate the statement of financial position value of one ordinary share.

17.32 | How is distributable profit calculated?

Distributable profits of the company
= accumulated realised profit unused – accumulated realised losses not written off
= Profit after interest and tax + retained profit from previous years – accumulated realised losses not written off

17.33 | Define:
a) Dividend policy

Dividend Policy Before a decision is made by the directors of a company to pay or recommend a dividend, the following factors must be considered:

1 That the company has sufficient distributable realised profits available.

2. That the company has sufficient liquid funds to pay the dividend.

3. Whether some of the profits should be ploughed back into the business as reserves to strengthen it.

4. It must be remembered that the company is not obligated to declare dividend. Having said that, a generous dividend policy may increase the value of shares on the stock exchange and a mean policy may have the opposite effect.

5. That there is a balance between dividend growth and capital growth. Share values should increase along with dividends for this to happen.

17.34 | What is a debenture?

A debenture represents a loan taken by the company from many debenture holders. A document called a debenture states the amount of the loan and the interest payable. It also includes the dates on which the loan is to be repaid by the company. Repayment is spread over a period and the dates of the start and end of the period are also included in the document. Debenture holders are not members of the company and cannot vote at annual general meetings. A Debenture is listed as a long term liability in the statement of financial position and not under share capital and reserves. If the debenture is due for redemption within one year, then it is shown as a current liability. Debenture holders are repaid before the shareholders of a company in the event of the company being wound up. Interest on debentures must be paid even if the company has not made a profit and this interest is debited as an expense in the income statement.

Note: Debentures are included as a deduction when calculating net assets.

17.35 | What is a secured debenture?

A secured debenture is one which is secured on all or some of the company's assets. If the company gets into financial difficulties, these assets are sold and the proceeds are used to repay the loans to the debenture holders.

EXHIBIT

On 1 January the directors of a company issued 40,000 ordinary shares of $1 each at $1.20 per share. The ledger accounts to record this if all the shares were taken up are:

Bank account (extract)

	$		$
Jan 1 Ordinary share capital	40,000		
Share premium a/c	8,000		

Ordinary share capital a/c

	$		$
		Jan 1 Bank	40,000

Share premium a/c

	$		$
		Jan 1 Bank	8,000

» EXERCISE 17.9

A newly formed company issues 100,000 shares of $1 at $3.00 each. It also issues $400,000 5% debentures. The operating profit was $340,000. The directors recommend an ordinary dividend of 6% for the year (disregard tax).

Required:
What is the retained profit for the year?
(Operating profit is also known as PBIT – Profit before interest and tax)

EXHIBIT
The Trial Balance of Molly and Co. at 31 December 20x6 is as follows:

	Dr	Cr
	$	$
Goodwill at cost	150,000	
Sales revenue		450,000
Purchases of ordinary goods	157,000	
Carriage outwards	12,000	
Property	158,750	
Motor Vehicles	80,000	
Machinery	76,000	
Provision for depreciation: Property		41,000
Motor Vehicles		20,000
Machinery		30,000
Inventory at 1 January 20x6	37,000	
Salaries	78,000	
General expenses	34,000	
Interest on debentures	5,000	
Trade receivables	75,000	
Trade payables		40,000
Cash and cash equivalents	41,000	
1,00,000 ordinary shares of $1		100,000
10% debentures 20x8/2010		100,000
*50,000 5% preference shares of $1		50,000
Share premium account		45,000
General reserve		20,000
Retained profit b/f		12,000
Interim dividends paid: preference	1,250	
ordinary	3,000	
	908,000	908,000

* The preference shares are non-redeemable.
Dividends payable on these preference shares is $2,500.

Additional information:

1) Inventory at 31 December 20x6 was $46,000
2) Depreciation for the year is to be provided as follows:
   Property $ 5,000
   Motor vehicles $2,000
   Machinery $ 3,000
3) Provision is to be made for taxation on the year's profits in the sum of $40,000.
4) A transfer of $52,000 is to be made to general reserve.
5) Debenture interest is payable on 1 June and 1 December.
6) Of the salaries, $50,000 was paid to sales staff.
8) The Motor Vehicles were used for delivery purposes.

Required:

a. Prepare Molly and Co's Income statement for the year ended 31 December 20x6 in as much detail as possible.

b. Prepare Molly and Co's Statement of Financial Position as at 31 December 20x6 in as much detail as possible.

SOLUTION

a) Molly and Co. Income statement for the year ended 31 December 20x6

	$	$	$
Sales revenue			450,000
Less Cost of sales:			
Inventory at 1 January		37,000	
Purchases of ordinary goods		157,000	
		194,000	
Less closing inventory		46,000	148,000
Gross Profit			302,000
Selling and distribution expenses:			
Sales staff salaries	50,000		
Carriage outwards	12,000		
Motor vehicles- depreciation	2,000	64,000	
Administration expenses:			
Administrative salaries	28,000		
General expenses	34,000		
Depreciation:			
Property	5,000		
Machinery	3,000	70,000	134,000
Operating Profit			168,000
Debenture interest			10,000
Profit before taxation			158,000
Taxation			40,000
Profit attributable to ordinary shareholders			118,000

STATEMENT OF CHANGES IN EQUITY

Retained profit b/f		12,000
Profit attributable to ordinary shareholders		118,000
Transfer to general reserve		(52,000)
Dividends paid:		
Preference	2,500	
Ordinary	3,000	(5,500)
Retained profit c/f		72,500

Note: IAS1 allows for alternative formatting of this statement, above, one of which is set out at the end of this page. Another alternative is The Statement of Recognised Income and Expenses which is less detailed and includes profit for the year and gains on revaluation of assets but not dividends and a new issue of shares

b)   Statement of Financial Position
             as at 31 December 20x6

Non-current Assets	$ Cost	$ Depreciation	$ NBV
Intangible: Goodwill	150,000	-	150,000
Tangible:			
Property	158,750	46,000	112,750
Machinery	76,000	33,000	43,000
Motor vehicles	80,000	22,000	58,000
	314,750	101,000	213,750
Total non-current Assets			363,750

Current Assets:		
Inventory	46,000	
Trade receivables	75,000	
Cash and cash equivalents	41,000	162,000
Total assets		525,750
Share capital and reserves:		
100,000 ordinary shares of $1 each		100,000
50,000 5% preference shares of $1 each		50,000
Share premium account		45,000
General reserve (20,000 + 52,000)		72,000
Retained profit		72,500
Non-current liabilities:		
10% debentures 20x8/2010		100,000
Current liabilities		
Trade payables	40,000	
Debenture interest	5,000	
Taxation	40,000	
Dividends: Preference	1,250	86,250
		525750

Alternative format for statement of changes in equity:
Statement of changes of equity for the year ended 31 December 20x6

	Share capital $	Retained earnings $	General reserve $	Share premium a/c $	Total equity $
Balance at start of the year	100,000	12,000	20,000	45,000	222,000
Profit for the year		118,000			118,000
Dividends paid		(5,500)			(5,500)
New share capital					
Transfer to general reserve		(52,000)	52,000		
Balance at the end of the year	100,000	72,500	72,000	45,000	289,500

» EXERCISE 17.10

The Trial Balance of Ben Trading Ltd. at 31 December 20x2 is as follows:

	Dr	Cr
	$	$
Purchases of ordinary goods	149,000	
Carriage outwards	5,250	
Property	158,750	
Motor Vehicles	77,000	
Machinery	79,000	
Sales revenue		370,000
Provision for depreciation: Property		38,000
Motor Vehicles		40,000
Machinery		30,000
Inventory of finished goods at		
1 January 20x2	47,000	
Salaries	65,000	
General expenses	47,000	
Interest on debentures	5,000	
Goodwill at cost	70,000	
Trade receivables	85,000	
Trade payables		50,000
Bank	35,000	
1,00,000 ordinary shares of $1		100,000
10% debentures 20x4/20x6		100,000
50,000 8% preference shares of $1		50,000
Share premium account		36,000
General reserve		10,000
Retained profit b/f		6,000
Interim dividends paid: preference	4,000	
ordinary	3,000	
	830,000	830,000

Additional information:

1) Inventory of finished goods at 31 December 20x2 was $50,000

2) Depreciation for the year is to be provided as follows:
   Property $ 5,000
   Motor vehicles $4,000
   Machinery $ 5,000

3) Provision is to be made for taxation on the year's profits in the sum of $10,000.

4) A transfer of $35,000 is to be made to general reserve.

5) Debenture interest is payable on 1 June and 1 December.

6) Of the salaries, $20,000 was paid to sales staff.

7) The Motor Vehicles were used for delivery purposes.

8) Accrued general expenses at 31 December 20x2 were $1,000

Required:

a) Prepare Ben Trading's Income statement for the year ended 31 December 20x2 in as much detail as possible.

b) Prepare Ben Trading's statement of financial position as at 31 December 20x2 in as much detail as possible.

c) Statement of changes in equity for the year ended 31stDecember 20x2

17.36 | What are bonus shares?

When a company capitalises its reserves by using them to issue shares to ordinary shareholders as fully paid up shares, these shares are called bonus shares. These shares are so called as the shareholders do not have to pay for them.

17.37 | Why are bonus shares issued?

A company issues bonus shares for the following reasons:
1) In the event of the issued share capital not adequately supporting the long-term assets of the company.
2) If the company distributed the reserves to their shareholders as dividend, then the shareholders would receive a very hefty rate of dividend that could cause problems with the workforce and the company's customers. The workforce would feel cheated if the shareholders were rewarded when they themselves received no increase in their wages. The customers would want the company to reduce their prices rather than shore up profits to pay excessive dividends to shareholders.

EXHIBIT
Kingston and company's summarised statement of financial position is as follows:

	$
Non-current assets	300,000
Net current assets	120,000
	420,000
Ordinary shares of $1	150,000
Share premium	50,000
Revaluation reserve	150,000
General reserve	50,000
Retained profit	20,000
	420,000

The directors have decided to make a bonus issue of three shares for every five shares already held. They also wish to leave the reserves in the most flexible form.

Required:
Kingston and company's statement of financial position immediately after the bonus issue.

> **Tip √** As any of the reserves could be used to issue bonus shares, directors prefer to use capital reserves and leave the revenue reserves intact

SOLUTION

Kingston and Company
statement of financial position immediately after the
issue of bonus shares.

	$
Non-current assets	300,000
Net current assets	120,000
	420,000
Ordinary shares of $1	240,000
Revaluation reserve	110,000
General reserve	50,000
Retained profit	20,000
	420,000

» EXERCISE 17.11

Barrington and company's summarised statement of
financial position is as follows:

	$
Non-current assets	400,000
Net current assets	130,000
	530,000
Ordinary shares of $1	200,000
Share premium	280,000
General reserve	30,000
Retained profit	20,000
	530,000

The directors have decided to make a bonus issue of four shares
for every five shares already held. They also wish to leave the
reserves in the most flexible form.

Required:
Barrington and company's statement of financial position
immediately after the bonus issue.

17.38 | What is a rights issue?

This is an issue of shares made to the existing shareholders of
the company. The offer price is generally below market price.

17.39 | What are the advantages of a rights
issue?

The advantages are:
1) The company can raise more capital.
2) A rights issue is a shorter and cheaper procedure than a
fresh issue of shares.
3) Shareholders are rewarded for their loyalty as rights issues
are generally made at a price that is cheaper than market price.
If shareholders do not wish to subscribe to a rights issue, they
may sell their rights.

EXHIBIT

What follows is a summary of the statement of financial
position of Ling and company as at 1 June 20x3:

	$
Net non-current and current assets	1,200,000
Share capital and reserves:	
Ordinary shares of $1	900,000
Share premium	100,000
Retained profit	200,000
	1,200,000

On 1 June 20x3, the directors made a bonus issue of one share
for every five held, leaving the reserves in the most flexible
form.

Required:
a)   Ling and company's statement of financial position
immediately after the bonus issue

SOLUTION

	$
Net Non-current and current assets	1,200,000
Share capital and reserves:	
Ordinary shares of $1	1,080,000
Retained profit	120,000
	1,200,000

Following the issue of bonus shares, Ling and company made a
rights issue on 10 June 20x3 of 108,000 ordinary shares of $1
at a price of $1.50 a share. All the shares were subscribed for
by the shareholders.

Required:
b.   Ling and company's statement of financial position
immediately after the rights issue had been completed.

	$
Net non-current and current assets	1,362,000
Share capital and reserves:	
Ordinary shares of $1	1,188,000
Share premium	54,000
Retained profit	120,000
	1,362,000

» EXERCISE 17.12

The capital structure of a company was as
follows:

	$
100,000 ordinary shares at $1 each	100,000
Share premium account	25,000

The financial year ends on 31 December. On 1 May 20x4 the
company made an issue of 30,000 shares for $ 54,000.
Subsequent to that, on 1 July 20x4 a bonus issue of one share
for every five in issue was made. The share premium account
was used for the purpose.

Required:

Calculate the balance on the share premium account at 31 December 20x4.

» EXERCISE 17.13

A company has issued 100,000 ordinary shares of $0.50 each. These are quoted on the stock exchange at $1.50 each. The company makes a rights issue on a 1 for 5 basis at a price of $1.10 each. The rights issue was fully subscribed.

Required:

Calculate the balance on the share capital account after the rights issue.

» EXERCISE 17.14

The following is an extract of a company's statement of financial position:

	$
500,000 ordinary shares of $1 each	500,000
Retained profit	300,000
10% debentures	200,000
	1,000,000
Total assets	1,000,000

A rights issue of 1 for 5 shares is made at $2 per share and 50% of the debentures are repaid at par. The rights issue was fully subscribed.

Required:

A statement of financial position extract reflecting the above mentioned changes.

» EXERCISE 17.15

The table below shows extracts from a company's statement of financial position at 31 December 20x2 and at 31 December 20x3:

	31 December 20x2 $m	31 December 20x3 $m
Ordinary shares of $1 each	200	231
Share premium account	40	73

On 1 April 20x3 there was a bonus issue of 1 ordinary share for every 10 held.
On 1 June 20x3 there was a rights issue
There were no other reserves.

Required:

Calculate the amount of cash received from the issue of shares in the year ended 31 December 20x3.

» EXERCISE 17.16

The following is a statement of financial position extract of a company

	$000
Capital and reserves:	
Ordinary share of $0.20 each	800
Share premium a/c	100
Revaluation reserve	150
Retained profit	100

The company makes a bonus issue of one share for every 4 held.

Required:

What is the position of the following after the bonus issue?
a)   The Share Capital Account
b)   The Share premium Account
c)   The Revaluation Reserve
d)   Retained profit

» EXERCISE 17.17

A company has an issued share capital of $250,000 of $1 ordinary shares. It makes a bonus issue of one $1 ordinary share for every five held. It also issues $60,000 debentures at a discount of 5%.
The company has $50,000 cash at bank before the issues.

Required:

Calculate the cash at bank after the issues.

» EXERCISE 17.18

Boseey Ltd has an authorised share capital of $800,000 and an issued share capital of $500,000 in $1 ordinary shares. It makes a 1 for 4 rights issue at $2 per share which is fully taken up.

Required:

Calculate the balance on the share capital account.

» EXERCISE 17.19

An extract from Kelston & co's statement of financial position is given:

	$
Ordinary share capital	40,000
General reserve	8,000
Retained profit	2,500
10% debentures	15,000

Required:

Calculate the ordinary shareholders' funds.

» EXERCISE 17.20

At 1 January 20x0 a company has authorised share capital of $0.50 ordinary shares and issued share capital of 100,000 $0.50 ordinary shares. During the year the company makes a further issue of 50,000 $0.50 ordinary shares at a price of $1.10 each.

Required:

Calculate the balance on the Share Capital Account at 31 December 20x0.

Q. What is a participating preference share?

Ans. It is a type of share that gives the holder the right to receive dividends equal to the normally specified rate that preference dividends receive as well as an additional dividend based on some predetermined condition. The additional dividend is triggered whenever the dividend for common shares exceeds that of the preference shares.

17.40 Give the journal entries to be passed when a debenture is redeemed.

When a debenture is redeemed or repaid, the following entries are passed.

a. If the debenture is redeemed at par.

	Dr	Cr
Debenture	xxx	
Bank		xxx

b. If a debenture is redeemed at a premium:

	Dr	Cr
Debenture	xxx	
*Share premium a/c	xxx	
Bank		xxx

(*or retained earnings, if there is no share premium a/c)

17.41 What are the other sources of finance available to a limited company?

Bank loans: Banks often lend limited companies money if they are satisfied that it will be used for legitimate purposes such as expansion, diversification or the acquiring of capital assets etc. They will usually ask for documentation proving that the company will be able to pay the interest and capital on time. The loan may be for a short-term, such as a few months or long term for more than one year and sometimes for as much as ten years. The bank will require assets to secure the loan on, usually called collateral. Interest charged may be fixed or variable.

Bank overdraft: This is a facility given to companies by banks by which they are permitted to withdraw more than they have deposited. Interest is calculated only on the amount overdrawn and the facility may be withdrawn anytime without notice.

Leasing: A Company can lease an asset form another business who then becomes the lessor. The lessor still owns the asset. The rental is shown as an expense in the income statement of the company (the lessee) using the asset. The lessor normally pays for repair and maintenance and this is a major advantage to the lessee.

Trade payables: This form of short-term finance becomes available when the company delays paying its trade and other creditors. The disadvantage is that the creditors may refuse to have future credit dealings with the company and insist on immediate cash payments. They may also limit or withdraw supplies or services.

Hire purchase: Assets can be bought by a company on the payment of a deposit, which is a percentage of the cost price. The remaining amount can then be paid in installments over the period of the agreement. Legally, the asset does not belong to the company till all the installments are paid but because of the principle of substance over form, the asset is included in the financial statements at its normal cost. The amount outstanding is shown as a liability. The advantage of this source is that the company can use the asset without having to pay the whole price in a lump sum.

17.42 What principles should a company follow when deciding on a suitable source of finance?

A company should match the purpose of the finance with the source of the finance. Basically, the purpose could be categorised as working capital or long-term capital.

Working capital: This capital is needed for the day-to-day running of a business and should only be financed by a short-term source such as an overdraft or a current liability.

Long-term capital: If a business needs finance to purchase non-current assets, it should use a long – term source such as a long-term loan or debentures. This would ensure that the time the asset is used to generate funds is matched with the period of finance during which it is serviced by those funds. If a short-term source of finance (e.g. a short – term loan) is used to finance a long-term requirement such as a non-current asset, the funds generated by that asset may not be sufficient in the short term to service and repay the short – term loan. It is advisable that all the non-current assets of a company be adequately covered by the shareholders' funds ((made up of share capital and reserves) and possibly, debentures.

17.43 What is a statement of cash flows?

A statement of cash flows shows what has happened during a financial year from the point of view of liquidity. It shows monies flowing into and out of the business during the financial year.

17.44 What is the difference between the income statement and a statement of cash flows?

The income statement takes into account non-cash items such as provisions to calculate profit. Accruals and prepayments are also taken into account. However, a cash flow only shows the actual movement of cash. e.g. If rent for a year is $1,000 but only $600 was paid during the financial year, the profit will be calculated after deducting $1,000. However, cash outflow is $600.

17.45 Which items normally affect the cash flow due to the differences outlined above?

The items in the statement of financial position that are affected are:
Depreciation for the year- It should be added back (treated as cash inflow).
Increase in inventories - It should be subtracted (cash outflow).
Decrease in trade receivable - It should be added (cash inflow).
Increase in trade payables - It is added (treated as cash inflow as the increase is available to finance the company's activities)
This year's tax - added back as it is not yet paid; Last year's tax paid this year - cash outflow, so subtracted.
Issue of new share capital - added back as it is a cash inflow
Increase in share premium account - added as it is a cash inflow
Increase in retained earning - added back as it is treated as a cash inflow.

EXHIBIT

Simran Ltd provides the following information. Prepare a cashflow statement outlining the cash inflows and outflows.

Statement of financial position

	at 31 December 20x5			at 31 December 20x4		
	$	$	$	$	$	$
Non- current assets	Cost	Depreciation	N.B.V	Cost	Depreciation	N.B.V.
Plant & equipment	11,500	5,000	6,500	11,000	4,000	7,000
Motor vehicles	6,000	3,000	3,000	6,000	2,500	3,500
	17,000	8,000	9,500	17,000	6,500	10,500
Current assets:						
Inventory		10,000			7,000	
Trade receivables		5,000			8,000	
Cash and cash equivalents		36,400	51,400		24,500	39,500
Total assets			60,900			50,000
Equity						
Ordinary shares		40,000			34,000	
Share premium		1,600			1,000	
Retained earnings		14,000			10,000	
		55,600			45,000	
Current liabilities:						
Trade payables		3,600			3,000	
Tax payable		1,700			2,000	
		60,900			50,000	

Solution:

Cash inflows	$	Cash outflows	$
Depreciation:			
Plant & equipment	1,000	Increase in inventory	3,000
Decrease in trade receivables	3,000	Tax paid	2,000
Increase in trade payables	600		
Tax owed	1,700		
Shares issued	6,000		
Premium on shares issued	600		
Profit	4,000		
	16,900		5,000

Net cash inflow = 16,900 - 5,000 = $11,900

This is reflected in the cash and cash equivalents balances: $

Net increase	11,900
At the start of the year	24,500
At end of the year	36,400

Exercise 17.21

Which of the following will result in a cash inflow?
a. New share issue
b. Purchase of some land
c. Increase in inventories
d. Decrease in trade receivables

17.1 | MULTIPLE CHOICE QUESTIONS

i) A company has an issued 100,000 ordinary share capital of $1 each. Their operating profit is $40,000. The company has issued $200,000 10% debentures. The directors have proposed a transfer of $10,000 to the general reserve. What is the maximum dividend that can be proposed on ordinary shares?
A) 3%   B) 10%   C) 30%   D) 5%

ii) Out of an authorised share capital of 200,000 ordinary shares of $0.50 each, the directors have issued 80,000 shares. If the proposed dividend is 60 cents in the dollar, what is the amount of the dividend?
A) $24000   B) $6000   C) $48000   D) $12000

iii) What follows is relevant information extracted from a company's statement of financial position:

	$000
Freehold premises at cost	*500*
Provision for depreciation of freehold premises	*240*
Ordinary shares of $1 each	*600*
5% preference shares of $1 each	*100*
Share premium a/c	*80*
Retained profit	*60*

It has been decided to revalue freehold premises to $800,000. What will be the statement of financial position value of the ordinary shares after revaluation?
A) $ 2.3   B) $1.3   C) $2.13   D) $1.5

iv) Adventure Ltd have an authorised share capital of 4,00,000 shares of $0.50 each and has issued 1,00,000 shares. They decide to make a bonus issue of 1 share of every 5 shares held. Which of the following shows the position of the company after the bonus shares issue:

	Authorised share capital	Ordinary share capital
A.	Increases by 80,000 shares	No effect
B.	No effect	Increases by 20,000 shares
C.	No effect	Increases by 80,000 shares
D.	Increase by 20,000 shares	Increases by 20,000 shares

v) A company has an ordinary share capital of 200,000 shares of $1 each. It makes a bonus issue of three shares for every two shares held. It follows that with a rights issue of one share for every five held at $1.50 a share. The rights issue was fully subscribed. What was the increase in the Share Premium account as a result of the bonus and rights issue?
A) $300,000   B) $100,000   C) $150,000   D) $50,000

17.2 | A newly formed company issues the following:
a) 1,000,000 ordinary shares of $1 at $2 each
b) $200,000 5% debentures.

Operating profit for the year was $390,000.
The directors recommend a 6% ordinary dividend for the year.
Required:
Calculate the retained profit for the year.

17.3 | A company's share capital consists of 100,000 ordinary shares of $1 each. It makes a rights issue of 1 ordinary share for every 4 held at $1.10 a share. It then makes a bonus issue of 1 share for every 5 held.

Required:
Calculate the amount shown in the statement of financial position for share capital.

17.4 | A company is financed by:
20,000 ordinary shares of $0.50 each.
$4,000 10% loan.
Its profit for the year before interest and taxation is $3,000.
Tax payable is $300
Required:
Calculate the maximum dividend payable per share from this year's profits.

17.5 | A company has an authorised share capital of 2 million $0.25 ordinary shares of which 1.5 million shares have been issued. Proposed dividend is $50,000.
Required:
Calculate the dividend as a percentage.

17.6 | After completion of the Trading Account section of the Income Statement the following balances were extracted from the book of Peter Jordan Plc on 30 April 20x6.

	$
Authorised and issued share capital :	
Ordinary shares of $1 each fully paid	1,500,000
7% Preference shares of $1 fully paid	200,000
Premises	2,300,000
Motor vehicles	500,000
Fixtures and fittings	170,000
Provision for depreciation on motor vehicles	375,000
Provision for depreciation on fixtures and fittings	102,000
Gross profit	1,620,000

	$
Inventory	204,000
Office expenses	460,000
Selling and distribution expenses	486,000
6% Debentures	100,000
Debenture interest paid	3,000
Profit on sale of motor vehicle	2,000
Retained profit - 1 May 20x5	143,600 Cr
Trade receivables	132,000
Trade payables	116,000
Bank	26,800 Cr
Cash	400
Share Premium	150,000
Interim dividend paid –	
ordinary shares	75,000
preference shares	8,000
Provision for doubtful debts	3,000

Additional information at 30 April2006 :

Office expenses prepaid $8000

Selling and distribution expenses accrued at $23,000

Provision for doubtful debts to be maintained at 2% of debtors.

Depreciation to be provided as follows:

Motor vehicles 50% per annum reducing (diminishing) balance

Fixtures and fittings 20% per annum on cost

The following are proposed:

Remaining dividend due is to be paid to preference shareholders.

REQUIRED

(a) Prepare Peter Jordan plc's Income Statement and Appropraition Account for the year ended 30 April 20x6.

(b) Prepare a statement of changes in equity for the year ended April 30 20x6.

(c) Prepare Peter Jordan Plc's statement of financial position at 30 April 20x6.

(Adapted from: UCLES, 2006, AS/A Level Accounting, Syllabus 9706/2, May/June)

17.7 Jellybeans Ltd. is preparing its statement of changes in equity.
Calculate its retained earnings from the following information:

Retained earning b/f	$40,000
Profit for the year attributable to equity shareholders	$30,000
Transfer to reserves	$15,000
Dividends paid during the year	$10,000
Proposed dividends	$5,000

17.8 Which of these statements are correct?

a. Preference share are included when calculating shareholders' funds.

b. A share premium account is classified as a reserve.

c. A revaluation reserve may be negative if a non-current asset decreases in value.

17.9 The following is an extract from a statement of changes in equity for the year ended 31 December 20x3

	Ordinary share capital	Share premium	General reserve	Retained earnings
	$	$	$	$
Balance at 1 Jan 20x3	67,000	14,000	30,000	45,000

During the year the following occurred.

1 An interim dividend of $5,000 was paid.

2 A final dividend of $10,000 was proposed.

3 $10,000 was transferred to the general reserve. What was the balance of retained earnings at 31 Dec 20x3?

17.10 The following is an extract from the statement of financial position of Mena Limited at 31 December 20x7.

	$
Equity:	
Share capital ($1 ordinary shares)	500,000
Share premium	15,000
Retained earnings 1	85,000
Non-current liabilities:	
7% debentures (2019-20)	90,000
Current liabilities:	
Trade and other payables	25, 000
Cash and cash equivalents	5,000
Total equity and liabilities	720,000

During the year ended 31 December 20x7 the following transactions took place.

1 January	Issue of 80 000 ordinary shares at $1.20 each.
30 June	Rights issue of 3 ordinary shares for every 10 shares held on this date at an issue price of $1.30. This was fully subscribed.
30 September	Bonus issue of 1 ordinary share for every 5 shares held on this date.

REQUIRED

(a) Prepare journal entries to record each of these transactions in the books of account. Dates and narratives are not required.

(b) Prepare a statement to show the effect that the transactions had on the total equity.

Analysis And Interpretation

18.1 | Why is it necessary to analyse and interpret accounting statements?

Analysis and interpretation of accounting statements like Financial Statements help stakeholders to assess the performance of the business. The liquidity, profitability and efficiency of a business can be ascertained by suitable analysis and subsequent interpretation.

18.2 | Who are the 'stakeholders' of a business and why would they be interested in a firm's performance?

The stakeholders are the parties who are interested in the firm's performance for one reason or another. They could be:

a) The owner. The owner of the business would like to know how his business is performing in comparison to another similar business or in comparison with targets set or in comparison with previous years.

b) Prospective investors. They would like to know how well the business is doing now, and its prospects for future profitability, in order to make good investment decisions.

c) A Bank manager. He/she will have to analyse and interpret accounting statements supplied by a business that has applied for a loan. The future liquidity position of the business will be the guiding factor in the manager granting loans and overdrafts to the business.

d) Creditors. Creditors, such as suppliers are also interested in a business's liquidity and its credit rating.

e) Members of a non-profit organisation. The members of a club, for example, will be interested it's financial position. They would like to know whether the club has a deficit or a surplus since this will affect the future of the club and consequently it's members.

18.3 | What is the need for ratios?

Accounting ratios form a basis of common measure so that comparisons become meaningful. It is impossible to compare absolute figures e.g. profits . What is needed is profitability, e.g. profit margins that are expressed in percentages and offer a platform for easy comparison.

18.4 | How can ratios be used?

Ratios can be used in the following ways:

a) Ratios of a business for the current year can be compared with those of a previous year to ascertain whether there has been an improvement.

b) Ratios of a business can be compared with those of another similar business

c) Ratios of a business for the current year can be compared with ratios derived from budgets and forecasts made to ascertain whether the targets were in fact achieved and if not, the reason why they were not achieved so that corrective action can be taken.

18.5 | What are the precautions to be borne in mind when making comparisons between two businesses using ratios?

The following points should be borne in mind when comparing ratios of two businesses:

a) The accounts may not be those of a typical year.

b) The financial years of the two businesses may end on different dates and hence this may affect the ratios, making interpretation difficult.

c) The two businesses may be different from each other. It is useless to compare the liquidity of a business selling electrical appliances with one selling vegetables and fruits.

d) The two businesses may be of a different size. There is no point in comparing a large business with a small one.

e) The businesses may operate using different accounting policies, for example, one business may be using the straight-line method of depreciation and the other business may be using the reducing balance method.

f) There may be differences that affect the items on the statement of financial position and the profitability of the businesses. For example, one business may own a certain non-current   asset and the other business may rent it.

Hence ratios should be used with caution.

18.6 | What are the limitations of accounting statements?

Accounting statements have the following limitations:

a) Due to the desire to keep to the money measurement concept, a lot of desirable information is excluded. For example, the following information is not revealed:
- Whether the firm has good or bad managers.
- Whether there are problems with the workforce that would affect the future of the business.
- Whether the government is about to introduce a law that would cause the firm additional expenditure.
- Whether there are competitors waiting to take over some of the firm's most valuable customers
- Whether the firm is able to adapt to changing market conditions.

b) Financial statements contain information about the past and may not be relevant for the future since change is an integral part of any business.

c) Since the historic cost concept is used, inflation is not factored in. This may make the value of non-current assets listed in the financial statements inaccurate.

d) Financial statements do not reveal pertinent information such as whether the firm is situated in a good location. If the location is fast becoming undesirable, for example, this would affect the profitability of the firm in the future.

18.7 | Define the following terms:
a)   Capital invested (or capital owned)
b)   Capital employed
c)   Working capital

a) Capital Invested is the amount owed by the business to the owner at that date. It is the amount of money or money's worth brought into the business by the owner from his outside interests.

b) Capital Employed is the amount of money effectively being used in the business. It is sometimes referred to as Net Assets.

Capital employed =
non-current assets + current assets – current liabilities
(Or)
Capital employed = opening balance of owner's capital
+ profit for the year – drawings + long term liabilities.

c) Working capital is the amount available for the day - to - day running of the business.
Working Capital = Current assets – Current liabilities.
*Profit for the year = operating profit = profit before interest and tax
**Capital employed = issued shares+reserves+non-current liabilities

18.8 | Name the different types of ratios used .

The different types of ratios used are:
a)   Profitability ratios
b)   Liquidity ratios
c)   Efficiency ratios

18.9 | Name and explain the profitability ratios.

The profitability ratios are:

1. **Return on capital employed (ROCE)**
It shows the operating profit earned for every $100 of capital employed. The higher the ROCE, the better since the capital is being more effectively employed.

$$\text{Return on capital employed} = \frac{*\text{Operating profit}}{**\text{Capital employed}} \times 100$$

2. **Gross margin**
This is also known as the Gross profit as a percentage of sales turnover. It shows the Gross profit for every $100 of sales. A higher rate indicates higher profitability.

$$\text{Gross profit as a percentage of sales} = \frac{\text{Gross profit}}{\text{Sales revenue}} \times 100$$

3. **Profit margin**

This measures the profit for the year for every $100 of sales. The higher the rate, the more profitable the business. It is an indication of the firm's efficiency, since it reveals how well the firm is able to control its expenses.

$$\text{Profit margin} = \frac{\text{profit for the year (after interest)}}{\text{Sales revenue}} \times 100$$

18.10 | What is the difference between 'profit' and 'profitability'?

'Profit' is an absolute figure and as such does not lend itself to comparisons. 'Profitability' is a ratio and can be easily used for comparison purposes. 'Profitability ratios' are more accurate measures of a firm's profitability. For example: a price – cutting policy may reduce the profitability of a firm even though the profit of the firm has increased.

$$\text{Profit as a percentage of sales} = \frac{*\text{Profit for the year} \times 100}{\text{Sales revenue}}$$

18.11 | What could be the possible causes for the reduction in the Gross Profit as a percentage of sales ratio?

The probable causes may be:
a)   Goods being sold at a reduced price due to a price - cutting policy.
b)   Seasonal 'sales'.
c)   Trade discounts being offered to customers who buy in bulk.
d)   Absorbing increased costs and not passing them on to the customers.
e)   The cost of sales may have increased due to inventory theft.

18.12 | How can the Gross margin be improved ?

The following measures could be used:

a) Increasing selling prices. This may improve the gross profit, if not balanced by a loss of sales due to customers changing to another cheaper product.

b) Taking measures to reduce cost due to theft of inventory

c) Using cheaper suppliers.

d) Increasing or changing product range.

18.13 | Name and explain the liquidity & efficiency ratios'.

The liquidity ratios are:

Current ratio. This ratio is also known as the 'Working Capital Ratio'. It measures the business's ability to meet its current liabilities . The ideal current ratio is 2:1. However, anything between 2:1 and 1.5:1 is considered desirable.

Current ratio = $\dfrac{\text{current assets}}{\text{current liabilities}}$

b) **Quick ratio.**

This ratio is also known as the 'Acid test ratio'. This ratio shows a comparison between assets in money or near money form with liabilities due for payment in the near future. The ideal current ratio is 1:1.

Quick ratio = $\dfrac{\text{current assets} - \text{inventory}}{\text{current liabilities}}$

The efficiency ratios are:

a) **Rate of turnover.**

It is the amount of times a business sells and replaces its inventory in a given period of time. The rate of inventory turnover can be calculated in two ways

1. Rate of inventory turnover = $\dfrac{\text{Cost of sales}}{(\text{opening inventory} + \text{closing inventory}) / 2}$

Rate of inventory turnover $= \dfrac{\text{Cost of sales}}{\text{average inventory}}$

This gives the number of **times** inventory is sold and replaced and is the more commonly used formula. The higher the rate, the greater the **efficiency** and gross profit (provided the profit margin is constant).

2. Rate of inventory turnover = $\dfrac{\text{Average inventory} \times 365}{\text{Cost of sales}}$

This gives the number of **days,** on an average, the inventory is being held before being sold. The lower the number, the greater the **efficiency** and gross profit (provided the profit margin is constant).

b) **Collection period for trade receivables.**

This is also know as trade receivables turnover. It is the average amount of time that trade receivables take to pay their accounts.

Collection period for trade receivables

$= \dfrac{\text{trade receivables} \times 365}{\text{credit sales}}$ ..... in days.

(or) $= \dfrac{\text{trade receivables} \times 52}{\text{credit sales}}$ .... in weeks

(or) $= \dfrac{\text{trade receivables} \times 12}{\text{credit sales}}$ ..... in months

c) **Payment period for trade payables.**

This is also known as trade payables turnover. It is the average amount of times a business takes to pay its trade payables.

Payment period for trade payables

$= \dfrac{\text{trade payables} \times 365}{\text{credit purchases}}$ ....in days

(or) $= \dfrac{\text{trade payables} \times 52}{\text{credit purchases}}$ .... in weeks

(or) $= \dfrac{\text{trade payables} \times 12}{\text{credit purchases}}$ ......in months

d) **Non-current asset turnover** $= \dfrac{\text{Net revenue}}{\text{Total N.B.V. of non-current assets}}$

This ratio shows how well the non-current assets are utilised.

18.14 | What does a current ratio over 2:1 indicate?

A ratio over 2:1 indicates inefficient management of resources. It means that the business may have:

a) Too much inventory and this means over trading.

b) Too many trade receivables and the consequent risk of bad debts.

c) Too much money in the bank(in a current account) earning little or no interest.

d) Too much cash in hand and this indicates assets not being put to economic use.

18.15 | Name two more profitability ratios

Mark-up = $\dfrac{\text{Gross profit}}{\text{Cost of sales}} \times 100$

(Operating) Expenses to revenue ratio = $\dfrac{(\text{operating})\text{Expenses}}{\text{Revenue}} \times 100$

18.16 | Why is over trading not desirable?

Too much inventory or over trading means:

a) Money tied up and this means the firm is not using its money to best effect.

b) The inventory requires a warehouse that indicates additional expenses by way of rent.

c) The inventory may expire or go out of fashion and be unsaleable.

d) The inventory may get stolen.

e) The inventory could get damaged.

18.17 | Why is inventory excluded from the Acid Test ratio?

Inventory is considered to be two steps away from being money and that is why it is not included in the Acid test ratio which measures immediate liquidity and the ability to pay off current liabilities immediately. The two steps are:
a)   Inventory has to be sold.
b)   Money has to be collected from debtors,
If inventory was included then the possibility of it having to be sold quickly, possibly at reduced prices, would arise.

18.18 | What would an Acid Test Ratio of more than 1:1 indicate?

An Acid Test Ratio of more than 1:1 indicates inefficient management of liquid assets. This would mean:
a)   Too many debtors with a consequent risk of bad debts.
b)   Too much money in the bank earning little or no interest.
c)   Too much cash in hand which again is lying idle.

18.19 | What would an Acid Test Ratio of less than 1:1 indicate?

An Acid Test ratio of less than 1:1 , 0.8:1, for instance, would be a very risky situation for the business. Many a business has had to close down due to its inability to pay off its creditors and thus being declared insolvent, even though it had a lot of money tied up in inventory that was not liquid.

18.20 | Which rate of inventory turnover is better : 53 times or 8 times?

The answer would depend on whether both figures refer to the similar businesses. If they do, then obviously, 53 times is better and indicates that the business is more efficient in selling its inventory. If 53 times represents business A that sells vegetables and 8 times represents business B that sells television sets then both rates are good. This is because the vegetable business should try to sell and replace it's inventory almost every week television sets are more difficult to sell and hence, a rate of inventory turnover of 8 a year would mean that it sells all its inventory and replaces it 8 times a year, an enviable accomplishment indeed!

18.21 | What would a higher trade receivables collection period indicate?

 This would mean that debtors take longer to pay their debts, thus increasing the risk of debts and liquidity problems. It indicates an inefficient credit control policy.

18.22 | What are the ways of improving the trade receivables collection period?

The ways are:
a)   employing a factor.
b)   offer cash discounts for early payment.
c)   charge interest on overdue debts.
d)   refuse further supplies until the overdue balance is paid.
e)   improve credit control (by sending regular statements of accounts, reminders etc.)

18.23 | Who are factors?

Factors are firms or people who advance money against debts and then collect the debts themselves for a fee.

18.24 | What would a higher trade payables payment period indicate?

This would indicate that the firm is paying its creditors quickly and has enough liquidity to do so. However, a longer payment period is more advantageous for the firm since it's liquidity improves and it enjoys interest free 'trade credit'. An efficient business would delay paying its creditors for as long it can without losing cash discounts for prompt payment and the goodwill of its suppliers.

18.25 | Why would the rate of inventory turnover vary from year to year?

The rate of inventory turnover may increase if the efficiency of the business increased. If the rate of inventory turnover has reduced, it may mean that the business has too much inventory or that sales are slowing down.

18.26 | Which ratio is known as the first or primary ratio?

The ROCE or return on capital employed is known as the first ratio. It relates **profit for the year** before tax to the capital employed in the business. The **Profit for the year** before tax is known as the 'bottom line'. Debentures and other long term loans are included in capital employed.

18.27 | How is profit before interest and tax as a % of sales revenue calculated?

Profit before interest and tax, or operating profit is calculated as a percentage of sales using the following formula:

Profit before interest and tax = $\dfrac{\text{profit before interest and tax} \times 100}{\text{sales revenue}}$

18.28 | Name the ratios showing utilisation of resources.

The following ratios show utilisation of resources:

1. Sales as a percentage of capital employed =
$$\frac{\text{sales x 100}}{\text{capital employed}}$$

This is a secondary ratio.

2. Utilisation of total assets = $\frac{\text{sales revenue}}{\text{total assets}}$

This ratio is expressed in times and measures the number of times the sales cover the capital invested in the assets of a business.

3. Non-current asset turnover = $\frac{\text{sales revenue}}{\text{total non-current assets}}$

This ratio is expressed in times and relates the revenue earned through sales with the non-current assets that are bought with the intention to earn revenue.

4. Current asset turnover = $\frac{\text{sales}}{\text{total current assets}}$

This ratio is expressed in times.

5. Net current assets (working capital) to sales = $\frac{\text{turnover}}{\text{net current assets}}$

18.29 | Name the financial ratios.

The financial ratios are:

1) Current ratio (mentioned earlier in the chapter)
2) Acid test or quick ratio, also known as the liquidity ratio (mentioned earlier in the chapter).
3) Trade receivables' ratio or trade receivables days (mentioned earlier in the chapter).
4) Rate of inventory turnover (mentioned earlier in the chapter)
5) Trade payables' ratio or trade payables' days (mentioned earlier in the chapter)

18.30 | What is meant by overtrading?

This is a situation where a business's turnover increases rapidly with a corresponding increase in trade receivables, trade payables and inventory. This situation may threaten the liquidity position of the business and the business could be in danger of being declared insolvent as they may not be in a position to pay their creditors.

18.31 | Explain the term 'The cash operating cycle'.

This cycle measures the time cash takes to circulate around the working capital system, the time between payment of creditors and receipt of cash from debtors. The interval marks the time when the company is paying its creditors with its own money. The formula is:

Cash operating cycle =
Inventory turnover in days + trade receivables days – trade payables days.

EXHIBIT
Merrick and company have arrived at the following figures :

	Inventory turnover	Trade receivables days	Trade payables days
20x4	20	29	37
20x5	19	37	43

Required:
Calculate the cash operating cycle for:
a)   20x4
b)   20x5

Solution:
Cash cycle for 20x4   = Inventory turnover + trade receivables' days – trade payables' days
= 20+ 29 – 37
= 12 days
Cash cycle for 20x5   = 19 + 37 – 43
= 13 days

» EXERCISE 18.1
A business gives you the following information:

	Inventory turnover	Trade receivables turnover	Trade payables turnover
20x2	22	25	34
20x3	24	28	34

Required:
Calculate the cash operating cycle for:
a)   20x2
b)   20x3

» EXERCISE 18.2

	Inventory turnover	Trade receivables turnover	Trade payables turnover
20x0	25	27	39
20x1	21	26	38

Required:
Calculate the cash operating cycle for:
a) 20x0
b) 20x1

Exhibit:
The final accounts of Mason for the year ended 31st December 20x7 are given below.

Mason's Income statement for the Year ended 31st December 20x7.

	$	$
Sales (all on credit)		130,000
Less Cost of sales:		
Inventory at 1st January 20x7	15,000	
Purchases of ordinary goods	65,000	
	80,000	
Inventory at 31st December 20x7	17,000	63,000
Gross profit		67,000
Less overheads -		
Selling and administration expenses		26,900
Profit for the year		40,100

Mason's statement of financial position as at 31st December 20x7

	$	$
Non-current assets at net book value		65,780
Current Assets:		
Inventory	17,000	
Trade receivables	25,000	
Cash at bank	4,520	
	46,520	
Current liabilities		
Trade payables	24,300	22,220
		88,000
Financed by:		
Capital at 1st December 20x7		90,000
Profit for the year		40,100
		130,100
Drawings		42,100
		88,000

Required:
a) Calculate the following :
1) Profit for the year as a percentage of sales
2) Profit for the year as a percentage of capital employed.
3) Percentage of gross profit to sales
4) Current ratio
5) Quick ratio
6) Rate of inventory turnover
7) Collection period for trade receivables
b) Mason compared some of the accounting ratios for his business with those for other similar businesses. These were:

Profit as a percentage of sales	16%
Percentage of gross profit to sales	40%
Quick ratio	1.1:1
Rate of inventory turnover	7 times

1) State whether each of Mason's four ratios is better or worse than that of other similar businesses.

2) Give a reason for each of your answers to (b) (1).
3) State whether or not Mason should be satisfied with the ratios for his business.

Solution:
a)
1) Profit for the year as a percentage of sales

$= \dfrac{\text{profit} \times 100}{\text{sales revenue}}$

$= \dfrac{40,100 \times 100}{130,000}$

$= 30.8\%$

2) Profit as a percentage of capital employed

$= \dfrac{\text{Net profit} \times 100}{\text{capital employed}}$

$= \dfrac{40,100 \times 100}{88,000}$

$= 45.6\%$

3) Percentage of Gross profit to sales

$= \dfrac{\text{Gross profit} \times 100}{\text{sales revenue}}$

$= \dfrac{67,000 \times 100}{130,000}$

$= 51.5\%$

4) Current ratio

$= \dfrac{\text{Current Assets}}{\text{Current liabilities}}$

$= \dfrac{46,520}{24,300}$

$= 1.9 : 1$

5) Quick ratio

$= \dfrac{\text{Current assets} - \text{inventory}}{\text{Current liabilities}}$

$= \dfrac{46,520 - 17,000}{24,300}$

$= 1.2 : 1$

6) Rate of inventory turnover

$= \dfrac{\text{Cost of sales}}{\text{average inventory}}$

$= \dfrac{63,000}{(15,000 + 17,000) / 2}$

$= 1.968$

$= 2$ times (approx.)

7) Collection period for trade receivables

$= \dfrac{\text{Trade receivables} \times 365}{\text{Sales revenue}}$

$= \dfrac{25,000 \times 365}{130,000}$

$= 70$ days (approx.)

b) 1) Mason's profit as a percentage of sales at 30.8% is better than those of similar businesses at 16%.
Mason's Gross profit as a percentage of sales at 51.5% is better than those of similar businesses at 40%.
Mason's quick ratio at 1.2:1 is worse than those of similar businesses at 1.1:1.

Mason's rate of inventory turnover at 2 times is worse than those of similar businesses at 7 times.

2) Reasons:

Mason has made $30.8 profit for every $100 of sales compared to $16 made by similar businesses.

Mason has made $51.5 gross profit for every $100 of sales compared to $40 made by similar businesses.

Mason has a slightly higher quick ratio(1.2:1) than those of similar businesses (1.1:1). The ideal ratio is 1:1 and all the businesses in the industry seem to be more liquid than the ideal. A business should have immediate liquidity of a value equal to its current liabilities to be considered efficient in managing its current assets.

Mason has sold and replaced his inventory only twice this year. Similar businesses have sold and replaced their inventory seven times, thus displaying strong salesmanship. Either Mason has too much inventory compared to the rest of the industry or his sales are too slow.

3) Comments:

Profitability Mason's gross profit as a percentage of sales is excellent compared to that of the rest of the industry. It is possible that he has good suppliers or that he is able to nose out bargains and buy goods more cheaply. Also, he might not be passing on his price increases to his customers. His profit as a percentage of sales is also almost double that of a similar business. This indicates efficiency in managing expenses.

Liquidity Mason is quite good at managing his liquidity too. Though his quick ratio is slightly over the industry's and also more than the ideal, it is not very much so. Mason has enough liquidity to pay off his creditors in an emergency and does not have a liquidity problem. He is therefore in no danger of being declared insolvent if faced with immediate payment of debts.

His rate of inventory turnover, however, is dismal compared to his competitors. He needs to revamp his sales policies and strategies. More promotions and advertising is recommended.

Tip √ *1) Always give the formula in your answer, even though it seems repetitive. That way, even if your calculation is wrong, you will get almost half the total marks for that question for a right formula.*

2) The inventory included in the quick ratio is closing inventory... from the statement of financial position.

» EXERCISE 18.3

1) The following information is given for two businesses:

	Business X	Business Y
	$	$
Sales	70,000	80,000
Gross profit	35,000	48,000
Profit for the year	21,000	26,667
Capital employed	84,000	133,335
Inventory	5,000	11,000
Trade receivables	4,000	5,000
Balance at bank	3,000	
Bank overdraft		2,000
Trade payables	5,000	6,000

a) For each of the businesses calculate:

I) Gross profit margin.
II) Profit margin
III) The expenses of running the business.
IV) Current ratio
V) Quick ratio
VI) Collection period for trade receivables.

» EXERCISE 18.4

2) Leela purchased Song's business on 1st December 20x4. Song's assets and liabilities at 1st December 20x4 were as follows;

	$
Machinery	12,000
Motor van	6,000
Equipment	4,800
Inventory	10,000
Trade receivables	4,500
Other receivables	650
Bank overdraft	3,250
Trade payables	1,900
Other payables	340

Leela took over all the assets and liabilities at the values shown above. Leela paid $ 40,000 for the business including goodwill.

a) Prepare the statement of financial position of the business as it appeared on 1st December 20x4 immediately after Leela had purchased it.

b) Calculate for the business:
1) the current ratio
2) the quick ratio

c) Leela hopes to earn 12% return on her capital. Calculate the profit she must earn.

Solution:

Leela's statement of financial position as at 1st Dec., 20x4

	$	$	$
Intangible Non-current Assets:			
*Goodwill			....
Tangible Non-current Assets:			
....			....
....			....
....			....
Current Assets:			
....		....	
....		....	
		....	
Less Current liabilities:			
....	....		
....	....		
....	....	....	....
			....
Financed By:			
Capital		40,000	

Working:

*Goodwill

= Purchase price – net assets

= 40,000 – [(12,000+6,000+4,800+10,000+4,500+650)-
         (3250+1,900+340)]

= $...................

b) Current ratio = ...

              ....

              =..............

Quick ratio   = ...

              ....

              = ...

c) Return on capital employed

    = $\dfrac{\text{Net profit}}{\text{Capital employed}}$ x 100

    $12 = \dfrac{\text{Net profit}}{40,000}$ x 100

    $............ = Profit for the year

» **EXERCISE** 18.5

You are given the following table:

Ratio	Average for the trade	Tony's ratios
Gross profit margin	46%	66%
Profit margin	25%	20%
Current ratio	2.2:1	3.2:1
Quick ratio	1:1	0.9:1
Collection period for trade receivables	56 days	70 days
Payment period for trade payables	37 days	26 days

Comment on the following:
Tony's comparative profitability

....
....
....
....
....
....
....
....
....
....
....

Tony's comparative efficiency

....
....
....
....
....
....
....
....
....
....

» **EXERCISE** 18.6

On 30 September 2001 a sole trader had the following assets and liabilities:

	$
Workshop premises	30,000
Inventory of raw materials	13,000
Trade receivables	7,000
Trade payables	10,000
Cash	1,800

Calculate, showing your workings:
a) the working capital

....
....
....
....
....

b) the quick ratio

....
....
....
....
....

» EXERCISE 18.7

The opening inventory of a business is $12,000 and the cost of sales is $240,000.
Using the average figure of opening and closing inventory, what value of closing inventory is needed to give a inventory turnover of 10

» EXERCISE 18.8

The following items appear in a statement of financial position:

	$
Inventory	14,000
Provision for doubtful debts	2,000
Cash at bank	500
Trade payables	10,000

The current ratio of 2:1.

Required:
Calculate the closing trade receivables.

» EXERCISE 18.9

Archie Palago's statement of financial position at 30 April 20x6 and 20x7 were as follows:

	30 April 20x6			30 April 20x7		
	$	$	$	$	$	$
Non-current assets						
(Net book value)						
Premises		100 000			100 000	
Equipment		75 000			56 500	
		175 000			156 500	
Current assets						
Inventory	7 500			6 800		
Trade receivables	10 800			8 900		
Bank	2 000			-		
Cash	400	20 700		400	16 100	
Current liabilities						
Trade payables	6 200			7 300		
Bank	-			1 200		
		6 200			8 500	
Net current assets		14 500			7 600	
		189 500			164 100	
Capital at 1 may 20x6		120 000			189 500	
Profit for the year/(loss)		83 500			(11 400)	
		203 500			178 100	
Less drawings		14 000			14 000	
		189 500			164 100	

REQUIRED

(e) For each year, calculate to be a maximum of two decimal places:
(i) the current ratio;
(ii) the liquid ratio

(UCLES, 2007, AS/A Level Accounting, Syllabus 9706/2, May/June)

18.1 | MULTIPLE CHOICE QUESTIONS

i) The closing inventory of a business was $12,000 and the cost of goods sold was $75,000. If the inventory turnover was 10 times, what was the opening inventory?
A) $6,000   B) $5,000   C) $ 3,000   D) $7,500

ii) With the following information, calculate the cash operating cycle:

	Days
Trade payables' days	37
Trade receivables' days	25

Inventory was turned over 14 times that year.
A) 14 days   B) 2 days   C) 12 days   D) 11 days

iii) You are given the following information:

	Gross profit	Sales
20x1	$ 412,000	$ 1,200,000
20x2	$ 480,000	$ 1,600,000

Which of the following is not the reason for the gross profit margin decreasing?
A) A rise in the price of good purchased may have been passed on to customers.
B) The goods were purchased from a different supplier at a lower price
C) The cost of sales may have been increased by the theft of stock.

D) The margin on sales may have been cut to increase volume of sales.

iv) *The following information has been extracted from the books of a company:*

	$
Trade receivables at the end of the year	20,000
Trade receivables at the start of the year	15,000
Credit sales for the year	120,000
Cash sales for the year	30,000

What is the Trade receivables collection period?
A) 61 days   B) 49 days   C) 37 days   D) 46 days

v. *Moneybags and company give you the following information:*

	$000
10% debentures	100
Ordinary shares of $1 each	300
10% preference shares of $1 each	60
General reserve	100
Retained profit	104
Authorised share capital	500
Profit before interest and tax	180
Profit after interest and tax	100

What is the Return on Capital Employed?
A) 8.59%   B) 15.46%   C) 27.11%   D) 15.06%

18.2 | A company has the following information in its statement of financial position:

	$000
Taxation due	45
Trade receivables	160
Bank overdraft	70
Inventory	100
Proposed dividend	80
Trade payables	70

Required:
Calculate the liquidity (acid test or quick) ratio.

18.3 | A business has cash sales of $70,890 and credit sales of $1,500,000 in a year (360 days).
The trade receivables' collection period is 12 days (approx).

Required:
Calculate the closing trade receivables' balance.

18.4 | The table shows an extract from a company's final accounts:

	$
Purchases	30,000
Cost of sales	25,000
Trade payables	5,000
Other payables	1,200

Required:
Calculate the trade payables' payment period for the year.

18.5 | A firm has $15,000 in the bank and buys inventory for $ 2,000 paying by cheque.
a) What is the effect of this on the current ratio?
b) What is the effect of this on he quick (acid test) ratio?

18.6 | A business has a current ratio of 1.25:1 and a quick (acid test) ratio of 1:1. The business sells inventory on credit at its usual mark-up.
What is the effect of this on the current and quick (acid test) ratio?

18.7 | During the year ended 31 July 20x6 a business made sales of $550,000 of which 20% were for cash. The trade receivables at 31 July 20x5 were $50,000 and at 31 July 20x6 they were $55,000.
What is the trade receivables' collection period based on average trade receivables?

18.8 | A company's income statement showed a profit before interest of $125,000. Interest paid was $5,000.
The table shows amounts included in the company's statement of financial position:

	$
Non-current assets	480,000
Net current assets	30,000
10% Debentures	70,000

How much is the return on the total capital employed?

18.9 | The following information has been calculated from the accounts of a business:

Days taken to pay creditors	40
Days taken by debtors to pay	56
Inventory turnover in days	14

Required:
Calculate the cash operating cycle.

18.10 | The following information is given for a business at 31 June 20x3:

Average inventory	$10,000
Trade receivables	$ 2,000
Trade payables	$ 6,000

The Current ratio is 3:1.

Required:
Calculate the value of inventory at 1 July 20x3.

Total or Absorption Costing

19.1 | What is meant by the term total or absorption costing?

Total or absorption costing is costing of products manufactured by a business based on the total costs of manufacture: direct and indirect.

19.2 | What are direct costs?

Direct costs are costs that are directly linked to the production process. They are also known as variable costs as they vary according to the volume of goods produced. If no goods have been produced then these costs are nil. They include direct materials, direct labour and direct expenses such as royalties.

19.3 | What are indirect costs?

Indirect costs are costs that cannot be linked to the production process. They are also known as overheads or fixed costs. They accrue and have to be paid even if no production has taken place. Examples of indirect costs are: salaries, rent, heating and lighting .

19.4 | What are cost centers?

A cost center is a center to which costs can be allocated. It can be a department, a process, a person or equipment e.g. machinery.

19.5 | What are production cost centers?

Production cost centers are ones that are involved in the production process. E.g. assembling, polishing, painting, molding.

19.6 | What are service cost centers?

Service cost centers provide services for the production departments. E.g. canteen, stores, repair and maintenance.

19.7 | What are allocated costs?

Costs which can be identified with cost centers are allocated to those centers. Direct expenses and some indirect expenses can be allocated. E.g. Food can be allocated to the canteen, paint can be allocated to the painting cost center, heating and lighting and power, when separately metered.

19.8 | What are apportioned costs?

Most fixed costs or overheads which are incurred by the business as a whole and cannot be allocated to specific cost centres are apportioned. E.g. rent, depreciation

19.9 | What is the basis on which costs can be apportioned?

Rent, insurance of building and heating and lighting (when not metered separately) can be apportioned on the basis of floor area occupied by the cost centre. Insurance of assets other than building are apportioned on the basis of replacement cost or on the historic cost of the asset. Depreciation of non-current assets is apportioned on the basis of cost or book value of the assets.

EXHIBIT

Delima & Co have three production cost centres: Assembling, painting and packaging. They give you the following information:

Allocated expenditure for the year ended 31 December 20x3 are as follows.

	Assembling	Painting	Packaging
	$	$	$
Direct materials	45,000	5,600	3,500
Direct labour	1,00,000	45,000	60,000
Indirect labour	20,000	6,000	8,000
Other information:			
Cost of non-current			
assets	40,000	60,000	20,000
	sq m	sq m	sq m
Floor area	1,000	500	1,000
Other overheads:		$	
Depreciation of non-current assets	12,000		
Factory rent	50,000		
Repairs and maintenance of			
non-current assets	6,000		
Insurance of non-current assets	5,000		
Heating and lighting	2,500		

Required:

a) Calculate the total cost of production for each department.

b) Calculate the total cost of production.

Solution

Cost Statement for the year ended 31 December 20x3

	Assembling	Painting	Packaging
	$	$	$
Direct materials	45,000	5,600	3,500
Direct Labour	100,000	45,000	60,000
PRIME COST	145,000	51,600	63,500
Indirect labour	20,000	6,000	8,000
Depreciation	4,000	6,000	2,000
Factory rent	20,000	10,000	20,000
Repairs and Maintenance	2,000	3,000	1,000
Insurance	1,667	2,500	833
Heating and lighting	1,000	500	1,000
a) COST OF PRODUCTION	19,3667	79,600	96,333

b) TOTAL COST OF PRODUCTION = $369,600

» EXERCISE 19.1

De Loy & Co have three production cost centres: Assembling, Varnishing and packaging. They give you the following information:

Allocated expenditure for the year ended 31 December 20x6 are as follows.

	Assembling	Varnishing	Packaging
	$	$	$
Direct materials	24,000	12,600	10,500
Direct labour	46,000	25,000	44,000
Indirect labour	30,000	16,000	28,000
Other information:			
Cost of non-current assets	50,000	30,000	20,000
	M2	M2	M2
Floor area	2,000	1,000	3,000
Other overheads:		$	
Depreciation of non-current assets		14,000	
Factory rent		10,000	
Repairs and maintenance of non-current assets		3,000	
Insurance of non-current assets		3,600	
Heating and lighting		2,100	

Required:

a) Calculate the total cost of production for each department.

b) Calculate the total cost of production.

c) If they manufactured 10,000 units, what is the overhead absorption cost of each unit?

19.10 | What are the uses of Absorption Costs?

There are two uses:

a) Profit/loss can be calculated when the selling price is fixed

b) Selling price can be calculated when the level of profit is predetermined.

EXHIBIT

In the exhibit, above, if Delima and Co had produced 10,000 units, Calculate:

a) The absorption cost of each unit

b) The profit/loss if the Unit selling price was $65

c) The Selling Price if a Profit for the year of 20% on sales was required.

SOLUTION

a) The absorption cost of each unit $= \dfrac{369,600}{10,000}$

$= \$36.96$

b) The Profit per unit $= 65 - 36.96$

$= \$28.04$

c) The Selling price @ 20% profit on sales $= \$44.35$

» EXERCISE 19.2

Using the cost of production per unit in Exercise 22.1, calculate:

a) The profit/loss per unit if the unit selling price was $40

b) The Selling price per unit if a Profit for the year of 10% on sales is required.

» EXERCISE 19.3

Abba & Co manufacture Prebits and produce 20,000 units a year at the cost of $65,000. Calculate:

a. The cost per unit

b. The Profit/loss per unit if the selling price was $ 30

c. The Selling price per unit if a Profit for the year of 25% on sales is required.

19.11 | What is meant by the term 'Overhead absorption'?

Overheads are added to the direct or prime cost to arrive at the total cost of production. The overheads are then said to be 'absorbed'.

19.12 | Enumerate the steps to be followed to calculate overhead absorption when there is more than one product being produced and each product passes through more than one department?

The steps are:
a) Allocate and/or apportion the overheads to the cost centres
b) Calculate the overhead absorption rates for cost units.

19.13 | What is meant by the term 'cost center'?

A cost center is an entity (may even be a machine or person) to which costs may be attributed. Examples of cost centres are: paint shop, warehouse, packing department, machine shop, foundry etc. A cost center may be a production cost center or a service cost center. Examples of service cost centres are: Canteens, Warehouse, Building maintenance, Plant and Machinery maintenance.

19.14 | What is the difference between allocations and apportionments?

Expenditure is allocated to a cost center when it is incurred specifically for that cost center. Eg. Expenditure on paint can be allocated directly to the paint shop, food to the canteen etc. Expenditure which is incurred for the whole business and cannot be allocated, is apportioned on some equitable basis. Examples of such expenditure are: rates, rent, insurance etc.

19.15 | How is expenditure apportioned?

Expenditure is apportioned on an equitable basis according to its individual characteristics. The basis chosen for each expenditure should be dependent on the nature of the expense and the impact of each cost center on the amount of the expense incurred or the relative benefit enjoyed by the cost center. Following are some of the usual bases of apportionment:

Overhead	Basis of apportionment
Heating and lighting	Floor area or volume of space occupied by cost center.
Rent, rates	Floor area of cost center
Depreciation of non-current assets other than property	Cost or book value
Depreciation/insurance of property	Floor area

Overhead	Basis of apportionment
Insurance of fixed assets other than property	Cost or replacement cost
Storekeeping costs	Number or value of stores requisitions raised by cost center
Canteen, personnel , administration costs	Number of personnel in each cost center
Property maintenance	Area occupied by each production cost center
Plant and machinery maintenance	Number or value of machines in each cost center

EXHIBIT

Mosambi Ltd. is a manufacturing company with four production departments: Foundry, Assembly, Finishing and Packing. You are given the following data:

	Foundry	Assembly	Finishing	Packing
Floor area (Sq, metres)	1,2 00	2,400	600	800
Plant cost ($000's)	50	20	10	20
Plant replacement cost($000's)	100	100	200	100
Number of stores requisitions	400	200	100	300

During the quarter ended 31 March, 20x4, Mosambi Ltd. incurred the following expenditure:

		$
Production materials –	Foundry	50,000
	Assembly	10,000
	Finishing	6,000
	Packing	12,000
Direct labour	Foundry	24,000
	Assembly	14,000
	Finishing	15,600
	Packing	20,000
Indirect labour	Foundry	5,600
	Assembly	4,600
	Finishing	3,400
	Packing	2,600
Plant depreciation		3,400
Plant insurance		1,500
Heating and lighting of plant		6,000
Factory rent		20,000
Storekeeping costs		5,300
Factory depreciation		5,500
Factory repair and maintenance		6,800

Required:

Show in tabular form the apportionment of Mosambi Ltd.'s overheads using the appropriate bases of apportionment.

SOLUTION

Cost	Basis	Total $	Foundry $	Assembly $	Finishing $	Packing $
Direct materials	Allocated	78,000	50,000	10,000	6,000	12,000
Direct labour	Allocated	73,600	24,000	14,000	15,600	20,000
Indirect labour	Allocated	16,200	5,600	4,600	3,400	2,600
Plant depreciation	Cost of plant	3,400	1,700	680	340	680
Plant insurance	Replacement value	1,500	300	300	600	300
Heating & Lighting	Floor area	6,000	1,440	2,880	720	960
Factory rent	Floor area	20,000	4,800	9,600	2,400	3,200
Storekeeping costs	Number of store requisitions	5,300	2,120	1,020	530	1,590
Factory depreciation	Floor area	5,500	1,320	2,640	660	880
Factory repair and maintenance	Floor area	6,800	1,632	3,264	3,816	1,088
Total Cost		216,300	92,912	48,984	34,066	43298

» EXERCISE 19.4

Merrick Ltd. is a manufacturing company with four production departments: Milling, Assembly, Finishing and Varnishing. You are given the following data:

	Milling	Assembly	Finishing	Varnishing
Floor area (Sq, metres)	1,500	3,000	500	1,000
Plant cost ($000's)	20	5	10	15
Plant replacement cost($000's)	200	200	100	100
Number of stores requisitions	100	400	100	100

During the quarter ended 31 March, 20x4, Merrick Ltd. incurred the following expenditure:

		$
Production materials –	Milling	40,000
	Assembly	20,000
	Finishing	3,000
	Varnishing	15,000

		$
Direct labour	Milling	22,000
	Assembly	12,000
	Finishing	13,500
	Varnishing	14,000
Indirect labour	Milling	4,700
	Assembly	3,900
	Finishing	2,100
	Varnishing	1,500
Plant depreciation		2,400
Plant insurance		1,200
Heating and lighting of plant		2,400
Factory rent		30,000
Storekeeping costs		3,500
Factory depreciation		3,000
Factory repair and maintenance		4,000

Required:

Show in tabular form the apportionment of Merrick Ltd.'s overheads using the appropriate bases of apportionment.

APPORTIONMENT OF SERVICE COSTS TO PRODUCTION COST CENTRES

19.16 | What is the quickest and simplest way of apportioning service costs to production cost centers?

The Elimination method is the quickest and simplest way of apportioning service costs to production cost centers.

19.17 | What are the advantages and disadvantages of the Elimination Method?

Advantage: The Elimination Method is very simple.
Disadvantage: It is illogical because it ignores the proportion of the second service department's overheads which should be borne by the first department to be eliminated. In the exhibit below, N's overheads which should be borne by M is ignored.

19.18 | What is meant by the term Reciprocal Services?

If two or more service departments are involved and they provide services for each other as well as for the production department, then the service departments are said to provide reciprocal services for each other. Departments M and N in the exhibit below, provide reciprocal services.

EXHIBIT

Indirect labour costs and other indirect expenses have been allocated to Production Departments X, Y and Z and Service Departments M and N as follows:

| | Production Departments | | | Service Departments | |
	X	Y	Z	M	N
Indirect labour	3,000	2,000	4,000	1,000	1,500
Other expenses	1,000	3,000	1,000	1,000	500
	$4,000	$5,000	$5,000	$2,000	$2,000
Number of staff	50	20	30	10	40
No. of stores requisitions	100	200	150		50

M is a Store and N is a canteen.

Required

Using the Elimination method, apportion the service department overheads to the production departments.

SOLUTION

| | X | Y | Z | M | N |
	$	$	$	$	$
Overheads	4,000	5,000	5,000	2,000	2,000
First apportionment*	400	800	600	(2,000)	200
	4,400	5,800	5,600	-	2,200
Second apportionment**	1,100	440	660		(2,200)
	5,500	6,240	6,260		-

Working:
*First apportionment of M's overheads is on the basis of number of stores requisitions as M is a store.

Dept. X	$\frac{100 \times 2000}{100+200+150+50}$	= $400
Dept. Y	$\frac{200 \times 2000}{100+200+150+50}$	= $800
Dept. Z	$\frac{150 \times 2000}{100+200+150+50}$	= $600
Dept. N	$\frac{50 \times 2000}{100+200+150+50}$	= $200

**Second apportionment of N's overheads is on the a basis of number of staff as N is a canteen.

Dept. X	$\frac{50 \times 2200}{50+20+30}$	= $1,100
Dept. Y	$\frac{20 \times 2200}{50+20+30}$	= $440
Dept. Z	$\frac{30 \times 2200}{50+20+30}$	= $660

» **EXERCISE** 19.5

Ballyho Ltd. has five departments for which the following information is available:

	Machining	Assembly	Paintshop	Stores	Premises maintenance
Number of stores requisitions	600	500	400		100
Floor areas (sq. m.)	2,400	2,000	1,200	1,400	600
Overheads	$96,000	$41,000	$26,000	$8,000	$14,000

Stores overheads are apportioned to the other departments on the basis of the number of stores requisitions raised by each department. Charges for premises maintenance are based on the floor area of each department.

Required:

Prepare a statement showing how the costs of the services departments are re-apportioned between the production departments.

» **EXERCISE** 19.6

Sample Ltd. provide the following information based on budgeted total departmental costs after all costs have been allocated or apportioned:

| | Production Departments | | | Services Department | |
	A	B	C	D	E
Overheads	$50,000	$30,000	$20,000	$10,000	$20,000

The service departments costs are to be apportioned as follows:

| | Production Departments | | | Services Department | |
	A	B	C	D	E
Dept. D	20%	30%	40%	-	10%
Dept E	25%	50%	20%	5%	

Required:

Prepare a statement showing how the costs of the services departments are re-apportioned between the production departments.

CALCULATION OF OVERHEAD ABSORPTION RATES (OAR) FOR COST UNITS

19.19 | What is meant by the term cost units?

A cost unit is a unit of production. The nature of the business determines the cost unit. Examples

Business	Cost Unit
Cereal manufacturer	100 boxes of cereal
Paving stones manufacturer	A Pallet of paving stones
Umbrella manufacturer	An umbrella
Bicycle manufacturer	A bicycle
Car manufacturer	A car
Passenger transport	A passenger-kilometre
Computer manufacturer	A computer

19.20 | What is meant by the term Overhead Absorption Rate (OAR)?

The overhead absorption rate determines the amount of a cost centre's overheads to be added (or absorbed) by each cost unit that passes through that cost center. These rates are predetermined and calculated on the basis of budgeted production and overhead expenditure. There are different bases for calculating OARs but the most common are the Machine hour OAR and the Direct Labour hour OAR.

19.21 | When is the Machine Hour OAR used?

The machine hour OAR is used when the means of production are capital intensive, the production process is predominantly mechanised and the machinery running costs are greater than the direct labour costs. This OAR will consider the amount of machine hours required to produce each cost unit. Machine hours will also include costs such as repairs, maintenance and depreciation of machinery.

EXHIBIT

Kelco Ltd. makes two products, M and N. The budgeted figures for the month of June are as follows:

	Units	Machine hours per unit
Product M	100	4
Product N	200	1

Budgeted overheads for June were $ 36,000.

The budgeted Machine Hour OAR = $\dfrac{36000}{4\times100 + 1\times200}$

= $ 60

OAR for each unit of M	= 60x4 = $240
for each unit of N	= 60x1 = $60

If budgets were met, the total overheads will be absorbed as follows:

	$
100 units of M (100x240)	24,000
200 units of N (200x60)	12,000
Total	36,000

» EXERCISE 19.7

Nordy Ltd. manufactures two products Alpha and Beta. Each unit of Alpha requires 3 machine hours to make while Beta requires 2 machine hours. Nordy Ltd. uses 10 machines in the manufacture of these products. Each machine is used for 50 hours per week. In a period of 8 weeks, it is planned to manufacture 500 units of Alpha and 1,500 units of Beta. Total budgeted overheads for the period are $76,000.

Required:

Calculate the overhead recovery rates for Alpha and Beta and prepare a statement showing how the total overheads will be absorbed by production.

» EXERCISE 19.8

Dewaar Ltd. manufactures 'Pyar' and 'Phool'.

The budgeted production for each product for the month of January is shown below:

	Units	Machine hours per unit
Pyar	1,500	2.5
Phool	4,000	3.5

Budgeted overheads for January are expected to be $350,000.

Required

Calculate:

a) the overhead absorption rate for each product, using the direct machine hour method

b) the total amount of overheads absorbed by each product if budgets are met.

19.22 | When is the direct labour overhead absorption rate used?

Direct Labour OAR is used when the processes are labour intensive so that machine involvement is small and machine costs low, but labour costs relatively high.

EXHIBIT

Dilwala Ltd. manufactures two products K and L. The budget for the month of July was as follows:

	Units	Direct labour hours per unit
Product K	3,000	0.5
Product L	5,000	1.5

Budgeted overheads for the month: $45,000.

SOLUTION

Total budgeted direct labour hours for July :

0.5x3000 + 1.5x5000 = 9000

Direct labour hour OAR = $\dfrac{45000}{9000}$

= $5

The OAR per unit:	K	= 5x0.5 = $2.50
	L	= 5x1.5 = $7.50

If the budgets are met, the total overheads will be absorbed as follows:

	$
3,000 units of K (3000 x 2.50)	7500
5000 units of L (5000 x 7.50)	37,500
	45,000

» EXERCISE 19.9

Jabali Ltd. manufactures chairs. The chairs are largely hand made and are of two designs: Comfy and Stylish. Comfy requires 6 hours of labour while Stylish requires 10 hours of labour. The company employs 40 staff to make the chairs and they work 40 hours a week each. In the 12 weeks to June 30, the factory overheads are estimated to be $65,000. It is planned to make 500 Comfy chairs and the balance of production hours will be utilised to make Stylish chairs.

Required

a) Calculate the Overhead Recovery Rate for each chair and state the number of Stylish chairs which it is planned to make in the period.

b) Prepare a statement showing how the overheads will be recovered in the period.

» EXERCISE 19.10

Delso Ltd. manufactures 'Peking' and 'Jijing'.
The budgeted production for each product for the month of January is shown below:

	Units	Direct Labour hours per unit
Peking	1,200	3.5
Jijing	3,000	0.5

Budgeted overheads for January are expected to be $380,000.

Required

Calculate:

a) the overhead absorption rate for each product, using the direct labour hour method

b) the total amount of overheads absorbed by each product if budgets are met.

» EXERCISE 19.11

Dingo Ltd. manufacture two products K and L. Both products require processing in Production cost centres: Machine Department and Assembly Department. The following budgeted information is available for the month of June:

		K	L
Production		1,000 units	3,000 units
Direct materials per unit		$7	$10
Direct wages per unit		$30	$40
Machine hours per unit:	Machine	4	2
	Assembly	1	1
Direct labour hours per unit:	Machine	2	3
	Assembly	3	2.33

	Machine Dept.	Assembly Dept.
Budgeted overheads	$45,000	$30,000
Budgeted machine hours	10,000	1,000
Budgeted direct labour hours	7,000	10,000

Required

a) Calculate an appropriate overhead absorption rate for each department.

b) Calcuate the overhead absorption rate for each unit of K and L, in each of the departments, and in total.

c) Pepare a statement to show how the overheads of each department is absorbed by production.

d) Calculate the total cost of each unit of K and L.

» EXERCISE 19.12

Balasite Ltd. process two substances N and M. Both products pass through two stages of electrolysis and filtration. Budgeted overheads for the month of July are as follows:

	$
Electrolysis dept.	25,000
Filtration dept.	12,000

Planned production for July is 1000 units of M and 1,000 units of N.
Other budgeted information for the month of July is as follows:

		M	N
Direct materials per unit		$4	$5
Direct labour per unit		25	25
Machine hours per unit:	Electrolysis	3	2
	Filtration	1	3
Direct labour hours per unit:	Electrolysis	1	2
	Filtration	2.5	3.5

Budgeted hours for July are:	Machine	Direct labour
Electrolysis	5,000	3,400
Filtration	4,500	6,000

Balasite Ltd. recover Electrolysis Department's overheads on a machine hour basis, and Filtration Department's overheads on a direct labour hour basis.

Required

a) Calculte the overhead recovery rate for M and N in each of the departments.

b) Prepare a statement showing how the total overheads are recovered by production.

c) Prepare a total cost statement for each of the two products.

19.23 | What are the other bases for calculating Overhead Absorption Rates?

The other bases for calculating OARs are: Direct Wages OAR, Direct Materials OAR, Prime Cost OAR, Cost Unit OAR.

19.24 | Write a short note on the Direct Wages OAR.

This OAR is calculated by expressing overheads as a proportion of direct wages.
Disadvantage: Direct wages may not be directly related to time taken in production, but to the different rates paid to skilled and unskilled workers, premium wages paid for overtime and shift work and bonus systems.

19.25 | Write a short note on the Direct Material OAR.

This OAR is calculated by expressing overheads as a proportion of direct materials.
Disadvantage: A product with a high material cost, taking less time to make, would have an unjustifiably higher OAR than one with lower material cost, taking more time to make; this despite the fact that the time required to manufacture the former clearly indicates that it should be loaded with less overheads and not more.

19.26 | Write a short note on Direct Prime Cost OAR.

This OAR is calculated by expressing overheads as a proportion of prime cost.
Disadvantage: This method combines the weakness of the Direct Wages OAR and the Direct Material OAR.

19.27 | Write a short note on Cost Unit OAR.

This OAR is calculated by expressing overheads as a proportion of Unit cost.
Disadvantage: This method can only be used if one type of good is produced with every unit using the same process.

OVER/UNDER RECOVERY OF OVERHEADS

19.28 | When does under-absorption take place?

Under-absorption takes place when actual expenditure is more than budgeted and/or actual production is less than planned. Under-recovery is debited in the cost income statement.

19.29 | When does over-absorption take place?

Over-absorption takes place when actual expenditure is less than budgeted expenditure and/or actual production is more than planned. Over-recovery is credited in the cost income statement.

EXHIBIT
Ballyho Ltd. budgets for overheads expenditure of $20,000 in July, and for an output of 5,000 units. The OAR is $3 per unit. Calculate the under-absorption or over-absorption of overheads in each of the following cases:
1) Actual output for July was 5080 units and actual expenditure equalled budgeted expenditure.
   Ans. Over-recovery of overheads = 80 x $3 = $240

2) Actual output for July was 4,800 units; actual expenditure equalled budgeted expenditure.
   Ans. Under-recovery of overheads = 200 x $3 = $600.

3) Actual expenditure was $22,000; actual output equalled budget.
   Ans. Under-recovery of overheads = $2,000

4) Actual expenditure was $17,000; actual output equalled budget.
   Ans. Over-recovery of overheads =$3,000.

» **EXERCISE 19.13**
Anisort Ltd. provides the following information about its overhead expenditure for the six months to June 30 and the next six months to 31 December as follows:

	Six months to 30 June	Six months to 31 December
Budgeted overhead	$250,000	$300,000
Planned production in units	80,000	100,000
Actual expenditure	$270,000	$280,000
Actual production	75,000	108,000

Required
Calculate the under-absorption or over-absorption of overheads in each of the two periods. In each case state clearly whether the overhead was under-absorbed or over-absorbed.
SOLUTION

Overhead Absorption rate	$\dfrac{250,000}{80,000}$	
		= $*......
	$\dfrac{300,000}{100,000}$	= $**.........
Overheads recovered	75,000 x $*.......	
	=$***..............	
	108,000 x $**........	
	= $#..........	
(Under)/Over-absorption	$(*** - 270,000)	
	= ($35,625)	
	$(# - 280,000)	
	= $44,000	

» **EXERCISE 19.14**
Bellinger Ltd. has provided the following information about its overhead expenditure for the six months to June 30 and the next six months to 31 December as follows:

	Six months to 30 June	Six months to 31 December
Budgeted overhead	$350,000	$200,000
Planned production in units	90,000	120,000
Actual expenditure	$370,000	$180,000
Actual production	85,000	128,000

Required

Calculate the under-absorption or over-absorption of overheads in each of the two periods. In each case state clearly whether the overhead was under-absorbed or over-absorbed.

19.30 What are sunk costs?

Ans. They are costs that are incurred and cannot be reversed.

19.31 What are stepped costs?

Ans. They are costs that increase to a new level in step with the significant changes in activity or usage.

19.1 | Multiple choice questions

i) Overhead Absorption Rates (OARs) are used to determine the
A)   total cost
B)   prime cost
C)   amount which is to be spent on overheads
D)   apportionment of services department overheads to production departments

ii) Overhead Absorption Rates need not be calculated if
A)   there is only one production cost center
B)   a variety of products are processed through all the company's production cost centres
C)   only one standard product is made
D)   the amount which will actually be spent on overheads is not known

iii) Which of the following could cause an over-absorption of overhead expenditure?
1)   overhead expenditure is less than budgeted expenditure
2)   actual production is more than the planned level.
3)   absorption rate calculated on actual production
4)   absorption rate calculated on actual number of units produced

A)   1 and 3
B)   1 and 2
C))   2 and 3
D)   2 and 4

iv. MLN Ltd. provides the following figures:

Actual direct machine hours taken	*1,000*
Budgeted direct machine hours taken	*1,300*
Actual overhead expenditure	*$ 45,000*
Budgeted overhead expenditure	*$ 50,000*

What is the Overhead Absorption Rate based on direct machine hours?
A) $50
B) $45
C) $38.46
D) $34.62

v) Malini & Co. provides the following information:

Budgeted overhead expenditure	*$100,000*
Actual overhead expenditure	*$115,000*
Planned production	*80,000units*
Actual production	*74,000 units*

Which of the following correctly describes the overheads absorbed?
A) Under – absorbed $75,000
B) Overabsorbed $75,000
C) Under-absorbed $ 22,500
D) Overabsorbed $22,500

19.2 | A company's overhead cost items for a year are illustrated by the following graphs. State which graph relates to the following overheads:

i)   Depreciation charged on the basis of cost per unit.
ii)   Factory rent of $45,000 per year.
iii)   Supervisors' salaries:
    under 5,000   units produced – two supervisors
    5,001 – 10,000 units produced – 4 supervisors
    10,001 – 15,000 units produced - 6 supervisors
iv)   Cost of a service was $3 per unit produced up to a maximum of $7,000 per year.
v)   Maintenance in the form of a standing charge of $3,500, plus a charge of $2 per unit produced to a maximum of $10,000 per year.

Note: OA represents Cost and OM represents output

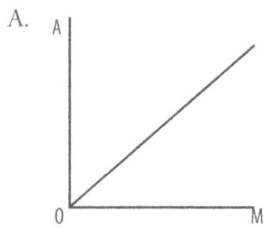

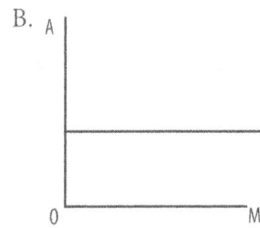

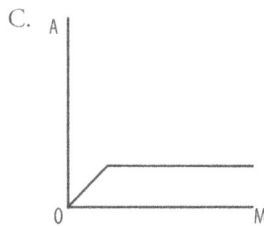

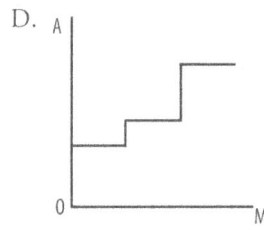

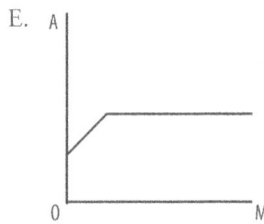

A.

B.

C.

D.

E.

19.3 | A hotel budgets for overheads totalling $12,000,000 for a financial year. It expects to have 20,000 guests in a year. Each guest stays an average of 10 days and the hotel absorbs overheads on a guest/day basis. Its direct costs for the year are budgeted at $20,000,000.
What is its overhead absorption rate?

19.4 | The following are figures for a week's production:
Expected production = 20,000 units
Expected production overhead = $100,000
Actual production overhead = $80,000
Over-absorption of overhead = $4,000
What is the actual amount of production in the week?

19.5 | A business uses a predetermined direct labour rate of $4.50 per hour to absorb production overheads. 5 direct labour hours are required to manufacture one unit of the product.
The following information is given:
Actual production overhead = $101,890
Under-absorption production overhead =$56,890
What was the actual output(in units) produced during that period?

19.6 A business provides the following data for the year:

Budgeted output (units)	10,000
Actual output (units)	8,000
Budgeted fixed production costs	$1,200,000
Budgeted variable production costs	$800,000
Budgeted fixed selling overheads	$600,000

What is the absorption cost per unit used for stocktaking?

19.7 What is meant by the term 'Currently attainable standard'?

Unit, Job and Batch Costing

20.1 | What is meant by the term continuous operations?

Continuous operations are those in which a single type of good is produced and the units produced are identical. Production may involve a sequence of continuous or repetitive operations.

20.2 | Explain: Continuous Costing

Continuous costing is used to find the cost of a single unit of production or service in a business that uses continuous operations.

20.3 | What is meant by Unit Costing?

This method of costing is used to find the cost of a single unit of production or service. A single unit may be a single item or a large number of items depending on the type of business it is. e.g. for a company producing thousands of packets of biscuits, the unit may be 100 packets.

EXHIBIT

Malassum Ltd. manufactures biscuits. Its cost unit is 100 packets of biscuits. They provide the following information:

Number of packets of biscuits produced	375,000
Expenditure: Direct materials	$250,000
Direct labour	$130,000
Overheads	$800,000

Required
Calculate the cost of one unit of biscuits.

Solution
Total cost = 250,000 + 130,000 + 800,000 = $1,180,000
Cost per unit = $\frac{1180000}{3750}$

= $314.67

» **EXERCISE** 20.1
Baltic Ltd. manufactures bricks. Its cost unit is a pallet of bricks. 1000 bricks make up a pallet. They provide the following information:

Number of bricks produced	675,000
Expenditure: Direct materials	$253,000
Direct labour	$127,000
Overheads	$350,000

Required
Calculate the cost of one unit of bricks.

SPECIFIC ORDER COSTING

20.4 | What is meant by Job Costing?

Costing for production which consists of special jobs for special orders which could be just one unit is known as Job Costing. E.g. A custom-made car, a contract for building a bridge.

20.5 | How is job costing carried out?

Each job is given a separate job number. Direct materials are charged to the job on the basis of LIFO, FIFO or AVCO etc. and direct labour is charged to the job as well on a piece rate or time rate basis. The job is thus a cost center and indirect expenses are allocated or apportioned appropriately. If the exact amount of the overhead is known, it is allocated, if not, it will be apportioned on a suitable basis.

20.6 | What is a job card?

A job card or job costing sheet is a record of the actual costs incurred by the company concerned to do a specific job. It is a useful source of information for job quotes on similar jobs in the future.

EXHIBIT

Klark Ltd. is asked for a quote to install a kitchen. They will base their quote on the following estimated costs:

	$
Materials	35,000

Labour: 2000 hours @ $50 an hour
Overhead Absorption rate = $75 per labour hour
Profit : 25% of total cost.

Required:

a) Prepare a statement to show the amount of the quote for this job No: M/25/156 .

b) Prepare a Job/Card Cost sheet for the job which started on 20 July 2007 and ended 31 August 2007.

Solution

a) $
Direct materials   35,000
Direct labour   100,000
Overheads   150,000
Total costs   285,000
Profit   71,250
Amount quoted   356,250

b)   Job cost sheet - Job no. M/25/156

	Started 20 July 2007 Budgeted $	Completed 31 August 2007 Actual $
Materials	35,000	28,000
Direct labour:	100,000	90,000
Overheads	150,000	135,000
Total costs	285,000	253,000
Profit	71,250	63,250
Total job cost	356,250	316,250

» EXERCISE 20.2

Mekalt Ltd. is asked for a quote to edit a book. They will base their quote on the following estimated costs:

Labour:1,000 hours @ $70 an hour
Additional labour: 350 hours @ $30 an hour
Overhead Absorption rate = $25 per labour hour

Required:

 Prepare a statement to show the amount of the cost for this job .

20.7 | What is meant by Batch Costing?

Batch production is when a number of units undergo the same production process together. E.g. printing of 4,000 copies of a book at a printer's establishment. Costing for this kind of production is called Batch Costing. All the costs incurred are charged to the batch and the cost per unit is found by dividing the cost of the batch by the number of units in the batch.

EXHIBIT

Wallim &Co prints books. It receives an order for printing 10,000 copies of books at an agreed price of $20,000 for the batch. They have three departments for which the following information is given:

Printing   OAR $14 per machine hour
Binding   OAR $45 per direct labour hour
Packaging   OAR $40 per direct labour hour

The costs incurred in the production of the batch were:
Direct materials $6000
Direct labour   Printing 10 hours at $25 per hour
                      Binding 20 hours at $35 per hour
                      Packaging 25 hours at $30 per hour

30 hours were booked against the batch in the printing department. Administration expenses were recovered at 10% of total cost of production.

Required

a) Calculate the production cost of the batch of 10,000 books.
b) Calculate the cost per book.
c) Calculate the profit per book.

Solution

Statement of Cost of Production for a batch of 10,000 books

	$	$
Direct materials		6,000
Direct labour: Printing (10 x 25)	250	
Binding (20 x 35)	700	
Packaging (25 x 30)	750	1,700
Prime cost		7,700
Production overheads recovered:		
Printing (30 x 14)	420	
Binding (45 x 20)	900	
Packaging (40 x 25)	1,000	2,320
Cost of production		10,020
Administration costs recovered(10%x10,020)		1,002
Cost of a batch of 10,000 books		11,022
Profit		8,978
		20,000

a) Cost of production per batch of 10,000 books   =$11,022

b) Cost per book = $\frac{11,022}{10,000}$

= $1.1022

c) Profit per book = $\frac{8,978}{10,000}$

= $0.8978

20.8 | What are the ways in which labour is paid?

Labour can be paid:

a. An hourly rate - The number of hours they work.
b. A piece rate - The number of units they produce
c. A fixed annual salary

Labour can, in addition to the above, receive overtime or bonus payments.

EXHIBIT

Kelly is given a job completing 500 units of a product. Her boss has offered her two options

1. She receives $1.10 for each unit she completes and a bonus of $300 if she completes the job in a 7 day week

2. She receives $1 for the first 200 units she completes and $1.60 for the next 300 units.

3. She gets $1 a unit for working on a weekday and overtime at a time an one third for working on a Saturday or Sunday

She will receive:
Option 1 (1.10 x 500) + 30 = $580 if she completes the job in a week.
Option 2 (1 x 200 + 1.60 x 300) = $680, with the second option. There is no time constraint with this option.

Option 3 If she works a 7 day week completing 400 units
Monday -Friday and the remaining on the weekend
$(400 \times 1) + (1^{1/}_{3} \times 100) = \$533.33$.

» EXERCISE 20.3

Ballyho &Co has three departments. It receives an order for
manufacturing 1000 units of its product at an agreed price of
$8,000 for the batch. They have three departments for which
the following information is given:

Department A	OAR $4 per machine hour
Department B	OAR $20 per direct labour hour
Department C	OAR $16 per direct labour hour

The costs incurred in the production of the batch were:

Direct materials	$3000
Direct labour	Department A 10 hours at $20 per hour
	Department B 20 hours at $30 per hour
	Department C 25 hours at $25 per hour

24 hours were booked against the batch in department A.
Administration expenses were recovered at 5% of total cost of
production.

Required

a) Calculate the production cost of the batch
of 1000 units.
b) Calculate the cost per unit.
c) Calculate the profit per unit.

» EXERCISE 20.4

Achieve Ltd guarantees its employees a weekly wage of $272.
They pay employees $6.80 per hour for a basic 40-hour week.
They also pay an overtime premium of 50% and a bonus of $0.25
per unit if the employees produce more than 350 units a week
and if the products met with established standards.
**If one employee worked 45 hours in a week, and produced
410 units, what was the employee's gross pay that week?**

20.1 | Multiple Choice Questions

i) Which of the following would involve specific order operations?
A) Oil refining
B) Passenger transport
C) Production of mineral water
D) Re-painting a house

ii) A car is hired for one job only.
A) The rental will be charged to the job as an indirect expense
B) The rental will be charged to the job as a direct expense
C) The rental and depreciation will be charged to the job as
direct expenses
D) The rental and depreciation will be charged to the job as
indirect expenses

iii) Which of the following refers to job costing?
A) a costing method that separates variable and fixed costs
B) a costing method used to calculates the cost of a job where a
customer orders homogeneous products.
C) a costing method by which fixed costs are absorbed into the
cost of the good being produced.
D) a costing method used to calculate the cost of giving a one-off
service for a customer.
20.2 Sandy's employer pays her $12 an hour for a 40-hour week
and a time and a half for overtime. She is expected to produce five
units an hour. She is paid a bonus of $1.50 per extra unit if she
produces more than this.
**If Sandy worked 42 hours and produced 225 units in a week,
what are her earnings?**

20.3   A job cost sheet showed the following estimates:

	$
Labour @ $10 per hour	720
Materials	200
Profit	150
Overheads @ $20 per hour	50

The price of the job was $ 1550.
Calculate:
The profit if the job actually took 20% more labour
hours than were estimated.

20.4 | The Bombay Ltd. company manufactures a product in batches of 400. 100 units were machined per hour

	Batch 445
	$
Raw materials per unit	1.70
Machinists' hourly rate	20.00
Machine hour overhead rate	4.30
Setting up of machine	23.00

Calculate:
1) The cost of Batch 45 in total.
2) The cost per unit

21 | Marginal Costing

21.1 | What are variable costs?

Variable costs are those costs which vary with the level of activity of a business. It increases proportionately with the level of production or turnover. Eg. Direct labour (if remuneration is paid on a piece basis, not on a time basis), commission based on turnover, direct materials etc.

21.2 | What are fixed costs?

Fixed costs do not vary with the level of activity and are time based. They remain 'fixed' or constant within given limits. Beyond those limits, they may vary. E.g. rent , heating and lighting

21.3 | What is meant by the term 'marginal cost'?

Marginal cost is the cost of making one extra unit of a product.

21.4 | Define: Marginal Cost of Production.

Since an additional unit of production entails only an increase in variable costs, the Marginal Cost of Production is the total of the variable cost of manufacture.

21.5 | Define: Contribution

Contribution is the difference between the marginal cost and the selling price. It is the contribution each unit of production makes towards covering the fixed cost and the profit, in that order.

Contribution per unit = Selling price per unit – total variable costs per unit.

EXHIBIT
Jumert Ltd. produces variable Jammets under licence and its budget for the month of July 20x5 was as follows:
Production : 2,000 Jammets.

	$	$
Direct materials		34,000
Direct labour		67,000
Royalties		20,000
Prime cost		121,000
Other production costs:		
Variable	13,000	
Fixed	25,000	38,000
Selling and distribution costs:		
Variable	6,000	
Fixed	18,000	24,000
Administration expenses (all fixed)		45,000
Total cost		228,000
Budgeted profit		100,000
Budgeted sales		328,000

Required
Draw up a marginal cost statement showing:
a) the cost of 2,000 Jammets.
b) the cost per Jammet.

Solution

Marginal cost statement

	Total cost of 2000 units	Marginal cost per unit
	$	$
Direct materials	34,000	17.00
Direct labour	67,000	33.50
Direct expenses- royalties	20,000	10.00
Production costs – variable	13,000	6.50
Selling and distribution costs – variable	6,000	3.00
Marginal cost	140,000	70.00
Contribution	188,000	94.00
Sales (selling price)	328,000	164.00

21.6 | Define: Contribution to sales (C/S) Ratio

Contribution to sales ratio is the ratio of the contribution to the selling price.

$$\text{Contribution to sales ratio (C/S)} = \frac{\text{Contribution x 100}}{\text{Sales}}$$

EXHIBIT

Calculate the C/S ratio from the exhibit, above

Solution

$$C/S = \frac{94 \times 100}{164} = 57.32\%$$

» EXERCISE 21.1

A company gives you the following information for the production of 5,000 units of a product:

	$
Marginal cost	165,349
Contribution	174,651
Sales revenue	340,000

Fixed costs: $ 59,000.

Required

Calculate:

1) The profit per unit if 5000 units were produced
2) The contribution to sales ratio at 5000 units of production
3) The profit or loss from the sale of:
   a) 3,000 units
   b) 6,000 units

4) **EXERCISE 21.2**
   A company gives you the following information for the production of 2,000 units of a product: $

Marginal cost	36,897
Contribution	63,103
Sales revenue	100,000

Fixed costs: $ 87,000.

Required

Calculate

1) The profit or loss per unit if 2,000 units were produced.
2) The contribution to sales ratio at 2,000 units of production
3) the profit or loss from the sale of:
   a) 3,000 units
   b) 1,000 units

EXHIBIT

You are given the following information:

C/S ratio	= 70%
Sales revenue	= $500,000
Fixed cost	= $ 90,000
Units produced	= 20,000

Required

a) The profit/loss for the year if 20,000 units were produced
b) The profit/loss for the year if 40,000 units were produced
c) The profit/loss for the year if 1,000 units were produced

Solution

		$'000
a)	Contribution = 70% x 500000	350
	less fixed overheads	90
	Profit for the year	260

b)	Sales revenue = $\frac{500000}{20000}$ x 40000	= $1,000,000

		$'000
	Contribution = 70% x 1000000	700
	Less fixed overheads	90
	Profit for the year	610

c)	Sales revenue = $\frac{500000}{20000}$ x 1000	= $ 25,000

		$'000
	Contribution = 70% x 25000	17.5
	Less fixed overheads	(90.0)
	Net loss	72.5

» EXERCISE 21.3

You are given the following information:

C/S ratio	= 60%
Sales revenue	= $50,000
Fixed cost	= $ 14,000
Units produced	= 2,000

Required

a) The Profit /loss for the year if 2,000 units were produced
b) The profit/loss for the year if 3,000 units were produced
c) The profit/loss for the year if 250 units were produced

» EXERCISE 21.4

You are given the following information:

C/S ratio	= 80%
Sales revenue	= $70,000
Fixed cost	= $ 34,000
Units produced	= 10,000

Required

a) The profit/loss if 10,000 units were produced
b) The profit/loss if 30,000 units were produced
c) The profit/loss if 5,000 units were produced

BREAK - EVEN

21.7 | Define: Break-even point.

It is the level of activity at which the business makes neither a profit nor loss. At this point total contribution will equal total fixed cost.

21.8 | How is break-even calculated?

The formula for calculating break – even point in units is:

Break even point (units) = $\dfrac{\text{Fixed cost}}{\text{Contribution per unit}}$

The formula for calculating break-even in terms of sales revenue is:

Break – even ($) = $\dfrac{\text{fixed cost x unit selling price}}{\text{Contribution per unit}}$

OR

Break-even point ($) = $\dfrac{\text{Fixed cost}}{\text{Contribution per $ of selling price}}$

21.9 | Define: Margin of safety

The margin of safety is the distance between break-even point and expected level of activity. It is the amount by which actual activity can fall short of expected activity before a loss is incurred. It is a measure of risk. It can be calculated by using any one of the following formulae:

Margin of safety (units)

= expected level of activity – break-even point

Margin of safety (%)

= $\dfrac{\text{Break-even point (units) x 100}}{\text{Expected level of activity}}$

Margin of safety = $\dfrac{\text{profit x 100}}{\text{C/S ratio}}$

EXHIBIT

You are given the following information:

C/S ratio = 70%
Sales revenue = $500,000
Fixed cost = $90,000
Units produced = 20,000

Required:

a) Calculate break-even point(in units)
b) Calculate break-even point in terms of sales revenue
c) Calculate margin of safety

Solution

a) Contribution per unit (70% x 500000) / 20000 = $17.5
   Break-even point = $\dfrac{90000}{17.5}$ = 5143 units

√**Tip** *When the break-even point results in a fraction of a unit of production, the answer should be rounded up to the next complete unit.*

b) Break –even point = $\dfrac{90000 \text{ x } 25}{17.5}$ = $128,571

(OR)

Break-even point = $\dfrac{90000}{0.70}$ = $ 128,571

c) Margin of safety (units) = 20000 – 5143 = 14,857 units
   Margin of safety (%) = $\dfrac{5143 \text{ x } 100}{20000}$ = 25.72%

   Margin of safety ($) = 500000-128571 =$ 371,429

» EXERCISE 21.5

You are given the following information:

Variable cost per unit   = $3
Selling price per unit   = $7
Planned production   = 25,000 units
Total fixed costs   = $23,000

Required:

a) Calculate the break-even point in units
b) Calculate the break-even point in terms of sales revenue
c) Calculate the margin of safety

» EXERCISE 21.6

You are given the following information:

Variable cost per unit   = $12
Selling price per unit   = $55
Planned production   = 35,000 units
Total fixed costs   = $70,000

Required:

a) Calculate the break-even point in units
b) Calculate the break-even point in terms of sales revenue
c) Calculate the margin of safety

21.10 | What is a break-even chart?

Break-even charts show sales revenue plotted against total cost and provide, within limits, useful information about various aspects of a product or service such as profit or loss at any particular level of activity, the break-even point, the margin of safety etc. Sales revenue and costs are plotted along the vertical axis and output is plotted along the horizontal axis.

EXHIBIT

Draw a break-even chart showing clearly:

i)   the fixed cost curve
ii)   the total revenue curve
iii)   the total cost curve
iv)   the break-even point in units
v)   the break-even point in sales revenue
vi)   the margin of safety
vii)   sensitivity
viii) area of profit
ix)   area of loss

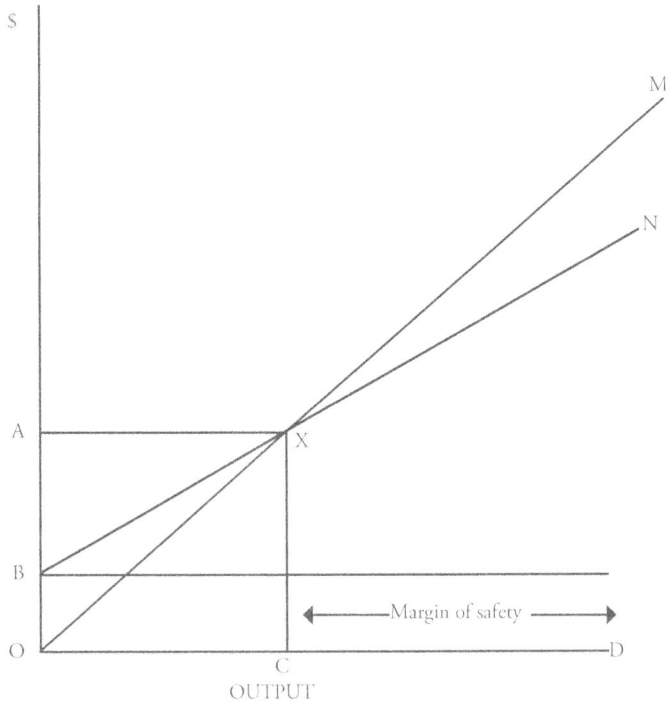

Solution

i)   The Fixed cost curve is at B
ii)   The total revenue curve is OM.
iii)   The total cost curve is BN
iv)   The break –even point in units is at C
v)   The break-even point in sales revenue is at $A
vi)   The margin of safety is depicted by CD where D is the planned output
vii)   The angle MXN depicts the sensitivity of the product to variations in the level of activity.
viii)   **Profit** at any particular of activity is to the **right of the break-even point** and is represented by the vertical distance between the sales revenue and the total cost line at that point.
ix)   **Loss** at any particular level of activity is to the **left of the break-even point** and is represented by the vertical distance between the sales revenue line and the total cost line at that point.

Note: 1. *If the angle MXN is large the product is more sensitive to variations in the level of activity compared to a product that has a smaller angle at the intersection of the Total Cost Curve and the Total Revenue Curve.*
2. A high fixed cost results in a high break – even point.

» EXERCISE 21.7

You are given the following information:

Variable cost per unit	= $12
Selling price per unit	= $55
Planned production	= 35,000 units
Total fixed costs	= $700,000

Required:
Using an appropriate scale draw a break-even chart showing:
a)   The break-even point in units
b)   The break-even point in sales revenue
c)   The margin of safety
d)   Fixed cost curve
e)   The Total Cost Curve
f)   The Total Revenue curve

21.11 | What are the limitations of break-even charts?

The limitations are:
1)   Costs are shown as straight lines. This is not realistic as variable costs can vary over a short period of time, for example.
2)   Again, fixed costs are more realistically depicted by a 'stepped' line as they may increase with the level of activity. E.g. with an increase in the level of activity the business may need two machines instead of one.
3)   Sales revenue are represented by a straight line. This is misleading as discounts are normally given to achieve optimum sales and this will 'flatten out' the sales revenue curve.
4)   Not all goods are sold. The chart does not allow for any closing stock as an unrealistic assumption is made that all goods produced are sold.
5)   Some costs may be semi-variable e.g. electricity: the fixed cost component would relate to meter charges which remain fixed and only the remaining cost is aligned to production activity. This would make up the variable cost component of electricity charges.

21.12 | What are the advantages of break-even charts?

Break-even charts are a useful visual aid for the study of the effect of changes in output, costs and revenue on the break-even point. Decision making is facilitated.

PROFIT/VOLUME CHARTS

21.13 | Explain: A Profit/volume chart

A profit/volume chart is also known as a Contribution/Sales Chart. Sales revenue is plotted along the horizontal axis and profit/loss are plotted along the vertical axis. The maximum loss occurs at zero sales and is equal to the total fixed costs. The break-even point is plotted on the horizontal axis when the profit is zero and the two plots joined by a straight line which represents the cumulative contributions. The profit /loss for any intervening level of sales may then be read from the chart.

Profit ($)

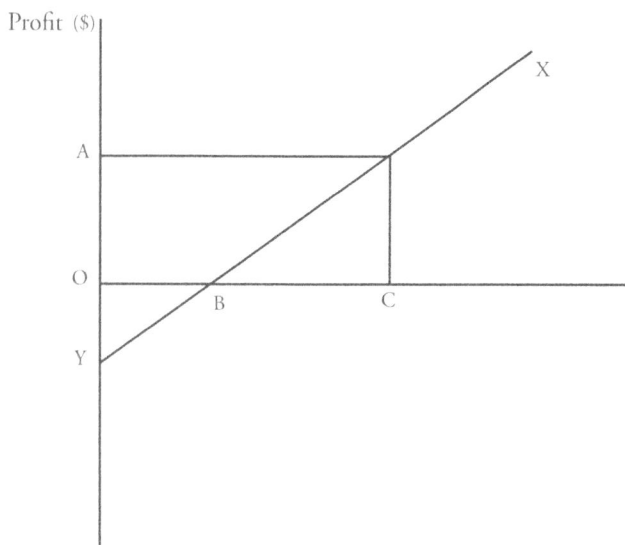

Loss($)

Y represents the Fixed Cost in $.

B represents the break-even point in units.

At C level of output, the profit is A

If the level of production activity falls below B then the business will make a loss which will fall between 0 and Y.

» EXERCISE 21.8

You are given the following information:

Beak –even point   = 20,000 units

Total fixed costs   = $70,000

Required:

Using a suitable scale, draw a profit/volume chart showing clearly:

a) Profit at 40,000 units

b) Loss at 15,000 units.

» EXERCISE 21.9

You are given the following information:

Beak –even point   = 10,000 units

Total fixed costs   = $20,000

Required:

Using a suitable scale, draw a profit/volume chart showing clearly:

a) Profit at 15,000 units

b) Loss at 5,000 units

21.14 | What are the factors that decide the selling price of a product?

The factors that decide pricing are:

a) Competition

b) Demand

c) Profit motive

d) Economic conditions

e) Political factors

f) Maximum utilisation of resources

g) Expansion and increased market share

21.15 | Explain: Marginal cost of sales

Some selling expenses may be variable e.g. sales commission. Marginal cost of sales = Marginal cost of production + variable selling expenses.

EXHIBIT

Comfy Ltd. is anxious to increase its market share. At present it sells 300 pairs of shoes a month at $55. The Sales Manager suggests that if the price of shoes was reduced to $52 a pair, the sales would rise to 500 pairs a month and if the price was reduced further to $48, the number of shoes sold would rise to 600 a month.

The following information is available for 300 pairs of shoes:

Direct materials	$9,000
Direct labour	$4,500
Variable selling expenses	$300
Fixed overheads	$2,000 per month.

Required:

Calculate the profit or loss from the sale of (i) 300 pairs (ii) 500 pairs (iii) 600 pairs and recommend which option should be accepted.

Solution

Per unit:	$	$	$
Selling price	55	52	48
Direct materials	30		
Direct labour	15		
Variable selling expenses	1		
Marginal cost of sales	46	46	46
Contribution	9	6	2
	300 pairs	500 pairs	600 pairs
Total contribution	2,700	3,000	1,200
Fixed expenses	2,000	2,000	2,000
Profit/(loss)	700	1,000	(800)

Recommendation:

Comfy Ltd. should reduce the price to $52 a pair.

EXERCISE 21.10

Belfast Ltd. is anxious to increase its market share. At present it sells 250 units of its product a month at $66. The Sales Manager suggests that if the price was reduced to $60 a unit, the sales would rise to 350 units a month and if the price was reduced further to $52, the number of units sold would rise to 400 a month.

The following information is available for 250 units:

Direct materials	$2,500
Direct labour	$5,000
Variable selling expenses	$1,000
Fixed overheads	$6,800 per month.

Required:

Calculate the profit or loss from the sale of (i) 250 units (ii) 350 units (iii) 400 units and recommend which option should be accepted.

EXERCISE 21.11

Abraham Ltd. makes two products: A and B. They give you the following information:

	Product A	Product B
Selling price per unit	$10	$12
Variable cost per unit	$3	$5
Maximum sales	5000 units	12,000 units

Fixed costs are $ 50,000
5,000 units of A are sold.
How many units of B must be sold to break even?

EXERCISE 21.12

Ye Ji Shin Ltd. has the following information:

	(Units)	(Units)
Output:	850	1000

	($000)	($000)
Sales	850	1000
Profits	200	250

Calculate: The contribution to sales ratio.

EXERCISE 21.13

Kai Ting Ltd manufactures two products Earl and Grey. Fixed costs are $50,000. Only 2500 units of Earl can be manufactured and sold.
You are given the following information:

	Selling price $	Direct labour $ per unit	Direct materials $ per unit
Earl	25	10	5
Grey	20	15	2

Calculate:
Number of units of Grey that should be manufactured and sold for the company to break even.

21.16 Explain: Limiting factor

Limiting factor is the factor that limits the quantity of goods that a business may produce. They could include a shortage of materials, a shortage of labour or a shortage of demand.

21.17 What should a business do when faced with a limited resources?

If the business is making more than one product, they should use the scarce resource in a way that produces the most profit.

21.18 What is a 'make or buy' decision?

It is a management decision that compares the costs and benefits of manufacturing a product against purchasing it.
EXHIBIT
Cost estimates for the manufacture of 8000 units of a product:

	PER UNIT	TOTAL
Variable costs	13	104,000
Fixed costs	6	48,000

Should the company make or buy if:

The supplier has offered to make the product at $16 a unit.
2/3rd of the fixed costs will continue regardless of the decision.

	PER UNIT		8000 UNITS	
	MAKE	BUY	MAKE	BUY
Purchase price		$16		128,000
Variable costs	$13		$104,000	
Fixed costs avoided	2		$16,000	
Total	$15	$16	$120,000	$128,000
Difference in favour of making	$1		$8,000	

The company should make the product.

21.19 What non-monetary factors should be considered?

The 'make or buy' decision should be considered in the broader perspective of available facilities and what the alternatives are: leaving facilities idle, renting out idle facilities, using idle facilities for other products.

Exercise 21.14

Niles Ltd. has 10,000 units of finished goods and budgets to produce 110,000 units, which, after sales will increase inventory to 20,000units.

	Resources required/unit	Resources available
Material(kg)	3	315,000
Direct labout(hrs)	2.5	300,000
Machine hours	0.5	110,000

Demand according to a market research survey will be for 90,000units.
Q. What is the limiting factor?

Exercise 21.15

McKenzie Sports manufactures four types of equipment that use the same raw material 'Droll' which costs $50 each. This raw material is in short supply and only 20,000 units are available. You are given the following information:

	Mackey	Drackey	Frackey	Backey
Demand (units)	10,000	4,000	3,000	500
Costs per unit	$	$	$	$
Droll	50	100	200	350
Additional raw materials	40	90	98	300
Direct labour	20	30	30	55
Fixed costs	60	80	40	70
Profit per unit	50	70	52	490
Selling price per unit	220	370	420	1,265

Required:
    a. Calculate the numbers of each type of equipment to be produced and sold that would maximise the profit.

    b. Prepare a marginal cost statement showing the profit for the year.

    c. Calculate the total annual sales revenue required by the company to break-even this year.

Exercise 21.16

The Cudo company manufactures parts for the computer industry. The company has two production departments and give you the following information:

OAR Department A based on machine hours $= \dfrac{25\ 886}{17\ 250} = \$1.50$

OAR Department B based on labour hours $= \dfrac{20\ 169}{12\ 605} = \$1.60$

The managers have been asked to cost a new job, reference 108/MJ.

The job would require:

6 kilos of materials costing $7.40 per kilo;

Other variable costs of $30.50.

The job would spend 14 hours in department A and a further 6 hours in department B.

The job would be marked up by 60% on cost to achieve the selling price.

    (a) Required:

Calculate the price to be quoted to the customer for job 108/MJ.

The Major company requires a special component for one of its computers. This will be a unique "one off" order.

The special component would take:

5 kilos of materials at $7.40 per kilo;

Variable overheads of $18.30;

It will require extra power estimated to cost $28.00.

The component will spend 10 hours in department A and 5 hours in department B.

The managers of the company have calculated a selling price of $170.08. Major company are only willing to pay $100.

    (b) Required:

Advise the managers of Cudo whether or not they should accept the order from Major at a price of $100. Support your answer with financial and non – financial data.

Adapted from (UCLES, 2009, AS/A Level Accounting, syllabus 9706/41,October/November)

Exercise 21.17

Kimnargh Ltd. Makes three products A, B and C. You are given the following details:

	Direct materials (kilos per unit)	Direct labour (hours per unit)	Direct expenses (per unit)	Selling price (per unit)
A	5	4	$7	$74
B	7	6	$4	$85
C	10	8	$9	$115

Additional information:
    a.   All three products are made from material Z.
    b.   Material Z costs $3 per kilo.
    c.   All three products require the same type of labour which is paid $7 per hour.
    d.   Total fixed costs amount to $70,000.
    e.   Budgeted production (based on maximum demand) is:
           A – 2000 units
           B – 2400 units
           C – 1800 units
The supply of material Z is limited to 38,000 kilos.

Required:
    a.   Prepare a production budget that would give maximum profit from the material available.
Adapted from (UCLES, 2005, AS/A Level Accounting, syllabus 9706/4, May/June)

21.1 | Multiple – choice questions:

i) The cost of manufacturing 500 units is given:

	$
Rent	4,000
Electricity	3,500
Direct Labour	24,800
Telephone	700
Indirect Labour	24,600
Materials	15,700

What is the marginal cost of each unit of the product?
A) $44   B) $81 C) $146.6 D) None of the above.

ii) A product has a selling price of $15. The following information is given to you regarding the costs per unit:

	$
Direct materials	1.00
Direct labour	1.10
Fixed factory overheads	2.00
Royalties	0.90
Fixed administration overheads	2.50

What is the contribution per unit?
A) $ 7.50   B) $10.5   C) $ 12.90   D) $12

iii) The following information is given to you regarding a product Meme:

	$
Fixed overheads	150,000
Unit selling price	50
Unit variable costs	10

What would be the new break-even sales volume if the fixed overheads increased by$10,000.
A)   3,750 units
B) $187,500
C)   4000 units
D) $ 200,000

iv) Lemmington manufactures 200 units of Amjifur a month. They give you the following information:

	$
Sales income	5600
Variable costs	2,400
Fixed overheads	8,000

What is the break-even point in Sales revenue?
A) $2.50   B) $250   C) $ 14,000 D) $500

v) A cost is classified as 'semi-variable' What effect will a 15% reduction in the level of production have on the cost of one unit produced by the manufacturer?
A) It will increase by less than 15%
B) It will decrease by 15%
C) It will decrease by less than 15%
D) It will increase by 15%

21.2 | Fernando manufactures 3 types of refrigerators for Household, Business and Factory use. The following data apply to the year ended 30 April 2007.

	Household	Business	Factory	Total
Sales (units)	2400	900	2250	5550
	$	$	$	$
Total sales value	240 000	108 000	360 000	708 000
Total costs				
Direct material	96 000	45 000	112 500	253 500
Direct labour	72 000	28 000	94 500	195 300
Variable overheads	24 000	13 500	45 000	82 500
Fixed overheads	57 000	27 000	67 500	152 100
	249 600	114 300	319 500	683 400
Profit (loss)	(9 600)	(6 300)	40 000	24 600

REQUIRED

(a) For the year ended 30 April 2007 calculate for each type of refrigerator:
(i) the contribution per unit;
(ii) the contribution as a percentage of sales.
Give answers to a maximum of two decimal places. Workings must be shown.

....
....
....
....
....
....
....

(b)   Calculate the break- even point for each type of refrigerator in both units and dollars.Give your answers to the nearest whole number. Workings must be shown.

....
....
....
....
....
....
....

(UCLES, 2007, AS/A Level Accounting, syllabus 9706/2, May/June)

21.3 | The break-even chart for a product is shown.

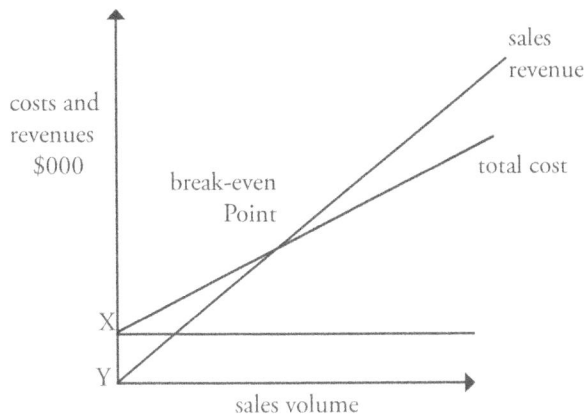

What does XY represent?

21.4 | Gerry Hatrick Ltd manufactures and sells video cameras. The unit selling price and production costs are as follows:

	$
Selling price	800
Direct material	100
Direct labour	90
Variable overheads	50
Fixed overheads	160

The fixed production overheads assume a monthly production of 2000 units.
The following monthly costs are also incurred :

Fixed administrative overheads	$80 000
Variable sales overheads	10% of sales value
Fixed sales overhead	$120 000

During the month of September 20x5 a total of 2400 units were produced, of which 1800 were sold. There was no stock on hand at the beginning of September.

REQUIRED
(a) Prepare profit statements for September 20x5 using
   (i) Absorption costing
   (ii) Marginal costing
(b) Explain why the profit found when using absorption costing differs from the profit found in marginal costing.
(c) Calculate the break-even point for September 20x5 in sales volume.

(UCLES, 2005, AS/A Level Accounting, Syllabus 9706/2, Oct/Nov)

21.5 A company manufactures three products: Alpha, Beta & Gamma. They are made from the same material.

Information given:	Alpha	Beta	Gamma
Planned production(units)	1000	2000	3000
Selling price per unit	$50	$45	$100
Direct material per unit	2kg	1kg	3kg
Direct labour hours per unit	3	2	5

Direct material costs $5/kg and direct labour is paid $10/hr
Fixed expenses amount to $50,000

Required:
Prepare a production plan that will make the most profit from

  i. 12,000 kg of material which is all that is available (labour is unlimited.

ii. 12,000 hours of labour that is all that is available (material is unlimited.

21.6 Abu & Sons expect sales to be 10,000 units. They fix their selling price at $5 and their variable costs at $3.50 a unit.

REQUIRED
Calculate their forecasted fixed cost if their margin of safety is one fifth of sales.

21.7 Calculate the profit using absorption costing if:

a. Profit using marginal costing is $75,000.
b. OAR is $5 a unit
c. Opening inventory is $10,000 and closing inventory is $15,000

21.8 Calculate the fixed cost from the following information.

A company's budgeted sales are 10,000 units and its margin of safety is 2000 units

Additional information	$
Selling price per unit	45
Direct labour per unit	10
Direct material per unit	15

22 The application of accounting to business planning

Q. List the benefits of accounting to businesses
Accounting helps businesses to:

1. Create tools of control such as budgets
Budgets are business plans in financial terms. They help businesses set financial goals and monitor them.
2. Make forecasts
Accounting help businesses make forecasts based on past financial data. e.g Future sales revenue. This helps businesses plan for the future.
3. Purchasing decisions
Accurate accounting help business to make good purchasing decisions. E.g When to purchase non-current assets.
4. Tracking expenses
With the help of accounting, businesses can monitor their expenses. This helps cash flow and liquidity.
5. Monitor financial health
Accounting ratios based on accurate accounting data, inform interested parties of the financial health of the business.
6. Personnel decisions
Businesses, with the help of accurate accounting records will know how much to spend on staff and when.
7. Taxation
Accurate accounting records will help a business at the time of preparing tax returns.
8. Loans and other sources of finance
Accurate accounting records can strengthen the negotiating power of businesses when they approach banks for loans.
9. Monitor business growth
Accounting keeps track of assets, liabilities and equity as well as sales revenue. Hence, interested parties can be kept informed of and managers will know if their strategies are successful.

Q. Why do businesses need to plan for the future?
Businesses plan for the future to achieve their objectives of growth, profitability, sustainability and survival in difficult economic periods. Accounting records are a good indication of growth and profitability. They also supply managers with accurate data on which to base good strategic decisions. Cash flow decisions can be made based on such data. Businesses can negotiate good finance terms with accounting data and this finance can be used to fuel future growth. Shareholders and other investors will also need this information to make decisions. Year-end financial statements help businesses to communicate with their interested parties. Finally, a business will know when it is time to exit an industry that is not doing so well.

Q. What are the advantages of a budget?
Budgets help managers in many of the following management functions:
1. Planning.
Budgets can translate strategic plans into activities that ensure these plans are implemented. Budgets force managers to think about the business' objectives and how to use the resources available to achieve these objectives.
2. Budgets ensure that organisational activities are recorded for future use.
3. Budgets are often a good tool of communication within a business between employees, between employees and managers and between top management and middle-level managers.
4. Control
Budgets can either be made by top management (called top-down budgets) or by departmental managers (called bottom-up budgets). In either case, these budgets can be used by managers to monitor performance. If actual figures do not equal budgeted figures, managers will have to find reasons for this variance and take corrective action. Actual performance could either be favourable, when it is better than budgeted revenue or expenditure, or adverse, when it is worse than budgeted figures.
5. Budgets can be used as a tool for corrective action when needed.
6. Co-ordination

Budgets help in the efficient allocation of resources. In the case of top-down budgeting, senior management can use budgets to co-ordinate resources so that there is no duplication. They can see the big picture and can therefore make use of their resources efficiently.

7. Identifying the limiting factor

A limiting factor, also called a key factor, is a resource that is available in limited supply to the business. Budgets help businesses identify these factors and can ensure that they are used profitably.

8. A form of responsibility accounting

Budgets can help identify managers who will be responsible for achieving budget targets. They can be a tool by which these managers can be held responsible for not achieving these targets.

9. Helps avoid management by crises

Management by crises is when managers have not been pro-active in identifying problems before they arise. Managers who adopt this style of management find themselves 'fighting fires'. Budgets can help mangers adopt a style that ensures 'fire prevention'. Managers are then prepared to identify and solve crises more efficiently.

10. Banks and other lenders may require budgets before they decide to lend.

Q. What are the disadvantages of budgeting?

Though budgeting can prove to be advantageous to a business, they may suffer from the following disadvantages:

1. If budgets are not flexible:
    a. They can be more of a problem than a solution. Resources may be in short supply as they may not have been budgeted for. A flexible budget can ensure change when needed.
    b. Rigid budgets may reduce innovation and initiative
2. Budgets may demotivate, especially in the case of top-down budgeting. Managers may not want to commit to them if they have had no say in their creation.
3. Budgets may encourage tunnel vision. Departments will work to achieve their own targets which may be counterproductive to that of the organisation's goals and vision.
4. Departments may have to compete for resources if company politics have influenced budgets.
5. Budgets may be perceived as being unfair especially if they are unattainable and unrealistic.
6. They cost time and money
7. They require specialist knowledge to prepare.
8. Managers may use 'budgetary slack'. This is when they either include extra costs or decrease expected revenue to ensure they achieve the targets set out in budgets.

TEST YOURSELF

» **22.1 Multiple choice questions**

i. What management function does budgeting **not** help with?

A. Planning
B. Coordinating
C. Control
D. Commanding

ii. You are given the following reasons for the actual cost of raw materials being more than budgeted:
    1. The materials are of poor quality
    2. The machinery used in the production line is outdated
    3. The costs of the materials have been recorded incorrectly in the budget

Which of the above will cause a variance between actual and budgeted costs?

A. 1 &2 only
B. 2 & 3 only
C. 1 & 3 only
D. 1, 2 & 3

iii. Which of the following is **not** a benefit of accounting to a business?

A. Accounting helps with purchasing decisions
B. Accounting helps by supplying data for the drawing up of departmental budgets
C. Accounting helps managers make personal decisions
D. Accounting helps interested parties monitor business growth.

Profitability Ratios:

Gross Margin = $\dfrac{\text{Gross Profit}}{\text{Revenue}}$ x 100

Mark up = $\dfrac{\text{Gross Profit}}{\text{Cost of Sales}}$ x100

Profit Margin = $\dfrac{\text{Profit for the year}}{\text{Revenue}}$ x100

It can also be expressed as:

$\dfrac{\text{Profit for the year (after interest)}}{\text{Revenue}}$ x 100

Return on Capital Employed = $\dfrac{\text{Profit for the year before interest}}{\text{Capital Employed}}$ x100

[Capital Employed = Issued Shares + Reserves + Non-Current Liabilities]

Expenses to Revenue Ratio = $\dfrac{\text{Expenses}}{\text{Revenue}}$ x 1000

Operating Expenses to Revenue Ratio = $\dfrac{\text{Operating Expenses}}{\text{Revenue}}$ x 100

Liquidity ratios:

Current Ratio = $\dfrac{\text{Current Assets}}{\text{Current Liabilities}}$

Liquid (acid test) Ratio = $\dfrac{\text{Current assets - Inventory}}{\text{Current liabilities}}$
(also known as 'Quick Ratio')

Efficiency ratios:

Non-Current Asset Turnover
= $\dfrac{\text{Net Revenue}}{\text{Total Net Book Value of Non-Current Assets}}$

Trade Receivables Turnover = $\dfrac{\text{Trade receivables}}{\text{Credit sales}}$ x 365 days
(also known as Average Collection Period)

Trade Payables Turnover = $\dfrac{\text{Trade payables}}{\text{Credit purchases}}$ x 365
(also known as Average Payment Period)

Inventory Turnover = $\dfrac{\text{Average Inventory}}{\text{Cost of Sales}}$ x 365

Rate of Inventory Turnover = $\dfrac{\text{Cost of Sales}}{\text{Average Inventory}}$
(answer given in times)